Michael Barry's

Radio Times

COOKERY YEAR

Michael Barry's

Radio Times

COOKERY YEAR

with photographs by
Nick Carman

BCA

LONDON   NEW YORK   SYDNEY   TORONTO

Note on the recipes

Recipes suitable for vegetarians (except puddings, breads and drinks, which are all vegetarian) are marked with a (V) symbol. Please note that these recipes may include cheese and other dairy products.

Each *Menu of the Month* was chosen to include complementary flavours and textures. Dishes featured here may differ from those in the photographs.

ACKNOWLEDGEMENT

I'd like to thank Susie Magasiner for her help in preparing the book. Her research into the spices and seasonal availabilities, her testing of so many of the recipes, her excellent advice and ideas and, not least, her unfailing good humour and support have been invaluable in both compiling and writing this book

This edition published 1994
by BCA
by arrangement with Network Books

Network Books is an imprint of BBC Books,
a division of BBC Enterprises Limited

Designed by Grahame Dudley Associates
Photographs by Nick Carman
Styling by Jane McLeish
Home Economist Janice Murfitt

Printed in Spain by
Printer Industria Gráfica, S.A., Barcelona

CONTENTS

INTRODUCTION

Thirty years ago, most of the foods we ate were seasonal. For strawberries you had to wait until the middle of June, when a trickle of the delicious red fruit would become a flow and then a flood towards the middle of July, only to dry up almost overnight in August. What began with strawberries and cream, progressed to strawberry tarts and shortcakes and culminated with a quick burst of jam-making to make the most of the flavour through the rest of the year. Not so any more. These days strawberries from Spain, Kenya and South America are available as much in January as in June. Dates, that once only put in an appearance, boxed, at Christmas, as a special treat to go on top of the fruit basket, now appear in fresh, preserved and candied forms throughout the year, as do tangerines and satsumas. What is more, lettuces, courgettes, peppers, aubergines – the fruit and vegetables of high summer – are now available the year round.

So, does a seasonal cook book actually make sense today? Well, for a number of reasons I think it does. However many strawberries we receive from Spain in February, nothing beats the succulence, flavour and sheer sumptuous pleasure of sun-ripened English strawberries in June. Nor, however practical and low-fat they are, do turkey portions in May replace the great festive bird in December. It isn't just flavour and freshness that seasonal foods boast, they are value for money too. The specialities grown *out* of season in exotic climes cost more to produce, to reach our supermarkets and finally to buy. There are, of course, some foods that will always remain seasonal – fish for example. Oysters are available these days even when there isn't the letter 'r' in the month, but they are simply not as good as when there is. Salmon, now that it's farmed, is available all the year round, as is trout, but most sea fish are still at their optimum at certain times of the year – sole in the winter, crab in the summer and sprats in the spring for example.

We, too, choose to eat certain things at specific times in the calendar: hot cross buns at Easter, fruit cake at Christmas and pumpkins at Halloween. You will find that several of the recipes in this book have been written with these traditional festivities in mind and I have also tried to include recipes for picnics, barbecues and other seasonal pastimes.

Here you'll find the year divided into monthly sections. Each month includes recipes that use ingredients at their seasonal best. There is, in each chapter, a selection of starters, main courses and puddings, many of which are suitable for vegetarians. For each month I have also included a list of best buys – ingredients that are either at their peak or are back in the shops in abundance after their annual absence. There's a preserve of the month too. Preserving's a habit that we now no longer have to practise in order to keep our families healthily fed, but there's still an enormous satisfaction in making your own preserves. Just a couple of hours a month will fill your store-cupboard with herb vinegars, potted cheeses, strawberry conserves and Christmas chutney – to name but a few. I hope, like me, you will find it's just one pleasurable aspect of seasonal cooking that this book contains. In addition, each month contains a bread and drink recipe as well as recom-mending a herb or spice to give added flavour to your monthly meals.

Whether you're cooking for family, friends, for a party or yourself, I hope this book will encourage you to take advantage of the vast array of fresh ingredients available throughout the year and will convince you of the real benefits and joys of seasonal cookery.

INTRODUCTION

January, the first full month of winter, always seems like a good time for wholesome and simple foods. Partly this is the weather, with the long haul up to spring still in front of us all, but also partly it's a reaction to the richness and inevitable self-indulgence around Christmas time.

In terms of supplies it's quite a good month, especially good for poultry, though once again Christmas may not make that seem the most attractive of options. But there's a lot of good fish, particularly British white fish – cod and coley, haddock and hake, bream and whiting – as well as the flat fish – sole, halibut, plaice, skate and brill.

Winter vegetables are still plentiful and in good condition, especially cabbages – savoy, with its crinkly leaves, and red – marvellous for making casseroles as well as for pickling, if that's your inclination. There are some newish potatoes coming in from the Mediterranean area – Cyprus, Egypt and the south of Italy – and brussels sprouts are still good, though it's important to look for ones that are small and tight and not open and loose-leafed. Jerusalem artichokes put in an appearance; they look a bit like knobbly potatoes and have a slightly hazelnut flavour. They make very good soups and are tasty mashed fifty:fifty with potatoes. They have an added advantage which is that they are genuinely not fattening, although their texture is very similar to that of potatoes when mashed.

On the fruit front there are good supplies from the southern hemisphere – grapes, apples, pears, kiwi fruit – but the particular speciality for January is oranges – both navels and Jaffas but most particularly Sevilles, the bitter orange that has always been used for making marmalade but also makes a marvellous sauce for duck.

The recipe suggestions for January combine some of these special ingredients with a number of the simple and wholesome foods that come from pulses and pastas – filling, warming and cheering against the weather's icy blast.

PREVIOUS PAGE

1 **Hungarian Fish with Paprika and Cream**

2 **Cooked Vegetable Salad**

3 **Steamed Ginger Pudding**

January

— PRODUCE AT ITS BEST —

Cabbages ● *Jerusalem artichokes* ● *Carrots* ● *Parsnips* ● *Turnip*
● *Swede* ● *Leeks* ● *Oranges* ● *Pink grapefruit* ● *Poultry* ● *Haddock*
● *Mussels* ● *Oysters*

STARTERS

LENTIL SOUP Ⓥ

This is a variation on the many lentil and split pea soups that used to be commonplace
in our diets at this time of year but have fallen slightly out of fashion. This is a pity
because not only are they cheap, easy to make and nutritious, they also have superb
flavour. In addition there's a very comforting quality that makes them perfect food
at this time of year for a light but filling lunch or the beginning of a cheering evening
meal. I've suggested using the little red lentils known as Egyptian lentils which are
readily available in our grocers and supermarkets, but you can, if you like, vary the
dish by using the green or slate-coloured French-style lentils; they take a little longer
to cook and produce a rather darker and richer soup, but equally good to eat.

SERVES 4

2 tablespoons cooking oil	a pinch of ground turmeric
225 g (8 oz) onions, roughly chopped	½ teaspoon dried thyme
225 g (8 oz) carrots, roughly chopped	salt and freshly ground black pepper
225 g (8 oz) lentils	1.2 litres (2 pints) water or stock
a pinch of ground ginger	2 tablespoons chopped fresh parsley

Heat the oil in a large pan and fry the onions and carrots gently until the onion
is translucent. Add the lentils, ginger, turmeric and thyme, stir well and season
generously with salt and pepper. Cover with the water, stir to mix thoroughly and
bring to the boil. Simmer gently for 25–30 minutes for red lentils and 35–40 minutes
for brown or green ones. Add the thyme and purée in a food processor or liquidizer.
Serve sprinkled with the parsley. Check for seasoning, it may need a little more salt.

COOKED VEGETABLE SALAD Ⓥ

This is a very simple dish but it uses ingredients which are unusual in salad: the root
vegetables that are so readily available and at their best at this time of year. We don't
normally think of them as salad vegetables, but dressed with a good sharp and well-
herbed dressing they make a marvellous and quite filling first course.

SERVES 4

225 g (8 oz) carrots	**FOR THE DRESSING**
225 g (8 oz) Jerusalem artichokes	4 tablespoons olive oil
1 large potato	1 tablespoon white wine vinegar
2 medium leeks	1 tablespoon chopped fresh dill
1 swede	1 tablespoon snipped fresh chives
	salt and freshly ground black pepper

Cut the vegetables into 1 cm (in) dice. Steam or boil the vegetables until just cooked, then drain. Mix the dressing ingredients together and stir into the hot vegetables. Leave to cool to allow the flavours to develop.

FRISEE SALAD WITH ROQUEFORT ⓥ

One of the unexpected items of produce that's available at this time of year is the frilly leafed frisée lettuce that the French call endive. It has a slightly bitter flavour and make marvellous salads with other strong-tasting ingredients. As an alternative to the frilly lettuce you can also at this time of year buy batavia, which looks like a soft lettuce with rather thick and succulent leaves. Like the frisée, it has a slightly bitter flavour. You can use them mixed together to provide a variety of textures, shapes and colours. This makes a good, elegant first course and an excellent light lunch.

SERVES 4

1 frisée or batavia lettuce	4 tablespoons salad oil
2 slices white bread	2 tablespoons lemon juice
50 ml (2 fl oz) cooking oil (not olive)	1 teaspoon sugar
	2 tablespoons milk
FOR THE DRESSING	
50 g (2 oz) Roquefort or Lanark blue	

Wash the lettuce and tear up the leaves into postcard–sized pieces. Dry them thoroughly and arrange in a bowl. Cut the bread into 1 cm (in) cubes. Heat the oil and fry the cubes until lightly browned. Do not let the croûtons go dark brown or they will burn, as they continue to cook after you've taken them out of the pan.

Put the dressing ingredients into a food processor and process until well blended but not necessarily completely smooth – the cheese may have a little texture. Add the croûtons to the lettuce, pour over the dressing, toss well and serve immediately.

Creamed Savoy Cabbage with Cashew Nuts

MAIN COURSES

JERUSALEM ARTICHOKES PROVENÇAL Ⓥ

Jerusalem artichokes have quite a crisp texture that holds together well when they're being cooked. They make a marvellous background for strong and rich-tasting sauces and here is a recipe which adds the flavours of a Provençal summer – a welcome and cheering thought for the middle of winter. This makes an excellent vegetarian dish or a side dish to grilled meats or sausages.

SERVES 4

450 g (1 lb) Jerusalem artichokes	350 g (12 oz) Italian tinned tomatoes
4 tablespoons olive oil	1 tablespoon tomato purée
225 g (8 oz) Spanish onions, thinly sliced	½ teaspoon dried thyme
1 garlic clove, finely chopped	½ teaspoon dried rosemary
salt and freshly ground black pepper	½ teaspoon dried basil

Wash the Jerusalem artichokes thoroughly, scrubbing them like new potatoes if necessary, but don't attempt to peel them. Cut them into 1 cm (½ in) slices. In a large, high-sided frying-pan, heat the olive oil and fry the onion and garlic gently until they are slightly translucent. Add the Jerusalem artichokes and turn gently over a medium heat for 5 minutes. Season generously with salt and pepper, add the tomatoes and tomato purée, and a little water if the mixture is dry. Cover and cook over a very low heat for a further 20–25 minutes until the artichokes are quite tender. The sauce should not be at all runny but should cling to the artichokes. Add the herbs, allow to stand for 2 minutes for the flavours to blend, then serve.

CREAMED SAVOY CABBAGE WITH CASHEW NUTS Ⓥ

The crinkly-leafed savoy cabbages are at their best at this time of year. They have a slightly stronger taste than their summer cousins but also quite a distinctive and crisp texture. When you buy one, discard any bedraggled leaves, but don't give up the dark green, large outside leaves, use those as well as the heart. They are combined here with cashew nuts to give a little crunch and contrasting colour and served with a creamy sauce with just a hint of mustard. It's a delicious dish on its own, served as a vegetable course, or with a combination of vegetables with or without roast meat.

SERVES 6–8

1 savoy cabbage, about 900 g (2 lb)	40 g (1½ oz) butter
salt and freshly ground black pepper	1 teaspoon made English mustard
300 ml (10 fl oz) water	100 g (4 oz) roasted salted (or unsalted) cashew nuts
150 ml (5 fl oz) milk	
40 g (1½ oz) plain flour	

Cut the cabbage in half and cut out all the stalk and hard parts from the centre. Slice each half across into 1 cm (½ in) ribbons. In a large pan, bring the water to the boil with a pinch of salt. Add the cabbage, cover and put it back over medium heat. Shake the pan, then leave for 1 minute, shake it again, leave it for another minute then remove from the heat. Drain the cabbage, reserving the cooking liquid. Mix that with the milk, flour and butter in a non-stick pan. Whisk thoroughly and heat gently until the mixture blends into a smooth, creamy sauce. Season generously and add the mustard, stirring until it's thoroughly blended. Stir the sauce into the drained cabbage, check for seasoning, add the cashew nuts and mix those in gently. You can, if you wish, pour the whole lot into an oval baking dish and flash under a hot grill for a golden surface, but don't cook for too long otherwise the cabbage will lose its green and succulent crispness.

LEEK AND MEATBALL PASTA

Pasta is a family favourite at any time of year, but at this time in the winter, green vegetables are really at a premium and leeks, with their rich yet mild flavour, make a wonderful pasta sauce. This recipe is derived from a New York Italian recipe, and was originally eaten with polenta, the cornmeal dough that comes from around Venice, but it's equally delicious and rather easier to make with the lovely bulky pasta that's available everywhere these days.

SERVES 4

450 g (1 lb) leeks	1 garlic clove, chopped
1 slice fresh white bread	450 g (1 lb) tin Italian chopped tomatoes
450 g (1 lb) minced turkey	2 tablespoons tomato purée
½ teaspoon freeze-dried thyme	½ teaspoon freeze-dried oregano
1 egg	½ teaspoon freeze-dried basil
salt and freshly ground black pepper	225 g (8 oz) shell or spiral pasta, cooked *al dente*
2 tablespoons olive oil	

Wash the leeks thoroughly to remove any grit or sand and slice across into 5 mm (¼ in) ribbons, green and white parts. Cut the bread into 2.5 cm (1 in) cubes. Put the turkey, bread, thyme and egg into a food processor or, if doing it by hand, into a large bowl. Season generously with salt and pepper and mix and knead until thoroughly blended. (If you're not using a food processor you may need to soak the bread in a little milk first to make it soft enough to work.) Divide the mixture into 16 equal amounts and roll these into balls. You may find wetting your hands between every few balls helps.

Heat the olive oil in a large, deep frying-pan. Fry the turkey balls gently until lightly golden. Add the leeks and garlic and fry for a further 3–4 minutes. Season again generously and add the tomatoes and tomato purée. Stir to mix thoroughly then cover and simmer for a further 15 minutes. If the mixture looks dry, add 1–2 tablespoons of water. Sprinkle on the oregano and basil, turn off the heat and allow to mature for 5 minutes before serving over the freshly boiled and drained pasta. You can use Parmesan cheese with this but it's not essential as the sauce is already very rich.

SPICED BAKED CHICKEN

This dish has roots in Anglo-Indian cookery, with a combination of spices and chutney in the sauce that produce a very rich and tangy set of flavours. I like it served in the Anglo-Indian way with plenty of boiled rice, popadoms, mango chutney and a salad made of finely chopped tomato, spring onion and cucumber dressed with lemon or lime juice.

SERVES 4

½ teaspoon ground ginger	25 g (1 oz) soft brown sugar
½ teaspoon freshly ground black pepper	4 generous chicken joints, breast or leg
½ teaspoon ground cardamom	100 g (4 oz) mango, finely chopped, or similar sweet chutney
½ teaspoon mustard powder	
½ teaspoon garlic salt	grated rind and juice of 1 lemon
½ teaspoon ground bay leaves	120 ml (4 fl oz) water

Pre-heat the oven to 180°C/350°F/Gas 4, 160°C fan, middle of an Aga roasting oven.

Mix all the dry spices and garlic salt with the sugar and coat the chicken pieces. You may find this easiest to do by shaking in a plastic or strong paper bag. Allow to stand for 30 minutes for the flavours to permeate the chicken. Put the chicken pieces into a baking dish in which they will all just fit. Mix together the chutney, lemon rind and juice, and the water and pour evenly over the chicken pieces. Bake in the oven for 15 minutes. Turn over, basting generously with the juices, and bake a further 15 minutes until the chicken is cooked through. Serve the chicken with a little of the juices poured over and the rest in a jug for people to pour over their chicken and rice.

HUNGARIAN FISH WITH PAPRIKA AND CREAM

A cuisine that's not much known in Britain is one that grew to a very high level of skill under the Austro-Hungarian emperors. It was a very rich and filling style, and some of the dishes we would find too heavy these days, especially without middle European winters to fortify ourselves against. But in our milder, but still chilly season, this dish of baked fish with a pink creamy and savoury sauce is just the thing to liven up a family dinner. I've suggested making it with haddock but any firm white fish will do very well, and large whiting fillets, which are available at this time of year, pollack or coley, all make excellent alternatives.

SERVES 4

1 tablespoon oil	150 ml (5 fl oz) soured cream
450 g (1 lb) Spanish onions, thinly sliced	150 ml (5 fl oz) single cream
15 g (½ oz) butter	1½ tablespoons finely ground paprika
675 g (1½ lb) haddock or white fish fillets	½ teaspoon caraway seeds

Pre-heat the oven to 180°C/350°F/Gas 4, 160°C fan, middle of an Aga roasting oven. Butter a pie or baking dish, about 5 cm (2 in) deep, into which the onions and fish will all fit comfortably.

Heat the oil in a large frying-pan and gently fry the onions for about 10 minutes until translucent. Into the prepared dish, put a layer of onion, a layer of fish, another layer of onion, a second layer of fish and the final layer of onion on top. Beat the two creams together with the paprika and the caraway seeds and pour over the fish. It should just come to the top of the fish, leaving the onions on top pretty well uncovered. Put a piece of foil over the dish and bake in the oven for 45 minutes until the fish is thoroughly cooked and the sauce bubbling. Serve with flat egg noodles or mashed potato. Any vegetable should follow as a separate course.

PUDDINGS

STEAMED GINGER PUDDING

Steamed puddings are a great comfort at this time of year and this one makes use of ginger, this month's spice, in more than one form. It uses ground ginger but also that marvellous preserved ginger in syrup that people are given at Christmas time. If you've got any left over from Christmas use that, if not, you can buy it all the year round in simple glass jars at most grocers and speciality shops. You can serve this pudding with cream or real custard if you prefer it and I have been known to serve it with home-made vanilla ice-cream at moments of true self-indulgence.

SERVES 4

75 g (3 oz) preserved ginger in syrup (3 tablespoons)	50 g (2 oz) caster sugar
100 g (4 oz) self-raising flour	2 eggs
75 g (3 oz) butter or vegetable margarine, softened	1 teaspoon ground ginger
	2 tablespoons milk

Finely chop the preserved ginger or put it and its syrup into a liquidizer or food processor and chop it. In a large bowl, mix together the flour, softened butter or margarine, sugar, egg, ground ginger, chopped ginger and milk. Beat with a wooden spoon until well blended. Butter a 1-litre (1¾-pint) pudding basin and pour in the mixture. Cover it with greaseproof paper and tie around with string or put an elastic band around it. Leave a little slack in the paper so that the pudding can rise. Steam it for 2 hours in a pan of water with a lid, or for about 45 minutes in a pressure cooker or 8 minutes in a microwave. To serve, remove the greaseproof paper, run a knife around the edge of the pudding and invert it on to a plate before cutting into wedges like a cake.

TREACLE TART

A great family favourite, this used to be made with a kind of treacle known as Liverpool treacle – half-way between golden syrup and molasses. Unfortunately it's not made any more in Liverpool or anywhere else, so you have to use a mixture of the two to get the dark and rich flavour that this tart requires. I think it's best eaten warm, neither hot nor cold, but it's perfectly pleasant either way if you prefer to eat it straight out of the oven or to keep it for a while. It's not improved by keeping in the fridge, though, as the filling tends to collapse a bit and the pastry goes soggy.

SERVES 4

2 eggs	50 g (2 oz) walnuts, chopped
a pinch of salt	20-cm (8-inch) pastry case (225 g (8 oz) shortcrust pastry in a 20-cm (8-inch) tin baked blind for 10 minutes) or a shop bought pastry case will do.
200 g (7 oz) golden syrup	
25 g (1 oz) molasses or treacle	
25 g (1 oz) butter, melted	

Pre-heat the oven to 200°C/400°F/Gas 6, 190°C fan, top of an Aga roasting oven.

Fill a mixing bowl with warm water and leave it to stand for a few minutes until the bowl is thoroughly warm. This will help very much in dealing with the treacle and syrup. Discard the water. Break in the eggs, add the pinch of salt, the golden syrup, treacle and melted butter. Mix thoroughly with a metal spoon until the mixture is well blended. Put the walnut pieces into the pre-baked pastry shell and pour in the treacle mixture. It should come to 5 mm (¼ in) below the rim. Don't fill it fuller than this as it will rise when it cooks. Bake in the oven for 25–30 minutes until the filling is risen and set. Allow to cool a little before removing it from the tin. The filling will sink a little as it cools but will taste none the worse for that.

HOT BAKED FRUIT SALAD

We tend to think of fruit salads as dishes to be eaten cold, and indeed you can eat this cold but only after it's been cooked. It's an unusual way of treating the classic fruits that are available in the winter in Britain, and one that brings out and emphasises some of the flavours that we take so much for granted. It's a great way also of emptying the remnants of the Christmas fruit bowl.

SERVES 4

2 apples	2 tablespoons soft brown sugar
2 pears	½ teaspoon ground ginger
1 large orange	½ teaspoon ground cinnamon
2 satsumas and/or tangerines	a pinch of ground cloves
2 bananas	25 g (1 oz) butter

Pre-heat the oven to 180°C/350°F/Gas 4, 160°C fan, bottom of an Aga roasting oven.

Core but don't peel the apples and pears and divide each one into 12 pieces. Cut the tops and bottoms off the orange and satsumas but don't peel them, and divide them into pegs, removing any obvious pips. Peel the bananas and cut across into 2.5 cm (1 in) pieces. Mix all the fruit together in a bowl, adding the sugar and spices, and stir to coat thoroughly. Put into a baking dish into which they will all just fit comfortably and dot with the butter. Bake in the oven for 25 minutes. Turn over thoroughly, spooning the juices over the fruit, and bake for another 20 minutes. The fruit should just have started to caramelize. You can eat it hot or allow it to cool and then chill before serving cold. Pouring cream is better than double cream with this.

PRESERVES

POTTED FOODS

The tradition in Britain for potting foods appears to be pretty well unique. It's very different from the French traditions of making pâtés or preserving foods for long periods of time in the *confit* style. These are the originals of our potted fish and meat spreads that used to play so large a part in sandwiches in the cricket pavilions of my youth. They are not, however, to be despised because of that. Freshly made and from good ingredients, they are one of the pleasures of the table. In Victorian times, and now, they are easy to make with small amounts of high quality left-overs. They keep in the fridge, sealed, for a week or more, making them ideal for unexpected guests. The technique in all of them is very similar and ideally needs a food processor as the old-fashioned method of pounding the ingredients through sieves is very arduous and time consuming.

POTTED TURKEY AND TONGUE

I must confess this is what I make with the remains of the festive board when no one else can face the left-overs any more. A week or so later, out of the fridge, it finds a new welcome.

SERVES 4

175 g (6 oz) boned cooked turkey	a pinch of cayenne pepper
175 g (6 oz) cooked tongue	salt and freshly ground black pepper
75 g (3 oz) butter, softened	1 tablespoon cranberry sauce (optional)
a pinch of ground mace	

Put the meat into 1 cm (½ in) cubes. Put into a food processor with 50 g (2 oz) of the butter, the mace, cayenne, salt and pepper and the cranberry sauce, if using. Process until smooth and well blended. Pack into small soufflé or china dishes. Melt the remaining butter and pour over the top to seal. This will keep for 7–10 days in the fridge if covered in cling film.

POTTED CHEESE Ⓥ

This can be used to rescue heels of cheese that have dried out too much to eat in the normal way. You can mix cheeses, but only hard cheeses should be used in this recipe.

SERVES 4

75 g (3 oz) butter	salt to taste
225 g (8 oz) hard cheese, finely grated	25 g (1 oz) snipped fresh chives or 1 teaspoon freeze-dried chives soaked in 2 teaspoons water
1 teaspoon made English mustard	
a pinch of mace	

Melt the butter in a pan, add the cheese to it and remove from the heat immediately. Put into a food processor with all the other ingredients and process until smoothly blended. Do not over-process otherwise the cheese will become stringy. Pack into china or glass pots, smooth the surface down and cover with cling film. Chill until set. This can be kept in the fridge for a week.

POTTED KIPPERS

Kippers have been going slightly out of fashion recently, despite the French passion for eating them raw, marinated in olive oil and black pepper. This recipe doesn't call for them to be eaten raw but cooks them in a way that gets rid of any problems with smell. What's more, the processing gets rid of any problems with bones too, so if kippers are something you like but can't cope with, this may be the answer.

SERVES 4

225 g (8 oz) kippers, whole or boned	½ teaspoon ground black pepper
75 g (3 oz) butter, melted	juice and grated rind of ½ small lemon
a good pinch of cayenne pepper	

Put the kippers into a jug into which they will fit completely and pour boiling water over them. Allow to stand for 5 minutes and then drain. Remove the skin and bones, put the kippers into a food processor, add the melted butter and all the other ingredients, and process until smoothly blended. You will not need to add any salt. Pack into pots and, if you wish to store for more than 2 or 3 days, cover with a little more melted butter. Sealed with cling film, these will then last for up to 10 days.

BREAD

CHEESE AND HERB BREAD

Flavoured breads like this one have suddenly become popular again in Britain. They've long had a great deal of popularity in America where a wide variety of recipes brought by the immigrant communities in the nineteenth century have persisted. This is the sort of bread that has sufficient flavour to be an ingredient in the meal, not just an accompaniment. A good rich vegetable soup is the perfect partner, or I like it with a ripe pear and some walnuts as the substantial end to a light meal. You can use a variety of cheeses, though some take better to cooking than others. My own favourites are Lancashire or Gruyère with some mature Gouda coming a very close second.

SERVES 4

½ cup of cut mixed green herbs (parsley, thyme, oregano, the green part of spring onions, marjoram or chives)	1 teaspoon salt
	250 ml (8 fl oz) water
10 g (½ oz) fresh yeast (or ½ a packet of dried yeast)	1 tablespoon sunflower or soya oil
	100 g (4 oz) grated cheese, Gruyère, Lancashire or mature Gouda
pinch of sugar	
350 g (12 oz) unbleached white bread flour	

re-heat the oven to 200°C/400°F/Gas 6, 180°C fan, top of an Aga roasting oven.

Chop the herbs finely and set aside. If using fresh yeast, mix it with a little warm water and a pinch of sugar and leave it to froth for about 10 minutes. Then mix the yeast (fresh or dry), the flour, salt, water and the oil together and knead either by hand or in a food mixer until the dough is smooth and elastic. Leave to rise in a warm draught-free place in a greased bowl until it doubles in size. This should take about an hour. Knead the dough again, adding the chopped herbs and half the grated cheese. Shape into a loaf, place in a loaf-tin and sprinkle the top with the remaining cheese. Leave to rise again in a warm draught-free place for about 35 to 40 minutes and then bake for 45 minutes. Make sure that the top doesn't burn. If it seems to be browning too fast, cover loosely with kitchen foil. To test that it's ready, tip out of the tin and tap the bottom. It should sound hollow. If not, replace on its side in the oven for another 5 to 10 minutes. Allow to cool on a rack before slicing and eating.

SPICE

GINGER

Ginger comes in a variety of forms, making it one of the most versatile spices, being used in both savoury and sweet dishes.

The ginger root is lemon perfumed, pungent and hot to taste. The woody, brown skin is removed and the inside either grated, chopped or thinly sliced. It is a staple ingredient in much oriental cooking. It is used in Chinese stir-fries, with fish and in many Indian and Thai dishes. It has medicinal qualities as a digestive, and is said to ease coughs and colds when made into a soothing hot tea. Simply boil up some peeled root in water for 20 minutes, strain and sweeten with honey.

Dried and ground ginger are used in baking, in cakes and biscuits.

Crystallized ginger is both hot and sweet. Being sugar-covered it is good eaten on its own and is also available covered in chocolate. It can be chopped and added to fools, ice-creams, biscuits, chutneys and preserves.

Stem ginger is bottled in syrup, this delicacy is delicious eaten on its own or on ice-cream.

GINGER FRUIT PUNCH

We tend to think of diluted fruit drinks these days as being just squashes but, in fact, the most marvellous flavours can be added to fruit to extend the quantity of the juice and to add to it a slightly tart or bitter edge. Punches are traditionally used at parties and on festive occasions and this one, with its combination of exotic flavours, makes an excellent and non-alcoholic contribution to many festivities.

MAKES OVER 1.5 LITRES (2¼ PINTS)

300 ml (10 fl oz) cold Earl Grey tea	juice of 2 lemons
150 ml (5 fl oz) pineapple juice	1 tablespoon caster sugar
300 ml (10 fl oz) fresh orange juice	600 ml (1 pint) ginger beer

Mix the tea and fruit juices together. Stir in the sugar and ginger beer. Taste – you may want to add a little more sugar. Chill well before serving. Ice cubes may be added just before serving.

MENU OF THE MONTH

STARTER
Frisée salad with Roquefort

MAIN COURSE
Leek and meatball pasta

PUDDING
Treacle tart

FEBRUARY

INTRODUCTION

February is the month for warming, generous foods but it's also a month in which it's important to make sure that you're getting all the vitamins and minerals you need from fresh fruits and vegetables. Our herb of the month, parsley, is particularly valuable in this respect. We tend to think of it only as something to add a little decorative colour but in fact it's rich in both iron and vitamins.

It's also a great time of the year for citrus fruits – lemons are particularly in good form and, with Seville oranges coming to the end of their season, now is the time to make marmalade. Fruit from the southern hemisphere and the tropics is also in good supply, particularly grapes, kiwi fruit and bananas. Of the winter vegetables, spring greens and cauliflower are at their best and, on the shelves of greengrocers and supermarkets, there's a wide range of beans – for example, the small, stringless varieties flown in from the Tropics.

On the fish front, it's domestic British fish that are at their best at this time of year, in particular the flat fish – sole and halibut, brill and skate, plaice and turbot – and the cheaper but extraordinarily delicious 'variety' soles like witch and megrim. For salads it's good to look for the unusual greens like the Chinese leaf which looks like a pale cos lettuce with a lovely crisp texture whether cooked or raw.

February, of course, is also a month in which St Valentine's Day and Shrove Tuesday, or Pancake Day, fall. Pancakes are worth eating at other times of the year than just Shrove Tuesday but there are a variety of different sorts here for you to try.

February

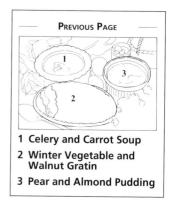

PREVIOUS PAGE

1 Celery and Carrot Soup

2 Winter Vegetable and Walnut Gratin

3 Pear and Almond Pudding

———— PRODUCE AT ITS BEST ————

Cauliflower ● *Green beans* ● *Chinese leaf* ● *Lemons* ● *Seedless grapes*
● *Bananas* ● *Forced rhubarb* ● *Poultry* ● *Cod*

STARTERS

CELERY AND CARROT SOUP ⓥ

Winter celery is at its best at this time of year, with an extra degree of crispness and flavour. Delicious eaten with cheese after a meal but also terrific made into a soup with a little texture left in. This dish can be augmented with a little chopped parsley or some crisp croûtons but is actually quite delicious eaten as it is with some crisp French bread.

SERVES 4

25 g (1 oz) butter	100 g (4 oz) onions, finely chopped
1 tablespoon oil	900 ml (1½ pints) chicken stock or water
450 g (1 lb) carrots, cut into chunks	salt and freshly ground black pepper
½ head celery, finely chopped	

Melt the butter in the oil in a pan and turn the carrots, celery and onions in the fat until well coated. Cook gently for 2–3 minutes. Add the stock or water and season generously. Simmer until the carrots are cooked through – about 15–20 minutes. Using a slotted spoon, remove the carrot pieces and purée them in a food processor with 1–2 cupfuls of the soup stock. When they are smooth, return them to the soup without puréeing the celery, which will retain its texture and a little bite. Check the soup for seasoning. You can, if you wish to enrich it, add a knob of butter or a little cream. Serve hot.

MINI SMOKED SALMON AND PARSLEY QUICHES

To make this dish you need what is known in Britain as a mini-Yorkshire pudding tin – a baking tin with four square-sided dents in it about 7.5 cm (3 in) across and about 2.5 cm (1 in) deep. We tend to use them for making individual Yorkshire puddings but in Europe they're used for making mini-sized quiches or tarts, and that's what I have in mind for them on this occasion. The filling of smoked salmon and parsley is pretty and delicate, and these are good for a special occasion or St Valentine's Day dinner. Off-cut pieces of salmon will do very well for this recipe.

SERVES 4

225 g (8 oz) shortcrust pastry	1 egg yolk
100 g (4 oz) smoked salmon	150 ml (5 fl oz) double cream
50 g (2 oz) fresh parsley, chopped	salt and freshly ground black pepper
1 egg	a pinch of freshly grated nutmeg

Pre-heat the oven to 220°C/425°F/Gas 7, 195°C fan, top of an Aga roasting oven.

Divide the pastry into four and either roll out and line the tart tins or divide into four and press the pastry into the tin until it fills the four indentations neatly. Cut the smoked salmon into small pieces about the size of a fingernail and divide between the pastry shells. Spread the parsley over the salmon. Beat the egg and egg yolk together with the cream and pour the mixture through a sieve into the tart cases. You may want to measure it into four cups first to make sure you get equal portions. Sprinkle with a little salt and pepper and the pinch of nutmeg and bake in the oven for 25 minutes until the pastry is lightly browned and the filling cooked and risen. Serve hot or warm.

CHINESE LEAF SALAD Ⓥ

This salad uses the crisp ingredients often found in a Chinese stir-fry vegetable dish but eaten as a salad without cooking. The dressing is one that's often used in South-east Asia with vegetables or vegetable salads, and although the ingredients may seem unusual, it's worth trying – you'll be converted without very much effort. It makes a good first course for a substantial meal or can be eaten with one or two other Chinese-style dishes as part of an Eastern dinner in its own right. You can use the large white radish, also known as dikon or mooli, instead of the bamboo shoots.

SERVES 4

450 g (1 lb) Chinese leaf, trimmed	100 ml (3½ fl oz) soy sauce
100 g (4 oz) tinned bamboo shoots, drained	50 ml (2 fl oz) cider or rice vinegar
225 g (8 oz) bean sprouts	2 teaspoons caster sugar
100 g (4 oz) carrots, cut into matchsticks	120 ml (4 fl oz) water
	a small bunch of fresh coriander or parsley
FOR THE DRESSING	a few coriander leaves to garnish
50 g (2 oz) roasted peanuts	

Cut the Chinese cabbage in half lengthways and then slice across into 1 cm (½ in) ribbons, discarding the heavy core at the base. Cut the bamboo shoots or radish into 1 cm (½ in) slices and then across again into matchstick-shaped shreds. Mix the cabbage, bean sprouts and shredded bamboo shoots and carrots together in a large bowl. Put the dressing ingredients in a food processor and process until well blended. Pour over the salad, toss, garnish with the coriander and serve.

MAIN COURSES

COD IN PARSLEY SAUCE

Many of us have bitter memories of fish cooked in parsley sauce from our schooldays, but properly made it can be a great treat – the fresh tang of the parsley balancing the richness of the white sauce and complementing the flaky meatiness of fresh cod. In fact, properly done, you realize why it was one of the most popular dishes in Victorian times and why it was emulated so widely and so catastrophically in so many school dining halls. It's particularly nice at this time of year because the bright green of properly made parsley sauce is not only very cheering but also full of nutritious goodness and vitamins.

SERVES 4

657 g (1½ lb) cod fillet, skinned	40 g (1½ oz) butter
1 tablespoon salt	salt and freshly ground black pepper
300 ml (10 fl oz) milk	generous pinch of freshly grated nutmeg
150 ml (5 fl oz) single cream	75 g (3 oz) fresh parsley, finely chopped
40 g (1½ oz) plain flour	juice of ½ lemon

Put the fish into a colander and sprinkle with the salt. Leave for 20 minutes over the sink and then rinse thoroughly. This firms up the fish. Put 5 cm (2 in) of water into a large pan into which the colander will fit without touching the water. Bring the water to the boil, place the fish, still in the colander, into the pan and put on the lid. Steam for 15 minutes until the cod is just done but still succulent.

Meanwhile, in a non-stick pan, whisk together the milk, cream, flour and butter and bring gently to the boil, whisking as you progress. Make sure you're whisking at the moment the liquid comes to the boil and you will wind up with a perfectly smooth and glossy sauce. Check for seasoning, add the nutmeg and then the parsley and lemon juice. The parsley should turn the sauce bright green. Carefully remove the cod and portion it on to warm plates. Coat thoroughly with the parsley sauce and serve with new potatoes or mashed potatoes and a simple vegetable like carrots or the stringless beans in all the shops at this time of year from Kenya and other exotic climes.

SPAGHETTI WITH PARMESAN AND PEAS ⓥ

We tend to think of pasta as something that has to be eaten with tomatoes in a sauce. This simply isn't true and many other countries, particularly those founders of pasta-eating – China and Italy – have recipes that have no tomatoes in sight. This is one of those, and combines some unusual ideas for eating pasta, but ones that will swiftly become firm favourites with you. It is most important to use tinned not frozen petit pois as they have a special flavour and texture.

SERVES 4

450 g (1 lb) spaghetti	50 g (2 oz) butter
400 g (14 oz) tin petit pois, drained	8 tablespoons freshly grated Parmesan
4 tablespoons light soy sauce	

Cook the spaghetti in plenty of boiling salted water until it is *al dente* (not too soft, with a little 'bite' left in it). Drain and stir in the rest of the ingredients. Serve immediately.

WINTER VEGETABLE AND WALNUT GRATIN

Gratins traditionally were dishes made with a sprinkling of breadcrumbs over the top but we've come to think of them as rather rich and creamy concoctions which are flashed under the grill or quick-baked in a hot oven. This is one of the latter kind, although there are breadcrumbs involved. It's a vegetarian dish with a variety of seasonal winter vegetables mixed into it to create a beautifully balanced and delicious meal in its own right.

SERVES 4

450 g (1 lb) parsnips	FOR THE SAUCE
2 teaspoons French Dijon mustard (not English!)	300 ml (10 fl oz) milk
25 g (1 oz) butter	40 g (1½ oz) plain flour
salt and freshly ground black pepper	40 g (1½ oz) butter
½ cauliflower	a pinch of freshly grated nutmeg
450 g (1 lb) spring greens	
1 large slice white bread, torn into pieces	
50 g (2 oz) walnut pieces	

Pre-heat the oven to 200°C/400°F/Gas 6, 180°C fan, top of an Aga roasting oven.

Peel the parsnips, cut them into 2.5 cm (1 in) chunks and cook in boiling salted water until tender. Drain them, reserving the cooking water. Mash them with the mustard and butter. Check for seasoning and use to line a gratin dish like a vegetable pastry. Break the cauliflower into small florets, add that to the water in which the parsnips were cooked, bring to the boil and simmer for 5 minutes then drain, reserving the cooking water. Arrange them on top of the parsnips. Wash the spring greens and cut them into 1 cm (½ in) ribbons. Put them into the boiling water in which the other vegetables have cooked and let them boil for just 1 minute. Drain them and reserve 150 ml (5 fl oz) of the water. Arrange the spring greens over the cauliflower pieces.

To make the sauce, mix the milk with the flour and butter and the reserved vegetable water, season well with salt, pepper and nutmeg and whisk thoroughly. Heat gently until the sauce thickens, whisking as you go. Pour the white sauce over the vegetables. Put the bread and walnuts in a food processor and process until they make a breadcrumb mixture. Sprinkle this over the top of the white sauce and bake in the oven for 15 minutes until the sauce is bubbling.

STUFFED CABBAGE

Although there is no tradition of stuffed cabbage in Britain, all over Europe there are different versions, ranging from the grand and complicated French ones – using a whole cabbage with the leaves opened and fillings laid into them – to the much simpler and more practical cabbage rolls of Eastern Europe. It's a very accommodating dish with all kinds of ingredients going in to stuff the cabbage, from vegetarian versions through to almost pure meat stuffings. The important thing is to make sure the filling is well flavoured, as bland stuffed cabbage has very few virtues. This version is not only in no danger of that problem but it's also very economical to make. Made in large quantities and served with rice or noodles – or equally well with lots and lots of mashed potatoes – it can cope with those occasions where you have to feed the horde but without damaging the purse too much. Use freeze-dried herbs if possible.

SERVES 6–8

4 large slices bread	18 medium to large green cabbage leaves, winter or savoy cabbage
675 g (1½ lb) lean minced beef	a few wooden toothpicks
175 g (12 oz) onions, finely chopped	2 pickled dill cucumbers, finely chopped
2 garlic cloves, finely chopped	250 ml (8 fl oz) water
1 teaspoon freeze-dried rosemary	500 ml (17 fl oz) passata
1 teaspoon freeze-dried thyme	1 tablespoon cider vinegar
1 teaspoon freeze-dried marjoram	1 tablespoon brown sugar
2 eggs	

Pre-heat the oven to 180°C/350°F/Gas 4, 160°C fan, bottom of an Aga roasting oven.

Turn the bread into breadcrumbs with a food processor or grater. Mix the breadcrumbs, meat, onions, garlic, and herbs together thoroughly, kneading them with your hands. Add the eggs and mix until the mixture moulds together. Dip the cabbage leaves into a pan of boiling water for 30 seconds then drain in a colander. Take a generous tablespoon of the meat mixture, place in the bottom of a cabbage leaf, roll up one turn, fold the sides in and continue rolling until the leaf is a complete cylinder. A toothpick may help hold the parcels together. Lightly oil a baking dish and lay the rolls in, fold side down so that they stay shut, packing them closely together so they don't move about. Mix the pickled cucumber with the water, passata, cider vinegar and sugar and pour over the cabbage rolls. Cover and bake in the oven for 45 minutes, basting with the juices once after about 20 minutes or so to prevent the cabbage rolls drying out at the top. Serve two or three rolls to each person with a spoonful of the sauce the cabbage rolls have cooked in poured over.

CHICKEN AND SWISS CHEESE BAKE

When this dish is made in Switzerland it's normally with the whole chicken with the cheese coating poured over it as it bakes. It's very pretty to look at but murder to carve, so I've made it a slightly crafty version by having the chicken portioned before I begin. The flavour, though, is unimpaired as the richness of the Swiss cheese (don't be tempted to use any other kind) perfectly complements the mild delicacy of the chicken. This is delicious with lightly roasted potatoes and plainly cooked vegetables as the cheese sauce is already rich enough.

SERVES 4

50 g (2 oz) butter	25 g (1 oz) plain flour
1 teaspoon paprika	salt and freshly ground black pepper
½ teaspoon ground bay leaves	2 teaspoons made French Dijon mustard
4 large chicken joints, breast or leg	1 teaspoon freeze-dried basil
300 ml (10 fl oz) milk	150 g (5 oz) Gruyère cheese

Pre-heat the oven to 180°C/350°F/Gas 4, 160°C fan, bottom of an Aga roasting oven.

Melt the butter in a pan, add the paprika and bay leaves and stir thoroughly. Dip the chicken pieces in the melted butter and lay them in a baking dish into which they will just fit. Bake them in the oven for 20 minutes. Using the remaining butter and, in the same saucepan, make a white sauce by whisking the milk, butter and flour together over a medium heat until the sauce thickens and goes glossy. Season generously, stir in the mustard and basil and then the grated Gruyère. Wait until the cheese is thoroughly melted and then, using a tablespoon, coat the chicken pieces. Return these to the oven to bake for another 20 minutes until the chicken is cooked through and the coating is browned and bubbling. Serve immediately, but warn your guests or family that the cheese sauce is extremely hot.

JUGGED HARE WITH RED CABBAGE

The cooking of hares seems to be surrounded with strange phrases and even jokes about catching it first. However, jugging was exactly what it sounds like – the hare was cooked in a tall jug with the minimum surface area available for evaporation so that the long slow cooking it required didn't leave the meat dried out. These days a jug is not essential as our ovens are rather more sophisticated and controllable, but the technique otherwise is unchanged and the marvellous accompaniment of casseroled red cabbage can be cooked in the oven at the same time. Many butchers have a game dealers' licence and can supply hare and almost all supermarkets do as well, though they may need 24 to 48 hours notice to get it. Ask whoever is supplying the hare to joint it for you and discard all the less salubrious bits like the head and the blood, despite what traditionalists say.

S E R V E S 4

FOR THE HARE	FOR THE RED CABBAGE CASSEROLE
1 hare, jointed	450 g (1 lb) red cabbage
25 g (1 oz) butter	225 g (8 oz) cooking apple
1 tablespoon oil	225 g (8 oz) onions, roughly chopped
1 large onion	1 tablespoon cooking oil
4 cloves	25 g (1 oz) brown sugar
2 bay leaves	2 tablespoons malt or cider vinegar
1 large sprig of fresh parsley	salt and freshly ground black pepper
900 ml (1½ pints) beef stock	
1 tablespoon redcurrant jelly	
2 teaspoons cornflour, slaked in a little water	
2 teaspoons made English mustard	

Pre-heat the oven to 170°C/325°F/Gas 3, 150°C fan, baking oven of an Aga. Fry the hare pieces in the butter and oil until lightly browned. Put them into a heavy casserole. Peel the onion, but don't cut it up, and stud it with the cloves. Place it in the casserole with the hare, bay leaves and parsley. Pour over the beef stock. Cover the casserole tightly; you may find a piece of foil helps if you've got a loose-fitting lid, and cook in the oven for 1½ hours.

Meanwhile, trim and wash the red cabbage and slice it across into 1 cm (½ in) ribbons. Core but don't peel the cooking apple and roughly chop that. Turn them in the oil until they are glistening and the onion has begun to go translucent. Add the sugar and malt or cider vinegar, season generously and cover. Place in the oven with the hare for the last 45–60 minutes cooking.

When the hare is cooked, remove the pieces from the liquid. Measure 300 ml (10 fl oz) of liquid into a pan and whisk in the redcurrant jelly, slaked cornflour and mustard. Bring to the boil over a medium heat, whisking as you go. It will thicken and take on a gloss. If the sauce goes too thick, as the mustard can thicken quite considerably as well, add a little more of the cooking liquid. Serve the hare with its sauce, plenty of mashed potato and the red cabbage direct from the casserole.

PUDDINGS

CRAFTY CREPES SUZETTE

This is a very crafty recipe made with the crêpes you will find the directions for in the bread section of this month's recipes. Crêpes Suzette were originally a very complicated and grand recipe that began with grating the rinds of oranges and lemons using lump sugar. It finished with a dramatic piece of flambéing in front of the diners by a maître d'hotel who'd been practising for years. I'm not in favour of any of those activities as they take an enormous amount of time for a result that's very little distinguishable from the crafty version given below. Just don't tell anybody you haven't been working for hours.

SERVES 4

50 g (2 oz) butter

120 ml (4 fl oz) fresh orange juice

2 tablespoons orange and lemon marmalade

grated rind of 1 lemon

8 crêpes (see p. 39–40)

1–2 tablespoons brandy or rum (optional)

In a large frying-pan, melt the butter until it foams. Add the orange juice and marmalade and stir gently until the whole mixture melts together. Sprinkle on the grated lemon rind and then add the crêpes one by one, making sure they are coated in the sauce. Fold them into quarters and pile them on one side of the pan as you go. You should just about be able to get eight pancakes into a 30 cm (12 in) pan using this method. If you feel like risking your eyebrows you can at this point flambé them with 1–2 tablespoons of brandy or rum, making sure that the whole of the alcohol is burnt off before you serve the dish otherwise it will taste terrible. If you just want to enjoy the pancakes as they come, serve them hot straight out of the pan on to warm plates, two to a person, with a good spoonful of the sauce that should still be swimming around a little bit in the bottom of the pan.

PEAR AND ALMOND PUDDING

One of the great unsung combinations in cooking are pears and almonds. Indeed, pears and most kinds of nuts seem to go especially well together. This is a very simple pudding to make and can be made, if you like, in individual soufflé dishes, in which case it comes as a rather grand piece of presentation as the pear pieces are buried in the golden almond confection.

SERVES 4

2 large, not too ripe, Comice or Williams-type pears	50 g (2 oz) self-raising flour
25 g (1 oz) caster sugar	75 g (3 oz) soft brown sugar
½ teaspoon vanilla essence	3 eggs
100 g (4 oz) ground almonds	175 ml (6 fl oz) milk

Pre-heat the oven to 190°C/375°F/Gas 4, 170°C fan, bottom of an Aga roasting oven.

Peel, halve and core the pears. Poach for 5 minutes in just enough water to cover with the caster sugar and vanilla essence. Take the pears out of the syrup and allow to cool. (The syrup makes a marvellous basis for a fruit salad.) Mix together the ground almonds, flour and soft brown sugar. Whisk the eggs with the milk and beat into the flour and almond mixture until you have a smooth batter. Place the pears in a buttered china soufflé or flan dish, or individual buttered flan or soufflé dishes, and pour the almond mixture over the top. Smooth down and bake in the oven for 30–35 minutes until the almond mixture is fully risen, set and golden on top with flecks of brown. Do not let it brown too much but make sure it is cooked through. The skewer test, pushing a skewer in and making sure it comes out without any smearing on it, will guarantee this. Serve the pudding immediately with a little pouring cream.

CHRISTINE'S BAKED AMERICAN CHEESECAKE

These days we tend to think of cheesecakes as a sort of cream mousse with a fruit topping. Certainly there is a tradition for cheesecakes of that sort, but there's another tradition, much older, for cooked cheesecakes, much richer in texture and taste than the chilled variety. This is one of those, preserved, as so many European recipes have been, by being transported across the Atlantic by immigrants in the nineteenth century. While this is eaten cold, it's a real *cheese*cake with a marvellous combination of sweet and savoury characteristics.

SERVES 4–6

225 g (8 oz) digestive or marie biscuits	120 ml (4 fl oz) single cream
75 g (3 oz) butter, melted	½ teaspoon salt
7 tablespoons caster sugar	2 eggs, separated
450 g (1 lb) curd cheese	finely grated rind of 1 lemon
25 g (1 oz) butter, softened	1 heaped teaspoon plain flour

Pre-heat the oven to 180°C/350°F/Gas 4, 160°C fan, bottom of an Aga roasting oven.

Crush the biscuits with a rolling pin. Stir in the melted butter and 1 tablespoon of the sugar. Use this to line a 23–25 cm (9–10 in) spring-form cake tin, pressing the mixture on to the bottom of the tin. Blend the curd cheese, softened butter, cream, salt, remaining sugar, egg yolks and lemon rind, then add the flour. Beat well. Whisk the egg whites until stiff then fold into the cheese mixture. Pour into the prepared tin and bake for 1 hour. Leave to cool before cutting into slices to serve.

PRESERVES

MARMALADES

February is the perfect month for making marmalade with Seville oranges (the bitter orange that grows in the south of Spain) still in generous supply, and both lemons and grapefruits at their peak. Marmalades can be made from a wide variety of combinations of fruit but I have three suggestions here: a classic straight Seville, Oxford-style marmalade, orange and lemon, and a multi-citrus fruit version. All marmalades are made by a similar technique which combines cooking the peel of the fruit first to tenderize it and then adding it to a jam made from the fruit juices. If you're making marmalade, try not to use an aluminium saucepan as the fruit is very acidic and it's widely held these days that aluminium and acid cooking is not the best combination. Marmalades need a little time to mature, so when you've bottled them try and keep them for at least a month before you use them. We have some in our store cupboard that go back four or five years and the flavour is quite remarkable.

A hint, by the way, on sterilizing bottles for marmalades and jams. It is possible to do them with boiling water and baking in ovens, but much the simplest way is using one of the commercial sterilizers supplied for babies' bottles. Rinse the bottle thoroughly with it and then swill out with a little boiling water to remove any lingering flavours. Warm the jars before filling with hot marmalade to prevent them from cracking.

Crafty Crêpes Suzette

SEVILLE OXFORD MARMALADE Ⓥ

MAKES ABOUT 2.25 kg (5 lb)

1.5 kg (3½ lb) Seville oranges

2 lemons (unwaxed if possible)

450 g (1 lb) dark Barbados or muscovado sugar

1.25 kg (2½ lb) preserving sugar

Halve and squeeze the juice from the oranges and lemons, keeping the pips aside. Cut the peel into thin or thick strips, depending on your inclination. Cover the peel with cold water, bring to the boil then drain, discarding the water. Measure the juices into a pan and make up to 1.75 litres (3 pints) with either fresh orange juice or water. Add the peel. Wrap the pips and any attached membranes in a piece of muslin or netting. Add to the peel and juices and simmer for 30 minutes until the peel is translucent. Remove the pips. Add the Barbados or muscovado sugar and stir, off the heat, until dissolved, then add the preserving sugar. (This is special sugar which helps clarify the marmalade; some contains pectin to help it set.) Stir until that is dissolved then bring the marmalade to a gentle simmer. Cook for a further 20 minutes and test for setting by dropping a teaspoonful on to a cold saucer. It should jelly and not be possible to pour it around the saucer. If it's still runny, cook for another 10–15 minutes or so until the jellying test works. Ladle into sterilized jars, cover with a circle of greaseproof paper and seal immediately.

ORANGE AND LEMON MARMALADE Ⓥ

This is often called St Clements marmalade.

MAKES ABOUT 2.25 kg (5 lb)

900 g (2 lb) unwaxed lemons

900 g (2 lb) Seville oranges

25 g (1 oz) fresh ginger root, crushed

1.25 kg (2½ lb) preserving sugar

Halve and squeeze the juice from the lemons and oranges, reserving the pips. Shred the peel very finely. Blanch the peel by placing in a pan of cold water, bringing to the boil and draining, discarding the water. Measure the juices into the pan, making up to 1.75 litres (3 pints) with water and/or bottled lemon juice if necessary. Add the peel and the ginger and the pips tied in a piece of muslin. Simmer for 30 minutes until the peel is tender and translucent. Remove the pips and stir in the sugar off the heat until it is thoroughly dissolved. Simmer the marmalade until setting point is reached, testing the mixture on a cold saucer for jellying. It should begin to set after about 30–40 minutes of simmering. Ladle into sterilized jars, cover with a circle of greaseproof paper and seal immediately.

MULTI-CITRUS MARMALADE Ⓥ

Almost any citrus fruit, and a number of other ingredients like rhubarb and ginger, can be turned into marmalade, but a combination of the more exotic citrus fruit makes an unusual and flavourful marmalade.

MAKES 1.75 kg (4 lb)

1 pink grapefruit	2 limes
1 sweet orange	1.75 litres (3 pints) water
2 lemons	1.5 kg (3 lb) preserving sugar, warmed

Pare the rind from the grapefruit then cut away the thick layer of pith. Cut the flesh into chunks, removing the pips. Place the flesh into a preserving pan and the pith and pips onto a large muslin square. Cut the orange, lemons and limes in half and squeeze the juice into the pan. Carefully cut the rind from the pith, putting the pith and pips onto the muslin. Shred the rind and add to the pan. Tie the pips and pith securely in the muslin and add to the pan along with the water. Simmer for 1½ hours until the liquid has reduced by half. Squeeze the muslin and remove. Add the sugar and stir until dissolved then boil rapidly for 20 minutes. Test for setting by placing a spoonful on a cold saucer – it should wrinkle on the surface when touched after a couple of minutes. Boil for another 5 minutes if it is still too runny. When ready, take off the heat and leave to stand for 15 minutes. Stir to mix the peel then ladle into sterilized jars, cover with a circle of greaseproof paper and seal immediately.

BREADS

PANCAKES

We don't tend to think of pancakes as bread, although in many parts of the world the technique we use for making them is the basis for bread-making. There are, however, far more pancakes than the ones we eat traditionally on Shrove Tuesday, although of course that day does fall in this month of February. So here are three traditional but very different kinds of pancake, one from Britain, one from France and one from America, although that is a British style which lost favour towards the end of the eighteenth century but the Americans continued, particularly at breakfast time.

CREPES

These are the French pancakes that originated in Brittany, or at least that's what the Bretons claim. Nowadays it's possible to buy all kinds of amazing electronic devices for making them, but the method is simplicity itself once you've realized that they are really meant to be so thin you can almost see through them. The secret is in making the batter and allowing it to stand for at least 30 minutes before you begin to cook. Any good, large frying-pan will do, and I myself favour either a really well seasoned, old, black iron type or a good, modern, thick, non-stick surface pan. You can toss them if you like but a fish slice serves the purpose equally well.

MAKES 16 PANCAKES

225 g (8 oz) fine plain flour	1 tablespoon oil (not olive oil)
a good pinch of salt	350 ml (12 fl oz) beer, water or orange juice
2 eggs, beaten	

Mix the flour, salt, beaten eggs and oil together and add the liquid of your choice: beer or water for savoury pancakes, orange juice for sweet ones. Whisk thoroughly until the batter is smooth then put to rest for at least 30 minutes in the fridge. Up to 1½ hours won't hurt it. Very lightly grease a heavy frying-pan and heat it gently but steadily until it is hot enough for a drop of water to dance on it. Don't be tempted to slosh oil into it – a good wipe with a piece of oil-impregnated kitchen paper is fine. Pour a generous tablespoon of the batter into the pan and swirl it round, covering as much area as you can. There should be just enough to cover the bottom of a 25 cm (10 in) pan. It will set and go curly at the edges and may be so thin that there are even a few holes in places where bubbles burst. Do not panic! Let it set for 30–45 seconds, gently ease the edges up with a fish slice or spatula and turn the pancake over. Cook it for another 45 seconds or so then place it on a warm plate. You can cook all the pancakes, one after the other, stacking them with a piece of greaseproof or silicone paper between them if you wish, or serve them as you cook them. They're delicious with a little icing sugar and lemon juice, equally nice with slivered almonds and apricot jam or grated chocolate and whipped cream.

OAT PANCAKES

In the north of England and Scotland there is a tradition for very substantial pancakes made with oatmeal. They were often made to be eaten with savoury foods like sausages or with eggs, or even just on their own with a knob of butter and some salt and pepper.

MAKES 8 PANCAKES

100 g (4 oz) fine oatmeal	300 ml (10 fl oz) water
50 g (2 oz) self-raising flour	2 tablespoons plain yoghurt
a good pinch of salt	1 tablespoon oil or melted butter

Mix together the oatmeal, flour and salt. Mix together the water and yoghurt then stir in the oil or butter. Combine the mixtures and stir well. Leave to mature for at least 20 minutes. Drop tablespoonfuls into a pan, spread with the back of a spoon and, cook for 2 minutes a side. Serve with honey and cream.

AMERICAN-STYLE PANCAKES

American pancakes are a very different business from the light, lacy French version. They are solid, slightly risen and never more than about 7.5 cm (3 in) across. They're eaten in what are known as stacks, sometimes ridiculously high, with maple syrup, butter, and often, at breakfast time, with what we would think of as a full English breakfast. I don't really recommend that, but the pancakes are delicious, and on their own are a slightly lower in cholesterol version of a substantial breakfast, even with a tablespoon of maple syrup and a knob of butter to help them along. They also make a good basis for very interesting puddings; they go well with ice-cream and/or berry fruits like strawberries and raspberries and sliced peaches or apricots.

SERVES 4

100 g (4 oz) plain flour	1 egg, separated
1 tablespoon sugar	1 tablespoon melted butter
a pinch of salt	a little butter for frying
250 ml (8 fl oz) milk	

Sift the flour with the sugar and salt. Make a well in the centre, add the milk and egg yolk and beat until smooth. Add the butter. Beat the egg white until stiff then fold it into the batter. Heat a little butter in a frying-pan and, when hot, add a small ladle full of batter. Cook gently until bubbles appear on the surface of the pancake. Turn over and cook for 30 seconds more. Keep warm whilst you cook the rest. These *are* delicious eaten with a knob of butter and maple syrup.

HERB

PARSLEY

Parsley is the most widely known herb in the world. It is rich in vitamins A, B and C. There are two varieties, curly and the flatleaf continental type.

It is eaten raw in salads and sandwiches, sprinkled on cooked vegetables and used as a garnish. Chewing parsley is said to help neutralize garlic breath.

It is a wonderful addition to many cooked dishes such as soups, stuffings and omelettes. Parsley sauce is a perfect accompaniment to poached fish and vegetables made by adding a generous amount of finely chopped parsley to a basic white sauce. The stalks help to flavour stocks and stews on their own or as part of a bouquet garni. The colour adds a brightness to the presentation of many dishes especially those without much green in evidence.

DRINK

LEMONADE

With lemons at their peak at the moment, this is a time to make lemonade. You may want to remember the recipe as well for high summer when lemons are again, from a different part of the world, in generous supply and the drink is exceptionally refreshing. Lemonade is a great source of vitamin C, something at this time of year we need for our well-being as well as for the drink's taste. The timing's important in this recipe – don't try and vary it or you'll lose on flavour and gain on bitterness.

MAKES ABOUT 1.2 LITRES (2 PINTS)

4 lemons, preferably unwaxed
175 g (6 oz) caster sugar
1.2 litres (2 pints) boiling water

Cut the lemons up into small pieces about the size of a hazelnut, skin, pip and all. Place in a large jug and pour the boiling water over them, stirring generously. Leave to stand for exactly 10 minutes. Strain through a wire or nylon sieve into a clean jug or container and stir in the sugar until it's dissolved. Do not be tempted to squeeze the lemon bits or to leave them to steep for longer. Allow the juice and sugar mixture to chill and then use it as the basis for fresh lemonade, diluted to taste. It will probably need at least a 2:1 dilution with still or fizzy water. It's also delicious drunk hot with a sprinkling of cinnamon and perhaps a small spoonful of honey.

MENU OF THE MONTH

STARTER
Chinese leaf salad

MAIN COURSE
Chicken and Swiss cheese bake

PUDDING
Crafty crêpes Suzette

CRAFTY TIPS FROM THE CRAFTY COOK

● Buy unwaxed lemons whenever possible – all you are losing is the artificial shine and you gain fewer pesticides in your diet.

● When frying in butter, add a little oil to the frying pan first. This stops the butter burning. When a recipe calls for butter only, use your ears! The moment the butter stops hissing, put in whatever you are cooking. If you delay, the butter will brown and you will have to start all over again.

● Good quality non-stick saucepans and frying pans will revolutionize your washing up as well as your waistline – you won't need to use so much fat or oil for frying. It really is not worthwhile buying cheap pans. Spend a bit more in the first instance and you will still happily be using them in ten years, not scraping bits of burnt food off a no longer non-stick surface! And buy the right cooking utensils to go with your non-stick cookware.

INTRODUCTION

Traditionally March was the month in which people planted the seeds that would provide the harvests of summer and autumn to tide them through next winter and spring. These days, with amazing fruits and vegetables shipped, or perhaps flown in would be a better description, from all over the world, March is another month of plenty. From the Tropics come an abundance of pineapples; the new green-skinned grapefruit known as sweeties, because of their lack of bitterness; kumquats, baby oranges that you can eat whole, rind and all; and kohlrabi, that extra-ordinary vegetable which is actually grown above ground but looks and tastes like a mild and delicate turnip. Mangetout peas are here from the Spanish greenhouses, and watercress, fresh radishes and the first appearance of the season of the famous lollo rosso lettuce enrich the salad bowls once again.

All kinds of native fish are still in generous supply with shellfish, particularly mussels and scallops, being at their most delicious. Sea trout, or sewin as it's known in Wales, which has pink flesh rather like delicate salmon, is on the menu again.

But if March contains some of the first real intimations of spring, it's also still the last month of winter. You need some comforting dishes as well. Pineapple milk shake, yes, but also warming dishes of baked Portuguese-style hake, stuffed baby chickens and traditional rice pudding to keep us cosy until the summer's warmth arrives.

PREVIOUS PAGE

1 Kohlrabi Stuffed with Chicken

2 Sorrell and Watercress Soup

3 Rhubarb Fool

──────PRODUCE AT ITS BEST──────

Kohlrabi ● *Watercress* ● *Radishes* ● *Chinese leaf* ● *Pineapples*
● *Grapefruit* ● *Rhubarb* ● *Kumquats* ● *Dates* ● *Poussin* ● *Mackerel* ●
Hake ● *Sea trout* ● *Scallops*

STARTERS

SORRELL AND WATERCRESS SOUP Ⓥ

Watercress soup, known as soupe cressonière, is one of the great classic dishes of French cuisine, and in certain great house traditions of English cookery it also puts in a frequent appearance. But often we forget how simple and delicious it is to make. Here I've added sorrel, with its lemony taste, to the watercress which has a lovely peppery flavour. It is a good idea to keep a little of the cress aside to purée with the cooked soup at the very end to give it a little extra punch.

SERVES 4

350 g (12 oz) potatoes	1 bunch of sorrel (5–6 leaves)
225 g (8 oz) onions	1.2 litres (2 pints) chicken stock or water
25 g (1 oz) each cooking oil and butter	50 g (2 oz) double cream
1 large bunch fresh watercress	

Peel the potatoes and onions and cut into cubes. Fry those gently in the oil and butter until the onion is translucent. Wash the cress and sorrel thoroughly and put aside a third of the cress. Add the sorrel and remaining cress to the potato and onion mixture and turn in the butter for a minute. Season generously, add the stock or water (water produces a lighter, clearer-tasting soup; stock a richer one) and simmer for 12 to 15 minutes until the potato is completely tender. Do not cook for longer than this or the cress will lose its impact. Put into a food processor, or liquidizer, with the retained third of the bunch of cress and process until you reach a smooth purée. Return to the saucepan, check for seasoning and stir in the double cream. Serve immediately. Small croûtons or toasted slivered almonds are delicious when floated on the top of this soup.

SOUSED MACKEREL

Oily fish, the herring and mackerel family, have become particularly popular, smoked in recent years but they're also perfect for delicate home pickling – not to preserve them for long periods of time but merely to add a little piquancy to their texture and flavour. They're also very good value as they are still some of the cheapest fish we can buy. This recipe makes a marvellous first course for family or friends and also, eaten with hot new potatoes and a cucumber salad, makes a delicious light lunch or high tea in its own right. Get your fishmonger or supermarket counter to fillet the mackerel for you, it saves a lot of time and makes the dish much easier to prepare. It's an English version of the French favourite, Maquereaux au vin blanc.

SERVES 4

175 g (6 oz) onions	juice of half a lemon
4 peppercorns	300 ml (½ pint) water
4 berries allspice	300 ml (½ pint) white wine or cider vinegar
1 small red chilli, fresh or dried	4 × 225–275 g (8–10 oz) mackerel, filleted
1 teaspoon of salt	

Peel and finely slice the onion. Crack the peppercorns and allspice berries, and put all the ingredients, except the mackerel fillets, into a saucepan with the cold water. Bring to the boil and simmer for 10 minutes. Place the mackerel fillets on a flat, non-metallic dish. Pour the warm, but not boiling, vinegar mixture over them. Cover the dish with clingfilm once the liquid has cooled and leave for a minimum of 24 hours and up to 3 days in the fridge, turning them once a day if you're keeping them. Serve them with brown bread and butter, adding a little of the onion to each drained fillet or with hot new potatoes and a cucumber salad.

GRATIN OF SCALLOPS AND MUSHROOMS

Scallops, those shellfish that look like fried eggs, are one of the great culinary treats. They're very rich and solid and you don't need a lot for a portion, which is just as well as they are in no way cheap. They are, however, worth the cost for the occasional special meal or moment of self-indulgence. Make sure you buy fresh not frozen ones, they are at their best now, and ask the fishmonger or fish counter to give you the deep half shell. Although it's perfectly possible to make this dish in china ramekins or individual dishes, serving it in the shell always seems to me to have a little extra charm.

SERVES 4

4 large fresh scallops	¼ teaspoon freshly grated nutmeg
150 ml (5 fl oz) milk	50 g (2 oz) Gruyère or Lancashire, grated
150 ml (5 fl oz) double cream	100 g (4 oz) button mushrooms, trimmed and halved
25 g (1 oz) plain flour	
25 g (1 oz) butter	

Gratin of Scallops and Mushrooms

rim the scallops, remove the orange coral and cut the white flesh into eight pieces for each scallop. Put the milk into a non-stick saucepan, add the scallops except for the corals, bring to the boil and simmer for 5 minutes. Remove the scallops from the milk and keep aside. Add the cream, flour, butter and nutmeg and whisk gently over a low heat until the sauce thickens and goes smooth. Add the cheese and allow that to melt without letting it boil and go stringy. Place the washed and dried scallop shells in a baking tray and pre-heat the grill. Put a tablespoon of the cheese sauce mixture into each one, then the scallops pieces, evenly divided, topped with a piece of coral. Lay the mushrooms around the scallops and pour the cheese sauce over the whole thing, making sure that the mushrooms and scallops are covered. Place under the grill for 4–5 minutes until the sauce is bubbling and brown. Serve immediately with plenty of French bread.

MAIN COURSES

PORTUGUESE HAKE

Hake is a fish we tend to associate with the West Country but it's very widely available at this time of year and if your fishmonger or fish counter doesn't have it, ask for it. It's a lovely meaty fish with a generous flavour that responds well to this combination of ingredients. It's a favourite fish of the Portuguese and they cook it in this marvellous mixture of onion, tomato and parsley. It can be eaten with rice, mashed potatoes or lots of crusty bread on its own with a vegetable to follow. If you can't find hake, thick cod steaks will make a very satisfactory substitute.

SERVES 4

750 g (1½ lb) hake fillet, skinned	juice of 1 lemon
450 g (1 lb) Spanish onions, thinly sliced	salt and freshly ground black pepper
4 tablespoons olive oil	50 g (2 oz) fresh parsley
450 g (1 lb) tin chopped tomatoes	

ut the hake into portion-sized pieces. Cook the onions in a large frying-pan with the olive oil very gently for 10 minutes until they are softened but not browned. Add the tomatoes and lemon juice, bring to the boil, season generously and simmer for another 5 minutes. Place the hake pieces on top of the tomato and onion mixture, spoon a little over, cover the pan and simmer for 10–12 minutes until the fish is cooked through and flakes when tested with a fork. Place the fish on individual plates for serving. Stir the parsley into the tomato and onion mixture. Check for seasoning and pour over and around the fish to serve.

FILLETS OF SEA TROUT IN CREAM SAUCE

Sea trout is at its early best in March and goes perfectly with this light cream, saffron sauce. If you can't find sea trout then some of the very excellent farmed salmon or giant pink-fleshed trout will do very well for the recipe, but if you're using salmon you may need to cook it for a minute or so longer. This dish is particularly delicious with one of the basmati and wild rice mixtures that you can now buy pre-packeted in most supermarkets. The combination of the delicate fish, rich sauce and slightly nutty rice makes a lovely balance. Save any other vegetables for a separate course either before or after the fish, as the flavours are so delicate that they might otherwise be overwhelmed.

SERVES 4

50 g (2 oz) butter
750 g (1½ lb) sea trout fillets, skinned
1 packet saffron powder or generous pinch of saffron strands (leave out rather than substitute)
250 ml (8 fl oz) double cream

In a frying-pan that will take all the fish in one go, heat the butter until it's foaming. Add the fish, skin-side up, and fry gently for 3 minutes. Turn over and fry for another 3–4 minutes until cooked through but not dry. Meanwhile, mix the saffron powder of strands with 2–3 tablespoons of boiling water and allow to steep. This will produce a fragrant and bright gold liquid. Transfer the fish to warm serving plates and season lightly. Add the cream and saffron liquid to the pan and stir to mix thoroughly. Bring to the boil then pour over and around the fish.

CHINESE VEGETARIAN NOODLES WITH BLACK BEAN SAUCE Ⓥ

While we're familiar with stir-fry vegetables, we don't know much about one of the most interesting and easily achievable techniques in Chinese cookery, using noodles to turn a simple stir-fry into a major meal. The one or two special ingredients are available in almost every supermarket and all speciality food shops. Look for Chinese noodles which tend to come in little tight crinkly bunches and are cooked in 3–4 minutes. Also look for jars of black bean sauce; there are a number of brands offering this rich and slightly pungent condiment. The other ingredients are vegetables that are in good shape at this time of the year and add a welcome crunch to the dish. This is a main course in its own right or can be served for a large Chinese meal as one of a number of dishes.

SERVES 4

1.2 litres (2 pints) water	2 tablespoons soy sauce
350 g (12 oz) Chinese egg noodles	1 garlic clove, finely chopped
3 celery sticks	100 g (4 oz) mushrooms, thickly sliced
1 bunch spring onions	175 g (6 oz) tin chopped tomatoes
5 tablespoons cooking oil (not olive)	3 tablespoons black bean sauce
225 g (8 oz) bean sprouts	

Bring the water to the boil in a large pan, add the noodles and simmer for 4 minutes. Drain well then run under cold water to stop them sticking. Trim the celery and spring onions. Split the celery into sticks and cut those across the grain into 1 cm (½ in) slices. Cut the spring onions into 2.5 cm (1 in) lengths, splitting any thick white ends in half lengthways. Put 2 tablespoons of the cooking oil into a large frying-pan or wok, add the celery and spring onions and stir-fry over a high heat for 3 minutes. Add the bean sprouts and cook for 1 minute. Add the drained noodles and the soy sauce and toss together until thoroughly mixed and hot. In a separate pan, heat the remaining oil and fry the garlic until pale gold. Add the mushrooms then the chopped tomatoes and finally the black bean sauce, and stir thoroughly together. Place the noodle mixture in an oval serving dish and pour the tomato and black bean sauce along the middle of the dish. Serve each person a portion of the main noodle mixture and some of the tomato and black bean savoury mixture on top.

KOHLRABI STUFFED WITH CHICKEN

Kohlrabi is a crisp, delicate vegetable with one of two coloured skins – green or purple. The colour on the outside makes no difference at all to the colour on the inside, which is creamy white, or to the flavour, which is half-way between crisp cabbage stalk and mild turnip. They are very pleasant steamed and eaten with a white sauce or fried gently with a little garlic and herbs, but they are also delicious when stuffed and baked. Because the flavour is so delicate, the stuffing itself needs to have quite mild flavours, and I have a combination of chicken and fromage frais that suits very well. These stuffed kohlrabi can be used either as a main course or as part of a larger hot buffet.

SERVES 4

4 medium-sized kohlrabi, about 175–225 g (6–8 oz) each	1 tablespoon snipped fresh chives or 2 teaspoons freeze-dried chives
225 g (8 oz) cooked chicken	250 ml (8 fl oz) low-fat fromage frais
50 g (2 oz) Mozzarella (Lancashire or Cheddar are okay substitutes)	salt and freshly ground black pepper
½ onion, finely chopped and sautéed	4 tablespoons fresh breadcrumbs

re-heat the oven to 180°C/350°F/Gas 4, 160°C fan, bottom of an Aga roasting oven.

Trim and peel the kohlrabi and cut each one in half. Scoop out the centre of the vegetable using a sharp knife and a spoon – a grapefruit knife is very helpful for cutting out the centre. Leave about a 5–10 mm (¼–½ in) thick shell. You can use the removed kohlrabi on another occasion steamed and covered in white sauce or buttered or herbed. Bone and skin the cooked chicken and cut it into 5 mm (¼ in) cubes. Cut the cheese into the same sized cubes and add the onions, chives, fromage frais, salt and pepper. Stir thoroughly and keep aside. Drop the kohlrabi shells into boiling salted water and let them simmer for 10 minutes. Remove and drain thoroughly in a colander. Fill with the chicken mixture and top with a few of the fresh breadcrumbs. Bake in the oven for 30 minutes until the kohlrabi are cooked and the filling is bubbling.

POUSSIN STUFFED WITH KUMQUATS AND PINE NUTS

Poussin are the small-size chickens that are available everywhere now. They're actually fully mature chickens grown specially for their size and have a considerable though delicate flavour. They are also quite substantial and a whole stuffed poussin is probably more than one person can eat on their own, especially if the meal has more than one or two courses. I find that half a poussin per person cooked in this way makes a wonderful main course in a dinner that has a starter and a dessert to go with it. This is particularly nice served with some of the green beans or mangetout peas that are newly arrived on the market. They are so out of season in Britain they make such a refreshing reminder of the pleasures of summer to come.

SERVES 4

100 g (4 oz) long-grain or basmati rice	salt and freshly ground black pepper
25 g (1 oz) butter	8 kumquats (tiny baby oranges the size of the first joint of your thumb), quartered and seeded
2 tablespoons olive oil	
50 g (2 oz) pine nuts	2 poussin, oven-ready
1 tablespoon orange marmalade	
1 bunch spring onions, finely chopped (white and green parts)	FOR THE SAUCE (optional)
a pinch of freshly grated nutmeg	250 ml (8 fl oz) fresh orange juice

re-heat the oven to 200°C/400°F/Gas 6, 180°C fan, middle of an Aga roasting oven.

Put the rice to boil in 600 ml (1 pint) of salted water for about 8–9 minutes until it's barely cooked. Drain it thoroughly. Melt the butter in the oil and fry the pine nuts gently for 2–3 minutes until golden. Add the marmalade and allow that to melt. Add the drained rice and the spring onions. Add the nutmeg and season generously with salt and pepper, remove from the heat and mix together thoroughly. Mix the kumquats with the rice. Stuff the poussin carefully with the rice, putting any extra stuffing into a baking dish. Season the poussin and roast them in the oven with the surplus stuffing, if any, in the baking dish alongside, for 50 minutes. Check if the chickens are done by putting a skewer or sharp knife into the thigh. If they show any pink juices allow them to cook for another 10 minutes and check again. To serve, split the poussins in half lengthways with a large sharp knife, pile the stuffing on to warm plates and cover with the half poussins, skin-side up.

If you with to make a little sauce to go with the chicken, add the fresh orange juice to the roasting pan, bring to the boil, stirring all the bits in, and serve separately.

PUDDINGS

RHUBARB FOOL

March sees the first of the delicate, forced pink rhubarb arrive. It's grown to be specially young and tender and, what's more, to keep that pretty pink colour when it's cooked. Older outdoor rhubarb goes rather a sludge green. Rhubarb is actually a very versatile ingredient, making everything from chutney to tarts, but at this stage, when it's new and delicate, it suits nothing quite so well as a fool – one of those lovely eighteenth century mixtures of fruit and cream that seem to be a British speciality. It makes a wonderful pudding, especially eaten with those thin, crispy, ginger-flavoured biscuits known as ginger thins.

SERVES 4

450 g (1 lb) forced pink rhubarb	150 ml (5 fl oz) double cream
2 tablespoons water	150 ml (5 fl oz) low-fat fromage frais
175 g (6 oz) caster sugar	Grated chocolate, to garnish

Trim the rhubarb, wash it and cut it into 2.5 cm (1 in) lengths. Put it in a pan with the water and simmer gently until it begins to break up into a pulp. Do this as carefully as you can so that the rhubarb doesn't dry out. When it's very well pulped, stir in the sugar and allow it to dissolve without boiling the mixture. Allow to cool. Beat the double cream until it's thick. Add the fromage frais, a spoonful at a time, whisking that in as well. You will find that the mixture stays thick and creamy but only has half the fat as the same amount of double cream. When the rhubarb is cool, stir that into the cream mixture. You can put it into a china basin or into individual wine glasses and chill for at least 1 hour before serving. Garnish with grated chocolate.

SPICED GRILLED GRAPEFRUIT

We always tend to think of grapefruit as a cold fruit, something to be eaten at breakfast time to clear the palate, but in fact it's substantial and well-flavoured enough to benefit from the occasional heating. This recipe turns it into a light and delicious pudding with more than a hint of the spices of the West Indian islands from which the fruit first came.

SERVES 4

2 large, ripe, preferably pink, grapefruit	½ teaspoon ground mace
50 g (2 oz) muscovado or soft Barbados sugar	1 teaspoon Angostura bitters

Cut the grapefruit in half and loosen the segments as though you were going to eat it cold at breakfast time. Mix the sugar with the mace and sprinkle that over the grapefruit and then sprinkle a few drops of Angostura bitters over each of them in turn. Pre-heat your grill to very hot, place the grapefruit on a piece of foil on the grilling tray and then grill for 5–6 minutes. The rind of the grapefruit may begin to char but the sugar should caramelize and protect the flesh itself. When the flesh is hot and before anything really burns, serve immediately in bowls that will keep the grapefruit steady while you eat them.

TRADITIONAL RICE PUDDING

While many countries eat rice, savoury and sweet, it seems to be only in Britain that we maintain the tradition of a simple milk pudding made with the very short Carolina rice that cooks almost to a mush. Don't be tempted to try this with any of the longer-grained rices as it simply won't produce the same result. There are regional variations to this recipe. In Wales they often include a couple of tablespoons of jam into the heart of the pudding, in the north of England they sometimes give it a couple of stirs as it's cooking to make sure the crust gets mixed in and has a chance to re-form two or three times. Try any of the variations, but try the basic method on its own first. It's one of those classic puddings where the flavour of nutmeg mixed into the milk adds just a hint of the exotic to what might otherwise be everyday cooking.

SERVES 4

40 g (1½ oz) short-grain pudding rice	25 g (1 oz) butter
600 ml (1 pint) rich Channel Islands-type milk	½ teaspoon freshly grated nutmeg
50 g (2 oz) caster sugar	

Pre-heat the oven to 160–170°C/300–325°F/Gas 2–3, 160–170°C fan, bottom of an Aga roasting oven.

Put the rice to soak in the milk for 5 minutes then bring gently to the boil. As soon as it reaches boiling point, decant the whole mixture into a pudding basin which will take it with 1–2.5 cm (½–1 inch) around the sides left free. Stir in the sugar until it dissolves, add the knob of butter and sprinkle the nutmeg over the top. Bake in the oven for 1–1½ hours until all the liquid is absorbed and the pudding has a golden skin on the top. It can be eaten hot or cold. It is so delicious you may consider making double the quantity.

PRESERVE

PICKLED RED CABBAGE Ⓥ

Pickled red cabbage is a very English tradition but a very good one nonetheless. This is the perfect time of year for it, with the last of the winter's red cabbages available. Pickled like this, with a touch of sugar added it makes an interesting addition to all kinds of cold meat plates and salads in the summer. There is also an excellent tradition of eating it with hotpots and Irish stew type casseroles in the North of England, a tradition which I find particularly attractive as the sharp and crunchy edge is a marvellous contrast to the rich juices and flavours of the stews. Make sure that you use jars without metal seals that will come into direct contact with the vinegar or pickle.

MAKES 4 × 450 g (1 lb) JARS

1 × 1.25 kg (2½ lb) red cabbage	25 g (1 oz) pickling spice
175 g (6 oz) salt	2 tablespoons caster sugar
1.5 litres (2½ pints) light malt pickling vinegar	

Cut the cabbage in half and remove the hard core and any discoloured outer leaves. Shred very finely across the grain. Put a layer of cabbage (about an eighth of the volume) in a glass or china bowl and then sprinkle with salt. Add the next layer of cabbage, then salt, and continue to do this until all the cabbage and salt has been used up. Leave to stand for 24 hours. This is called dry brining and removes the water from the cabbage so it doesn't dilute the pickling vinegar. Pour off the liquid that comes out of the cabbage and rinse it thoroughly, straining it in a colander and leaving it to stand for 5 minutes. While the cabbage is being salted, bring the vinegar to the boil with the pickling spice wrapped in a piece of muslin or a spice ball. Add the sugar and simmer for 5 minutes. Allow to cool. Put the cabbage into the jars and pour the cold vinegar over the cabbage, ensuring that it comes right to the top. Seal the jars. This pickle will keep well in a cool dark place and is at its best about two to three months after bottling.

HERB AND ONION BREAD

This is a very savoury loaf, delicious enough to eat on its own and especially good with a bowl of soup. You can vary the ingredients to suit what you happen to have on the pantry shelf, or growing in the garden, and you can use spring onions instead of the ordinary round ones I've suggested. Indeed, they give a lovely green fresh flavour to the whole loaf. Do experiment – a clove of garlic, a little celery leaf, all produce breads of a surprisingly delicate yet rich flavour.

SERVES 4

1 onion, peeled and chopped	½ cup fresh mixed green herbs (parsley, thyme, oregano and marjoram) chopped, or, for dried herbs a generous teaspoon of each, with a double one of your favourite
1 tablespoon oil	
350 g (12 oz) white bread flour	
½ packet (1 teaspoon) instant dried yeast	1 teaspoon salt
	250 ml (8 fl oz) water

Pre-heat the oven to 200°C/400°F, Gas mark 6.

Fry the onion very gently in the oil until translucent, but not brown. Set aside. Mix the flour, yeast, onion, herbs and a teaspoon of salt and knead or process together. Add the warm water. Knead for about a minute and a quarter, making sure half way through, that all the ingredients are blended in thoroughly. Leave to rise, in a greased bowl, in a warm draught-free place for about an hour. Knock the air out of the dough and knead again for 1 minute. Place in a loaf tin and allow it to rise to double its volume. Then bake it for 45 minutes. Test to see if it is cooked by tipping it out of the tin and tapping on the base. It should sound hollow. If it's not done, give it another 5 or 10 minutes. I have been known to put a layer of cheese slices along the top of this loaf about half way through cooking. After it's had a chance to rise and set properly in the oven, it makes cheese, herb and onion loaf, but that's a personal self-indulgence and I suggest you only do it the second time you try.

SPICES

NUTMEG AND MACE

A whole nutmeg is hard and brown, shaped like a small chocolate egg with a woody texture. The spice is available both whole and ground. Freshly grated from the whole nut is best. It has a scented, more characterful flavour that should be used sparingly as an addition to many sweet and savoury dishes.

Try grating a little into a basic white sauce or into mashed potatoes. It will enhance spinach, moussaka and Brussels sprouts.

Its exotic flavour lends itself to baking, milk and rice puddings, egg custards and stewed fruit, especially rhubarb.

Mace is the golden filigree casing surrounding the nutmeg. It is available as blades or ground. Although it is less widely used nowadays it was often used as an addition to dishes in the eighteenth century. Try adding a couple of blades to a lamb stew or to pickled eggs or mushrooms. The addition of ground mace to puddings, spiced cakes and rice pudding is also good.

DRINK

PINEAPPLE MILK SHAKE

Pineapples, particularly from the West African area – the Ivory Coast, Nigeria and Ghana – are plentiful at this time of year and in very good condition. As well as eating them in the conventional way, you might like to consider making a milk shake out of some of the bits left over when making a fruit salad. It's delicious and refreshing, and a pinch of salt added to it makes it a surprisingly adult flavour as well. Make it just before you drink it as the froth dies away fairly quickly.

MAKES ABOUT 1.5 LITRES (2½ PINTS)

225 g (8 oz) fresh pineapple	a pinch of salt
1 banana	a dusting of freshly grated nutmeg
175 g (6 oz) ice cubes	For those with a sweet tooth:
250 ml (8 fl oz) fromage frais	50 g (2 oz) caster sugar
450 ml (15 fl oz) milk	

Cut the fruit into 2.5 cm (1 in) cubes and place with all the other ingredients in a liquidizer or food processor. Turn on slowly at first until the mixture begins to become a purée, turning up to full speed at the end to produce a froth. Make sure it's been whisked enough for all the ice to have been crushed completely. Pour into glasses and serve with straws.

MENU OF THE MONTH

STARTER
Sorrell and watercress soup

MAIN COURSE
Poussin stuffed with kumquats and pine nuts

PUDDING
Rhubarb fool

CRAFTY TIPS FROM THE CRAFTY COOK

● Here's a tip for peeling oranges so you get rid of as much pith as possible. First, roll the fruit around gently on a hard surface under the palm of your hand then, using a sharp knife, cut down into the orange's skin with the tip to a depth of not more than ½ cm (¼ inch) so it is marked in quarters. When you peel back the skin on each quarter, the pith will come off with it.

● Invest in a liquidizer. Better still, buy a food processor/liquidizer. A number of manufacturers make machines that combine these two with juice extractors. The perfect situation is to have one of these machines and a small electric or battery-operated mixer or whisk.

● Instead of fiddling around trying to weigh one ounce (25g) of something, use a tablespoon. One slightly rounded tablespoon is roughly equal to one ounce.

APRIL

INTRODUCTION

Easter tends to dominate April as Christmas does December, although there are fewer traditional foods to eat at Easter-time. There are old traditions for eating lamb, but in fact British lamb hasn't arrived by April, and it's a tradition that's not surviving very well against the onslaught of a second serving of turkey. The small turkeys that are widely available at this time of year are ideal for a small family or celebratory meal, and here you will find a slightly unusual way of serving one as a centrepiece for a buffet.

Although it's spring, there are comparatively few vegetables around to prove it, although some of the first baby carrots are available and make marvellous but simple dishes, in their own right. Fish supplies tail off in April as well, except for the shellfish – crab, crayfish and lobster – which are at one of their peaks both for flavour and supply. They often combine well with the flavours of lemons and limes which are also readily available and in good condition at this time of year.

Salads are just starting to come into their own with especially good supplies from our southern European neighbours, particularly Spain and Portugal: cos lettuces, salad cresses and cucumbers all emerging newly refreshed from the winter. Spring greens, appropriately enough, are a good choice at this time of year and there's a marvellous soup called Caldo Verde that makes use of them in a slightly unusual way. We have a similar tradition in Britain of soup made not with spring greens but with nettle tops, an interesting alternative if you fancy experimentation. Wear gloves to pick the nettles, but once they're exposed to cooking there's no sting left in them at all, but they do have a nice bright green flavour.

On the bakery side, there are two very traditional Easter choices – simnel cake and hot cross buns – both traditions surviving from medieval times but still current favourites well worth making at home to recover the real flavour.

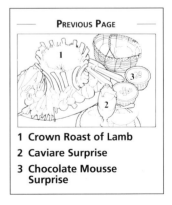

PREVIOUS PAGE

1 **Crown Roast of Lamb**
2 **Caviare Surprise**
3 **Chocolate Mousse Surprise**

April

PRODUCE AT ITS BEST

Spring greens ● *Nettles* ● *Cos lettuce* ● *Limes* ● *Poultry* ● *New season's lamb* ● *Salmon* ● *Monkfish* ● *Crab* ● *Lobster*

STARTERS

HOT POTTED CRAB

Cleaning a crab is quite hard work because it's so fiddly, but it is very rewarding because of the wonderful taste of really fresh crab meat. One good medium-sized crab will feed four people if handled the right way, and this hot potted version is most certainly one of the right ways. If you don't have a fresh crab you can buy frozen or ready-prepared crab meat which is also good for this dish. Serve it in individual-sized ramekins or mini soufflé dishes. You can prepare it in advance and put it into the oven at the last minute just before serving.

SERVES 4

100 g (4 oz) brown crab meat	40 g (1½ oz) Parmesan, grated
175 g (6 oz) white crab meat	175 g (6 oz) fromage frais
2 teaspoons Dijon or Bordeaux made French mustard	juice of ½ lemon
salt and freshly ground black pepper	

Mix the brown crab meat and the mustard together, check for seasoning and use to fill the base of four individual soufflé dishes or ramekins. Mix 25 g (1 oz) of the Parmesan with the white crab meat, fromage frais and the lemon juice, check for seasoning and pile on top of the brown crab meat, smoothing the top down. Sprinkle with the remaining Parmesan. This can be kept in the fridge for up to 6 hours.

Pre-heat the oven to 200°C/400°F/Gas 6, 180°C fan, middle of an Aga roasting oven. Fifteen minutes before eating, place the ramekins on a baking tray in the hot oven to heat through until they are bubbling on the surface. Eat with lots of wholemeal or granary bread and butter.

TUNISIAN CARROT SALAD Ⓥ

This is a bright, vivid salad both in appearance and flavour and makes a tasty though not too substantial starter for a meal with other exotic flavours or tastes in it. As with so many similar dishes, there are variations and versions for almost every household in North Africa, but this crafty version incorporates the British liking for vegetables that still have a little crispness and bite to them.

SERVES 4

750 g (1½ lb) carrots	1 teaspoon caster sugar
2 garlic cloves, chopped	½ teaspoon salt
120 ml (4 fl oz) olive oil	grated rind and juice of 1 lemon
½ teaspoon ground turmeric	few mixed salad leaves to garnish
½ teaspoon ground cumin	

Peel the carrots and cut them into 5–7.5 cm (2–3 in) lengths and then split those lengths into batons about 5 mm (¼ in) across. Heat the garlic in the olive oil in a heavy pan, add the spices and cook gently until the garlic is pale gold but not burned. Add the carrots, turn them thoroughly in the mixture and cook over a very gentle heat for 2 minutes. Barely cover the carrots with water, add the sugar and salt, and bring to the boil. Simmer for 7–8 minutes, checking to make sure you don't overcook the carrots; they should still retain a little crispness. Allow them to cool in their liquid then drain them, sprinkle with the lemon rind and pour over the lemon juice, turning them thoroughly. Chill for 1 hour before eating. Serve on some mixed salad leaves.

CALDO VERDE Ⓥ

This soup comes from Portugal, a country with a surprisingly different style of cuisine from its Iberian neighbour. In its origins, Caldo Verde was one of those solid, everyday peasant soups that constituted a central part of a main meal in a basically agricultural community. In a slightly refined version, however, it makes a delicious and refreshing soup, light enough to be served as a first course, substantial enough in larger quantities to make a meal in its own right with some bread, cheese and fruit. You need to use spring greens or the dark green spring cabbages, not the white ones, for this dish.

SERVES 4

3 tablespoons olive or cooking oil	salt and freshly ground black pepper
225 g (8 oz) onions, diced	1.2 litres (2 pints) light chicken stock or water
450 g (1 lb) potatoes, diced	450 g (1 lb) spring greens

Heat the olive oil and fry the onions and potatoes gently for 4–5 minutes. Season generously and add the chicken stock or water. Bring to the boil and simmer for 15–20 minutes until the vegetables are soft. Purée or mash the soup so that the potatoes and onions are mixed to a rough paste. Wash, trim and shred the spring greens into ribbons not more than 5 mm (¼ in) across. Discard any lumpy or heavy pieces of stalk. Bring the puréed soup to the boil and add the spring greens. Cook vigorously for 3–4 minutes until the greens are as brightly coloured as possible. Serve immediately with, if you care for it, a knob of butter in each serving bowl. This soup doesn't re-heat well as the bright colour and flavour of the spring greens vanishes on a second cooking.

CAVIARE SURPRISE

This is a crafty adaptation of a very grand dish served in three-star French restaurants. There it is made with real caviare but while I quite like the real stuff I've never really reconciled myself to the price it costs for a mouthful, and in fact I prefer the pink salmon caviare and trout caviare that are available very widely at a fraction of the price. This recipe makes a really special first course for a dinner party and, in its French form, is known as 'surprise eggs' because of the form of presentation. If you've got pretty eggcups it makes the whole thing look even more attractive.

SERVES 4

4 large free-range eggs	50 ml (2 fl oz) soured cream
50 g (2 oz) butter	1 × 25 g (1 oz) pot caviare – sturgeon, salmon or lump fish roe
juice of ½ lemon	

Cut the tops off the eggs at the pointed end very carefully with a sharp knife, leaving a lid of about 2.5 cm (½ in) in each case. Tip the eggs into a bowl and rinse and lightly dry the emptied egg shells. Place those ready in egg cups. Five minutes before you are ready to eat, scramble the eggs in the butter and lemon juice until they're cooked and beginning to go grainy but still slightly soft. Pile back into the egg shells, leaving a little space at the top. You may have some scrambled egg left over. Put 2 teaspoons of soured cream on top of each egg and then a teaspoon of your chosen caviare on top of that. Cover the egg with the reserved shell lid and serve immediately with thin, hot buttered toast.

MAIN COURSES AND VEGETABLES

PINK AND WHITE FISH KEBABS

April is the last month for a while for fish from British waters to be at anything like their best. This recipe celebrates and makes use of that end-of-season availability with some delicate fish kebabs. You can substitute other fish for the salmon and monkfish in the recipe but it doesn't work nearly so well, as the fish needs to have a certain density in its flesh to stay and cook well on the kebab sticks. These kebabs look especially good on a dish of long-grain or wild rice into which you've stirred a tablespoon or two of chopped parsley with a knob of butter before serving. The combination of colours is extremely attractive and needs no other vegetable served with it. Try a salad afterwards or the Moroccan carrots before it.

SERVES 4

350 g (12 oz) salmon, boned and skinned	1 teaspoon freeze-dried oregano
350 g (12 oz) monkfish, boned and skinned	1 teaspoon freeze-dried basil
grated rind and juice of 1 lime	1 garlic clove, chopped
2 tablespoons olive oil	8 bay leaves
1 teaspoon freeze-dried rosemary	

Cut the fish into 2–2.5 cm (¾–1 in) cubes. Stir the lime rind, lime juice, oil, dried herbs and garlic together and marinate the fish in the mixture for at least 2 hours.

Pre-heat the grill and line the grilling tray with foil, both for heat reflection and reduced washing up. Thread a cube of salmon, a cube of monkfish, a bay leaf, another of salmon and monkfish, another bay leaf and another salmon and monkfish on to each of four skewers. If you have more fish, add more cubes in between the two bay leaves Pack them closely together and as close to the sharp end of the skewers as you can. Grill the kebabs for 2–3 minutes a side, turning at least twice. The fish should be seared brown on the outside but still moist in the middle. You may want to brush them with a little more marinade as they grill. Serve hot on wild or long-grain rice mixed with parsley and butter. You may, if you wish, bring the marinade to the boil and pour a little of that over the kebabs and rice as you serve them.

CHICKEN TAGINE WITH PRESERVED LEMON

Tagines are the great speciality dishes of Morocco and its North African neighbours. They're a kind of casserole, usually vividly flavoured and eaten in comparatively small quantities as part of a multi-coursed meal. There are special dishes for cooking them in, with lids rather like tall pointed hats, and as many variations as there are cooks. For our pattern of eating, however, they make a lighter style of casserole eaten with some rice or couscous, that rice-like wheat grain that is the staple food of North Africa. It's widely available in Britain and most of the packs are pre-cooked and have simple instructions for preparing the couscous itself. This tagine is flavoured with the pickled lemons that are our main preserve this month but if you haven't got preserved lemons you can use fresh lemon zest – the flavour's not the same but is still delicious.

SERVES 4

packet or pinch of ground saffron or saffron strands	1 garlic clove, finely chopped
	1 preserved lemon (see p. 75)
300 ml (10 fl oz) chicken stock made from the chicken carcass or stock cube	25 g (1 oz) green olives (optional)
50 g (2 oz) butter	½ teaspoon ground cinnamon
1 × 1.5 kg (3 lb) chicken, cut into 9 portions	salt and freshly ground black pepper
100 g (4 oz) onions, finely chopped	

re-heat the oven to 170°C/325°F/Gas 3, 160°C fan, top of an Aga roasting oven.

If you are using the saffron strands, crush them with a pestle and mortar or a bowl and a spoon, and place them in a teacup. Heat the chicken stock and add 3–4 tablespoons of that to the saffron and allow to steep. It will go bright gold and give off a wonderful aroma. Heat the butter in a flameproof casserole dish into which all the chicken will just fit. Add the chicken and turn in the butter for 2–3 minutes until lightly golden. Add the onion and garlic and continue to cook gently for another 3–4 minutes. Split the preserved lemon into quarters, strip away any flesh and cut the preserved rind into 5 mm (¼ in) dice. Add those to the chicken and onion mixture with the olives, if using. Pour over the stock and then the saffron mixture, stirring thoroughly to make sure that the whole of the chicken is flavoured and coloured. Season with cinnamon, salt and a little black pepper. Cover and cook gently in the oven for 45–50 minutes. It's a good idea to stir the dish half-way through to make sure all the flavours blend.

STEAK AU POIVRE

There are many versions of this classic French dish, from grilled steaks to ones flambéed in brandy, using variations on green, black or even red peppercorns. Some of them can be overpoweringly flavoured and this crafty recipe, while still redolent of the rich aromas of pepper, is a moderate version that suit most palates. Do make sure you buy well-hung steak; the meat should be almost maroon in colour and should (ask your butcher) have been aged for 2–3 weeks before you buy it.

SERVES 4

2 tablespoons black peppercorns	25 g (1 oz) butter
4 sirloin steaks, about 175–225 g (6–8 oz) each	150 ml (5 fl oz) double cream
1 tablespoon oil	25 ml (1 fl oz) lemon juice

ut out on your work surface a large piece of greaseproof paper and grind the peppercorns through a pepper grinder or spice mill and spread them evenly on the greaseproof. Trim the steaks, cutting off any surplus fat and making sure you sever the line of sinew along the back of the steak which can make them curl as they cook. Lay each one gently on to the greaseproof and turn over to coat lightly with the ground pepper. You will probably have some surplus pepper left over – discard this with the greaseproof paper. Heat the oil in a large frying-pan into which all the steaks will fit. Add the butter and as soon as it sizzles, lay in the steak. Cook for 2 minutes, turn and then cook for 2 minutes more for rare, 3 minutes for medium and 4 for ruined. Transfer the steaks to hot plates. Add the cream and lemon juice to the pan and stir the mixture round thoroughly. Bring to the boil then pour over the steaks and serve immediately with new potatoes and a side salad.

CROWN ROAST OF LAMB

A crown roast is a butcher's invention but a very handsome and spectacular one. It's one of the easiest of roasts to prepare and serve, and yet without question the most spectacular to look at. It consists of two best ends of necks that have been chined and tied around together so that they look like a crown. When roasted they can be carved simply by separating out the individual chops and serving two or three to a portion. It can be roasted as it comes, although there is a tradition of putting the kidneys into the centre of the crown under a little lid of fat and roasting them too. However, I much prefer my rather fruity and nutty stuffing which is more to the modern taste. Roast or mashed potatoes and a simple vegetable like baby carrots or tropically grown string beans is ideal. To get a crown of lamb ask your butcher at least 24 and preferably 48 hours in advance. Any supermarket with a butchery counter will also be able to obtain or prepare a crown of lamb for you but will also need similar notice. Be prepared to pay a little extra for the skill in preparation above the price of just the meat.

SERVES 6

175 g (6 oz) dried apricots	100 g (4 oz) shelled walnut pieces
1 bunch spring onions, finely chopped	1 egg
175 g (6 oz) fresh breadcrumbs	1 crown of lamb
25 g (1 oz) chopped fresh parsley	

Soak the apricots in water or tea overnight or for about 6 hours.

Pre-heat the oven to 190°C/375°F/Gas 5, 170°C fan, middle of an Aga roasting oven.

Mix together the spring onions, breadcrumbs and parsley. Roughly chop the apricots and crush the walnuts in your hands leaving a number of quite reasonable-sized pieces. Mix those into the breadcrumb mixture and add the egg to bind it. Place the crown of lamb in your roasting tray and, with it in position, stuff with the breadcrumb and apricot mixture. You might want to put a piece of foil over the top as this not only helps the stuffing to cook but also prevents the bones from burning. Roast in the oven for 60–70 minutes if you like your lamb pink and 70–80 if you like it well done. To serve, slice the crown down into individual chops and serve a good spoonful of the stuffing with each helping. You can make gravy in the normal way with the pan drippings.

TURKEY ROSE

Turkey has become a popular meat at Easter, the only time apart from Christmas we really cook whole birds. This is a suggestion for a small bird that makes a very attractive centrepiece for a cold buffet, allowing the cook a little time to enjoy the holiday celebrations as well. As it's to be eaten cold, perfect accompaniments are a rice salad, an orange and watercress salad and perhaps a green salad tinged with red from the lollo rosso and oak leaf lettuces that are available now. It makes for effortless, and with this centrepiece spectacular, dining.

SERVES 4

1 × 4 kg (9 lb) turkey	300 ml (10 fl oz) tomato juice
1 lemon	25 g (1 oz) gelazone or gelatine
large bouquet garni consisting of 2 sticks of celery, 25 g (1 oz) fresh parsley, 4 bay leaves and 4 sprigs of fresh thyme	celery or parsley leaves
	25 g (1 oz) red peppercorns
600 ml (1 pint) water	

Pre-heat the oven to 170°C/325°F/Gas 3, 160°C fan, bottom of an Aga roasting oven.

Make sure the turkey is thoroughly defrosted if it's a frozen one. Remove all the giblets and bits and pieces and place it on a rack in a baking tray. Put the lemon cut in half into the turkey. Put the bouquet garni ingredients in the baking tray underneath it, pour in the water and, using a large sheet of foil, cover the turkey and seal the foil to the edges of the baking tray. It does not need to be hermetically sealed, but the intention is that the turkey should steam as much as roast. Cook in the oven for 15 minutes per 450 g (1 lb). Check at the end of this time that the turkey is cooked through by inserting a skewer at the thickest part of the thigh. If the juices run clear the turkey is cooked, otherwise cook longer and check again. Remove it from the tray and the foil and allow to cool. Strain the juices left in the pan and add to the tomato juice. Follow the instructions on the packet of the gelazone or gelatine and mix with the tomato juice and cooking juices. Keep this warm. When the turkey is cool, use a ladle or a thick clean kitchen brush to spread the gelatine mixture over the turkey. Pop it back into the fridge immediately and wait until the coating sets. Do this three or four times, building up a pink coated layer over the turkey – it will make it look glossy and rosy. When it's sufficiently coated, decorate in the appropriate places with some greenery – celery leaves or parsley and the red peppercorns. Allow the remaining gelatine mixture to set in the fridge and, using a non-porous chopping board, chop it into rough cubes. Put in as a dressing around the turkey and keep the whole thing chilled until ready to present and then carve. Serve a little of the highly flavoured chopped jelly with each portion of turkey.

FIFFINES POTATOES (V)

I'm indebted for this recipe, as with so much of my early enthusiasm, to Robert Carrier, in whose long-past restaurant in Islington in London I first discovered this dish. This is a very simple way of cooking potatoes but the addition of the bread cubes and herbs makes them not only an ideal accompaniment to simply cooked meats but also a delicious course in their own right, or part of a tapas-style meal. You can shallow or deep-fry these – I'm not sure it makes any difference to the calorie or cholesterol count.

SERVES 4

750 g (1½ lb) yellow-fleshed potatoes, Desirée, Cyprus, etc.	1 teaspoon fresh or freeze-dried thyme
4 thick slices white bread	1 teaspoon fresh or freeze-dried oregano
oil for frying	salt and freshly ground black pepper

Peel the potatoes and cut into 1 cm (½ in) cubes. Trim the crusts off the bread and cut those slices likewise. In a deep-fryer or in a large frying-pan with a 5–10 mm (¼–½ in) of oil in it, fry the bread cubes until they are crisp and golden. Do not let them go more than gold or they will burn as they continue to cook when you remove from the pan on to kitchen paper. Keep them aside and add the potatoes to the oil. Fry those for 7–8 minutes until gold and crispy on the outside. Drain those thoroughly, mix with the herbs, and season generously with salt and black pepper. Mix in the bread cubes and serve immediately – they do not improve with keeping.

Apple Slices with Apricot

PUDDINGS

CHOCOLATE MOUSSE SURPRISE

Chocolate mousse is one of the favourite puddings on every dining table. It's extremely easy to make at home but it tends to be regarded as rather a complicated and restaurant-orientated process. Here is a recipe that includes the basic way of making chocolate mousse but adds an unexpected additional ingredient that produces the justification for the name of 'surprise' in the title. It is some finely chopped orange peel coated in chocolate, a Belgian speciality that is now available in almost all good confectioners and chocolate shops. For making the mousse itself by the way, do try to find some of the excellent cooking chocolate that's available, not the stuff that's called cake coating but chocolate that has at least 50 per cent chocolate solids in it (check the ingredients list on the wrapper).

SERVES 4

100 g (4 oz) top quality bitter chocolate	4 eggs, separated
juice of ½ orange	25 g (1 oz) orange peel in chocolate, chopped
25 g (1 oz) butter	

Melt the chocolate very carefully over a low heat in a non-stick pan with the orange juice. As it melts, stir it. It will go glossy and thick. When it is all completely melted but not boiling, add the butter and stir till that has melted thoroughly too. Allow to cool slightly. In a mixing bowl, beat the egg yolks until pale and lemon-coloured. Add to the chocolate mixture off the heat and stir carefully until well mixed. Beat the egg whites until absolutely stiff but not grainy. Fold carefully into the chocolate – try to lose as little air as you can from the beaten egg whites. Half-fill individual soufflé or ramekin dishes, sprinkle on the chopped orange peel in chocolate and cover with another layer of chocolate mousse mixture. Chill for at least 2 hours in the fridge before serving.

APPLE SLICES WITH APRICOT

One of the simplest recipes to make, if you have a fruit bowl in the house and a jar of apricot conserve or jam you can have this on the table even for unexpected guests within ten minutes. No need to admit how simple it is, though, as people really enjoy it. The best apples for this at this time of year are the excellent Cox's or Braeburns that come from New Zealand.

SERVES 4

50 g (2 oz) butter	100 g (4 oz) apricot conserve or jam
4 eating apples	25 g (1 oz) slivered almonds
½ teaspoon ground cinnamon	

In a large, preferably non-stick frying-pan, melt the butter gently until it foams. Core the apples but don't peel them and divide them into 12 segments. An apple cutter is ideal for doing this in a few seconds. Add to the butter before it browns and sauté gently for 3–4 minutes, stirring occasionally. Sprinkle with the cinnamon and add the apricot jam, stirring carefully not to break the apples but to spread the jam throughout the pan. Bring to a high heat until the jam bubbles. Serve immediately sprinkled with the slivered almonds and, if you like, with a little single cream.

SIMNEL CAKE

Simnel cake's named, so legend has it, after one Lambert Simnel. He was a pretender to the throne of Henry VII, the first Tudor king, who, after he defeated the coup attempt, instead of executing Simnel decided really to get rid of him by a more humane method and put him into the kitchens to be a kitchen boy. He appeared to have an aptitude for it, however, and rose to be a famous pastry cook. This cake, now eaten traditionally at Easter, is supposed to be named after him. I ought to say that the legend has a number of holes in it but it's a nice enough story and the cake is delicious. It certainly features one of the aspects of medieval cookery that would have been in evidence at the time of Henry VII and that is the love of almonds and marzipan. It has been eaten at Easter time ever since.

SERVES 4

175 g (6 oz) butter	1 egg yolk
100 g (4 oz) caster sugar	1 teaspoon vanilla essence
175 g (6 oz) self-raising flour	
50 g (2 oz) ground almonds	**TO DECORATE**
1 teaspoon baking powder	225 g (8 oz) marzipan
2 eggs	milk or apricot jam

re-heat the oven to 170°C/325°F/Gas 3, 160°C fan, bottom of an Aga roasting oven. Grease and line a 20 cm (8 in) cake tin, preferably loose-bottomed.

Cream together the butter and sugar. Sift the flour, add the ground almonds and baking powder, and mix with the butter and sugar mixture. Beat the eggs and egg yolk with the vanilla essence and add those to the mixture. Put the mixture in the prepared tin and bake in the oven for about 1 hour. Test the cake to see that it is done using a skewer; it should come out clean if it's cooked. If it's still smeary, cover the cake with a butter paper or a piece of foil and cook for another 10 minutes or so then test again. Allow to cool for 5 minutes and then turn out on to a rack. When it's cold, roll out the marzipan and, using a little milk or apricot jam brushed over the cake to help it adhere, cover the cake across the top and, if you like, around the sides. Traditionally the cake was gilded using an egg yolk mixed with a little saffron powder and was decorated with rolls of marzipan to resemble Easter eggs.

BREAD

HOT CROSS BUNS

Being Easter, hot cross buns are the obvious bakery item for the month. They come from a tradition that goes back to Renaissance time and they are a delicious mixture even if you don't choose to mark them with a special pastry cross on the top. They're also very good split and toasted, rather like a highly spiced tea bun.

MAKES 8 BUNS

15 g (½ oz) fresh yeast	25 g (1 oz) mixed peel
300 ml (10 fl oz) warm water	½ teaspoon ground cinnamon
50 g (2 oz) demerara sugar	½ teaspoon ground cloves
25 g (1 oz) butter	½ teaspoon ground mace
450 g (1 lb) unbleached white flour	25 g (1 oz) caster sugar
a pinch of salt	50 ml (2 fl oz) water
25 g (1 oz) currants	
25 g (1 oz) sultanas	

ix the yeast with a couple of tablespoons of the warm water and a teaspoon of the demerara sugar and leave to froth. Rub the butter into the flour and salt until it resembles fine breadcrumbs. When the yeast is frothy add that with the remaining warm water and knead to a supple dough. You can do this in a food processor or by hand. As flours absorb different amounts of water you may need a little more flour or a drop more water to make the dough firm and soft but not sticky. Put to rise in a warm place for 45–50 minutes.

Knead the dough again, adding the remaining demerara sugar, the fruit and spices. Divide into eight portions, roll these into bun shapes and place on a greased baking sheet. If you wish to mark them you may do it by slitting the top in a cross with a knife or putting thin matchstick-sized strips of pastry on the top of the bun in a cross shape. Allow to rise for another 30 minutes.

Pre-heat the oven to 220°C/425°F/Gas 7, 190°C fan, top of an Aga roasting oven. Mix the caster sugar and water together, warming gently to make a glaze, and brush the buns with the glaze. Bake in the oven for about 15 minutes. Check after this time. The buns should be golden and risen but not burnt at all on the top. Remove and place on a cooling rack and allow to cool completely before eating.

PRESERVE

PRESERVED LEMONS Ⓥ

Pack as many lemons as you can fit into two clean preserving jars. Empty them out and add 2 or 3 more to the pile. Wash the lemons very well. Cut the lemons lengthways almost to the bottom, turn and cut again to quarters, again not cutting to the bottom, so that the lemons are still held intact by a sliver at one end. Pour about 1½ teaspoons of salt into the cut in each lemon and place into the jar, squashing to fit in all the lemons. Top up with a cool brine solution made by dissolving 25 g (1 oz) of salt to every 600 ml (1 pint) of boiling water.

It is most important that the lemons are totally submerged in the liquid. You will need to weight them down or secure them in place by means of an improvised wedge. They will be ready to use in a couple of weeks.

To use: scrape the flesh from the rind. It is the rind that you keep. Chop it and add it to stews and use in the recipe for Chicken Tagine (see pp. 66–7).

SPICE

PEPPERCORNS

Pepper was one of the first spices to be introduced into Europe. There are many colours of peppercorn available and each has an individual delicate flavour.

Black pepper, the most commonly used, is best freshly milled and is an essential part of everyday seasoning of food. It is even said to be an interesting addition sprinkled on to strawberries.

White pepper is less pungent, usually bought as a fine powder. It is best for white sauces and delicate dishes.

Red, pink and green peppercorns are available freshly preserved in brine and dried. They are highly perfumed and good in casseroles and stews. For grills, the peppercorns can be freshly milled or crushed and gently rubbed on to the outside of meat or fish.

Crushed fresh peppercorns are delicious as an addition to cream sauces for chicken, turkey, duck or steak.

DRINK

LIME CORDIAL

Limes from the Tropics are fresh into their new season in April and make a marvellous, sharp drink that can be made now and drunk right the way through the summer. Though it keeps quite well it's probably best to keep this cordial in a bottle in the fridge as it's processed as little as possible to retain both flavour and vitamins.

MAKES 900 ml (1 ½ pints)

12 limes	350 g (12 oz) caster sugar
600 ml (1 pint) water	100 g (4 oz) soft brown sugar
1 cinnamon stick	

Halve and squeeze the limes, retaining the juice. Place the squeezed shells in a large china jug and pour over the boiling water. Allow to marinate with the cinnamon stick for exactly 10 minutes. Strain and stir in the sugars to the hot water and allow to stand until thoroughly dissolved. Bring the mixture rapidly to the boil and, as soon as it's boiling, add the squeezed lime juice and remove from the heat. Bottle in a bottle or bottles that you have sterilized with baby bottle solution and then rinsed in boiling water. The drink is okay immediately but matures after two or three days. It can be diluted with still, fizzy or hot water or used as the basis for more complex punches or fancy concoctions.

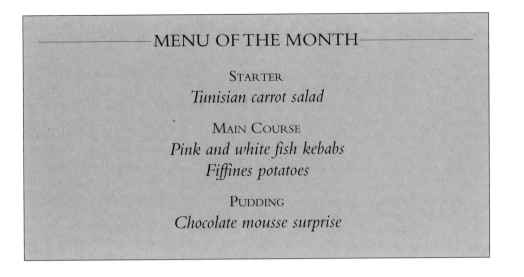

MENU OF THE MONTH

STARTER
Tunisian carrot salad

MAIN COURSE
Pink and white fish kebabs
Fiffines potatoes

PUDDING
Chocolate mousse surprise

CRAFTY TIPS FROM THE CRAFTY COOK

EASY REFERENCE OVEN TEMPERATURES:

Hot – 210°C, 425°F, Gas 7, 190°C fan oven, or the top of an Aga roasting oven

Pretty hot – 190°C, 375°F, Gas 5, 170°C fan oven, or the bottom of an Aga roasting oven

Medium – 180°C, 350°F, Gas 4, 160°C fan oven, or the bottom of an Aga roasting oven

Low/cool – 150°C, 300°F, Gas 2, 140°C fan oven, or the top of an Aga simmering oven

MAY

INTRODUCTION

May has always been the beginning of summer's plenty. May Day was a celebration as much of the end of winter shortages as it ever was of the lover and his lass. For domestic produce, though, we have always had to wait until towards the end of the month really to enjoy the marvellous new foods – spring lamb, asparagus, home grown new potatoes – even, if we're lucky and the weather flatters us, cherries. These spring treats still provide some of the most delicate and delicious flavours of the year but we're even more fortunate these days because they're joined by all the other foods that modern transportation and refrigeration bring to us.

For fish it's really a time for flat fish with brill, Dover and the other soles, plaice, skate and turbot all still in good supply. Cockles and squid reappear on the market as does a whole sudden range of spring vegetables. As well as the new potatoes from Jersey, Pembrokeshire, Kent and Cornwall, the baby carrots arrive and the first of the courgettes, calabrese and aubergines. These last tend to come from overseas at this time of year.

There is also a good range of salads, plus a whole variety of tomatoes that over the last few years have become available in the shops. Cherry, beef, salad, plum and yellow tomatoes are usually to be found in the more aspiring greengrocers and well stocked supermarkets by the end of May. For fruit we still have to depend mostly on the southern hemisphere but with South Africa, Chile, Australia and New Zealand all doing their best to supply our needs – with pears and pineapples, grapes and kiwi fruits – we don't suffer too much hardship! It's also the time for the first and perhaps the most English of all fruit, gooseberries, which, with that other peculiarity of English cooking, elderflowers, combine to make some of the most extra-ordinarily delicious puddings, pies and preserves.

May

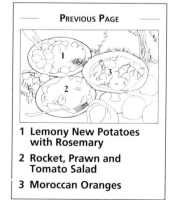

— **PREVIOUS PAGE** —

1 **Lemony New Potatoes with Rosemary**

2 **Rocket, Prawn and Tomato Salad**

3 **Moroccan Oranges**

-PRODUCE AT ITS BEST-

Asparagus ● *New potatoes* ● *Baby spinach* ● *Baby courgettes*
● *Aubergines* ● *Baby carrots* ● *Calabrese* ● *Cherry tomatoes* ● *Rocket leaf*
● *Gooseberries* ● *Lamb* ● *Skate* ● *Squid* ● *Cockles*

STARTERS

ASPARAGUS WITH CRAFTY HOLLANDAISE ⓥ

There is simply no equal of young fresh British asparagus cooked in the most straightforward way and eaten with a simple sauce. To eat asparagus hot, hollandaise has no challenger and here's a crafty way of making it. If you prefer your asparagus cold or, by some chance have any left over from eating it hot, you can always use a well-made light vinaigrette.

SERVES 4

750 g (1½ lb) asparagus	1 egg yolk
salt	juice of ½ lemon
1 whole egg	175 g (6 oz) butter, cubed

Trim the base off the asparagus and, if they are very thick or woody, carefully peel the bottom end of the stalk with a potato peeler until your thumbnail will sink easily through the skin. The thumbnail test is a good basic test for whether it needs peeling at all. Find a tall pan into which you can put the asparagus standing up, if possible. Fill it so that the water comes to within 5 cm (2 in) below the top of the asparagus. Salt it lightly, place in the asparagus tied in a bundle with a bit of string if that helps, so that they remain standing up with their heads out of the water. If you don't have a pan that will do this you may have to lie them down, in which case you need to watch the cooking time very carefully so that the heads don't overcook before the stalks are done. Bring the water to the boil, put on the lid and cook at a gentle, rolling boil for 10 minutes if the asparagus is standing up and about 8 if it's lying down. Drain it carefully and serve it with hollandaise which you've made while it's cooking.

Mix together the whole egg and egg yolk in a liquidizer or food processor. Add a pinch of salt and lemon juice and process for 5 to 10 seconds until thoroughly blended. In a non-stick pan, heat the butter until it foams. At the moment it stops hissing, pour it, with the motor on, into the processor through the feed tube. Allow to process for 10 seconds after all the butter has been poured in. Tip the mixture back into the pan

but do not replace on the heat. There will be enough heat in the pan to finish thickening the hollandaise, which can be kept warm for up to 10 minutes before serving.

WELSH COCKLE CHOWDER

In fact, in the parts of Wales where this is eaten, it's known as Cockle Broth or Cockle Soup. The tradition of chunky shellfish soups for most of us, however, is deeply rooted in the chowders of North America that this closely resembles. Cockles are still widely available in Britain though they can often do with a little soaking in fresh water before cooking to get rid of any residual sand. They usually arrive shelled and cooked and therefore need little additional cooking in the broth itself. This is a substantial soup that can be eaten as a first course but is very good as a main dish with fruit and cheese or pudding to follow.

SERVES 4

275 g (10 oz) potatoes	600 ml (1 pint) cockles, cooked and shelled
300 ml (10 fl oz) milk	salt and freshly ground black pepper
300 ml (10 fl oz) water	25 g (1 oz) butter
275 g (10 oz) onions, roughly chopped	25 g (1 oz) fresh parsley, chopped
2 sticks of celery	

Cut the potato into 1 cm (½ in) cubes and poach it in the milk and water with the onions for 10 minutes. Trim and slice the celery into 5 mm (¼ in) rounds across the grain, add that to the soup and simmer for another 2 minutes. Add the cockles and season generously. Put the butter and parsley in a soup tureen or bowl and pour the hot soup over it, mixing until the butter is thoroughly melted. Serve immediately.

ROCKET, PRAWN AND TOMATO SALAD

Rocket is a salad vegetable that we used to be very familiar with in Britain in the seventeenth century but has fallen out of use until recently when it became fashionable as an imported salad leaf. It's now readily available at this time of year and has an oak leafy sort of shape and a slightly spicy flavour and texture. Used in small quantities as it is in this first course salad, it adds colour and bite to the mixture. The tomatoes to use are the smallest cherry tomatoes you can find. These are often sold under names like Gardeners' Delight or Flavia but the thing to look for is small tomatoes with a bright, full colour.

Asparagus and Crafty Hollandaise

SERVES 4

100 g (4 oz) rocket leaf	1 tablespoon red wine vinegar
225 g (8 oz) cherry tomatoes, halved	a pinch of salt
175 g (6 oz) shelled prawns	a pinch of sugar
	1 teaspoon made Dijon mustard
FOR THE DRESSING	
3 tablespoons salad oil	

Wash and dry the rocket leaves and tear them into pieces. Discard the stalks of the tomatoes and cut them in half. Put the dressing ingredients into a jar or bowl and shake or whisk until smoothly blended. Mix the rocket, tomatoes and prawns together and pile into individual cups or serving dishes. Pour the dressing over and chill for about 30 minutes for the flavours to blend before serving.

VEGETABLES

SPINACH WITH ORANGE Ⓥ

Around May, the first of the new season's crop of fresh spinach starts arriving, although there have been supplies through the winter from abroad. This dish, an unusual way of handling spinach, makes full use of the fresh texture and flavour. You can add some lightly browned pine nuts or baby croûtons at the end to add crunch if you're eating it as a dish on its own.

SERVES 4

50 g (2 oz) butter	a pinch of freshly grated nutmeg
900 g (2 lb) picked spinach	salt and freshly ground black pepper
120 ml (4 fl oz) freshly pressed orange juice	

Melt the butter in a large pan into which the spinach will all fit. Wash the spinach and place it in the pan with the butter. Turn the vegetable gently over a low heat until it wilts and forms a compact mass. Add the orange juice and turn the heat up to maximum, stirring the spinach around. The orange juice and juices will dry out fairly rapidly. Do not let them dry out completely; the spinach should remain moist and flavoured with the orange. After 2–3 minutes, remove from the heat, season with nutmeg, salt and pepper and serve. The spinach will have reduced enormously in volume but be quite dense and filling.

LEMONY NEW POTATOES WITH ROSEMARY Ⓥ

For many people – and I must say it usually includes me – new potatoes are a pleasure in their own right. With their fine texture and delicate flavour, just cooking them and eating them with a little mint, seasoning and butter is enough of a treat. But towards the end of the month when we've got used to them again, this Greek style of cooking them offers an interesting and refreshing alternative. The combination of rosemary and lemon is remarkably successful and the method of cooking produces a richness of flavour in the potatoes as well.

SERVES 4

750 g (1½ lb) new potatoes	2 teaspoons rosemary sprigs
3 tablespoons olive oil	salt and freshly ground black pepper
1½ lemons	

Scrub the potatoes thoroughly and make sure they're all evenly sized. Choose a frying or sauté pan into which the potatoes will all fit in one layer and with a good lid. Heat the oil until it's hot but not smoking, add the potatoes and turn them in it thoroughly. Turn the heat down and allow them to cook gently for 15 minutes with the lid on. Turn them and cook for another 5 minutes. Cut matchsticks of rind from the whole lemon and add those to the potatoes with the rosemary and the juice of the whole and half lemon. Bring rapidly to the boil, season and allow to cook until all the liquid has evaporated. Put the lid back on and allow to stand for 1–2 minutes for the flavours to blend before serving. The potatoes, of course, should be cooked right through.

BAKED AUBERGINES AND ALMONDS Ⓥ

Aubergines are plentiful in May; it's the beginning of their season in the Mediterranean and they are imported from there. On their home turf they're a bread and butter vegetable, part of the basic food of everyday life, but for us they're still a little more exotic than their common colleagues courgettes and peppers. This is a dish derived from Middle Eastern origins but with some very modern nutrition involvement in it. The almonds that provide crunch are also one of the best sources of vitamin E, currently believed to be a major factor in helping to prevent heart disease. The oil used in the recipe is also a mono-unsaturate, olive oil, so altogether, although the dish tastes delicious and indulgent, it's still very healthy eating.

SERVES 4

2 small to medium-sized aubergines, about 225–275 g (8–10 oz) each	25 g (1 oz) fresh parsley, finely chopped
1 garlic clove, crushed	juice of ½ lemon
salt	75 g (3 oz) slivered almonds
85 ml (3 fl oz) olive oil	

Pre-heat the oven to 180°C/350°F/Gas 4, 160°C fan, middle of an Aga roasting oven. Grease a baking dish.

Split the aubergines in half and put them in the prepared baking dish. Bake in the oven for 45 minutes until the aubergines are soft. Very carefully spoon out the centre, leaving the shells. Crush the garlic with a little salt and mix it with the aubergine flesh, 2 tablespoons of the olive oil, the parsley and the lemon juice. Pile the mixture back in the shells and top with the slivered almonds. Sprinkle the remaining olive oil over the top and return to the oven for 10 minutes until the almonds are just crisping. This can be served on its own with plenty of bread or rice or with grilled kebabs.

MAIN COURSES

CRISP FRIED SQUID WITH SWEET AND SOUR SAUCE

Squid are one of those ingredients that divide people, especially when seen on the fishmonger's slab complete with tentacles. This dish, however, makes use of them in their most simple and universally appealing form as neat, snow-white rings fried to a crisp crunchiness. You can buy the squid ready prepared in this manner from supermarkets and fishmongers or, if you prefer, clean the squid yourself in the few moments it actually takes. To do this just wash the squid thoroughly under running water until all the purple, filmy skin comes off. Remove and discard the head, tentacles and the pen-like transparent cartilage. Rinse the squid thoroughly and cut across into 1 cm (½ in) rings.

SERVES 4

350 g (12 oz) squid rings prepared as above or bought prepared	**FOR THE SAUCE**
50 g (2 oz) seasoned plain flour	2 teaspoons cornflour
1 egg	120 ml (4 fl oz) orange juice
50 ml (2 fl oz) milk	1 tablespoon soy sauce
175 g (6 oz) fine fresh breadcrumbs	1 tablespoon soft brown sugar
oil for frying	1 tablespoon wine vinegar
1 lemon, cut into wedges	

inse the squid rings and allow to drain. Roll the squid rings in the flour. Beat the egg into the milk and dip the squid into the mixture and then roll carefully in the fine breadcrumbs. Allow to set on a dry plate for a few minutes.

To make the sauce, mix the cornflour with a little water until it's thoroughly dissolved, add to the other sauce ingredients and bring the whole mixture to the boil gently, stirring as you go. The sauce will thicken and go glossy. Deep-fry the squid rings in oil for 3–4 minutes until golden brown. Drain on kitchen paper and serve with a wedge of lemon and the sweet and sour sauce. They do not improve with keeping.

SKATE IN BLACK BUTTER

Flat fish are at their best at this time of year and one of the kinds that's terrific value but often neglected is skate. In Europe it's a great treat but in Britain it's still in that strange position where it's a cheap luxury. Buy some skate wings then and enjoy what the French have known about for a long time.

SERVES 4

750 g (1½ lb) skate wings, 1 portion per person	75 g (3 oz) butter
50 g (2 oz) plain flour	1 teaspoon capers
1 tablespoon oil	50 ml (2 fl oz) white wine vinegar

rim the skate wings and shake them in a plastic or paper bag with the flour. Heat the oil in a frying pan into which the skate will all fit in one go. Add half the butter and when it foams add the floured pieces of skate. Fry over a medium heat for 4–5 minutes, turn and fry again for 4–5 minutes until the skate is cooked through. Do not let the butter or the flour burn. Transfer the skate to warm plates. Wipe out the pan carefully with a piece of kitchen roll and add the remaining butter. Allow this to heat till it turns just hazelnutty – this is known as black butter – add the capers and pour over the skate. Tip the vinegar into the pan, swill round and pour immediately over the skate then serve with new potatoes.

ROMAN LAMB WITH GARLIC AND ROSEMARY

In the days of my youth in Soho there used to be a famous Italian restaurant to which all Italian football teams repaired immediately on arrival to Britain to fortify themselves with home-style cooking. The restaurant has long since gone and no football team is ever more than a kilometre from Italian food almost anywhere in the British Isles these days, but the chef had a way of cooking spring lamb which has remained firmly fixed in my memory. You need quite a small joint for this so the new season's lamb is quite essential. Fortunately, playing for AC Milan before you can enjoy it is not!

SERVES 4

2 tablespoons olive oil	1 sprig of fresh rosemary
1 leg spring lamb, about 1.25 kg (2½ lb)	4 ripe tomatoes, cut into 8
2 garlic cloves, finely chopped	salt and freshly ground black pepper

Pre-heat the oven to 180°C/350°F/Gas 4, 160°C fan, bottom of an Aga roasting oven.

Heat the oil in a roasting tin and roll the leg of lamb in that till lightly browned. Remove the lamb and make a bed of the garlic, rosemary and tomatoes. Place the lamb on top, season with salt and pepper and either put a lid over the roasting tin or cover with foil, sealing the edges as tightly as you can. Bake in the oven for 1 hour. Remove the foil and allow the meat to brown for another 10–15 minutes. When ready to serve, carve in thick slices and stir the contents of the pan together, remove the sprig of rosemary and serve a spoonful or two of the mixture with the lamb.

PUDDINGS

GOOSEBERRY TURNOVER

Gooseberry turnovers come from a tradition of bakestone cooking where a large iron or stone baking griddle was heated by the side of the fire and food was cooked on top of it, particularly pastry and cake dishes. A turnover was a very easy way of using pastry to make a fruit pie on it without a tin, though these days it's much more practically cooked in an oven on a baking tray. Made in small sizes, about half the size of the recipe recommended below, they make excellent teatime treats for a children's party, but the combination of tartness and sweetness, and the crispness of the pastry turns out to be pretty popular amongst adults.

SERVES 4

450 g (1 lb) gooseberries, topped and tailed	450 g (1 lb) puff pastry (you can use a packet variety)
100–175 g (4–6 oz) caster sugar (adjust according to sweetness of gooseberries and your tooth)	1 egg, beaten
1 pinch allspice	25 g (1 oz) granulated sugar

Pre-heat the oven to 210°C/425°F/Gas 7, 190°C fan, or the top of the Aga roasting oven.

Put the gooseberries and the caster sugar into a non-stick pan with the pinch of allspice and cook gently until just starting to break up but not puréed. Roll out the puff pastry until quite thin and cut into six circles the size of large tea plates. Using the back of a knife, draw a fine marking line across the centre of each pastry circle and fill one half with three tablespoons of the gooseberry mixture, leaving a half-inch edge. Brush that edge with a little of the beaten egg, fold the remaining pastry over the top and, using a fork, press the edges together. Cut a slit in the top of the pastry and sprinkle with a little of the granulated sugar. Bake for 20–25 minutes until the pastry is golden brown. Allow to cool a little before serving as the fruit inside will be hot.

MOROCCAN ORANGES

May is the season when the best of the Moroccan oranges begin to arrive. They're slightly different from oranges from other parts of the world in that they have a very thin skin and a quite intense flavour. They make a marvellous pudding eaten in the way that's traditional in their country of origin, involving using the peel to temper the sweetness of the caramel marinade.

SERVES 4

4 oranges	250 ml (8 fl oz) water
75 g (3 oz) sugar	2 cloves

Using a zester, take the outer skin off 2 of the oranges in matchsticks and retain. Peel all 4 oranges and discard the remaining skins. Blanch the orange peel matchsticks by putting into a little cold water, bringing to the boil then draining and discarding the water. Put the sugar in a non-stick pan with 1–2 teaspoons of water and cook gently until the sugar has melted and started to go pale brown and caramelize. Remove from the heat and very carefully add the water, cloves and blanched orange peel and then simmer together for 4–5 minutes until the caramel is completely dissolved. Slice the oranges into 1 cm (½ in) slices and arrange in a flat layer in an attractive bowl. Pour the caramel and orange rind mixture over and allow to marinate for at least 2 and up to 12 hours before serving. They're delicious on their own but if you would like cream, the thin pouring type is the best to add.

STICKY BANANA PIE

Over the last few years, banana pies in various forms – some with and some without butterscotch covering – have become extremely popular. There's no getting away from the fact that they're high in calories but they are also very high in family appeal. The original was supposed to have been invented in Canada of all places at a ski lodge in the Rockies. This version makes a substantial close to a light or delicate meal. It uses marmalade, which adds a good contrast with the sweet bananas and rich cream.

SERVES 4

FOR THE SHORTBREAD	FOR THE TOPPING
50 g (2 oz) caster sugar	3 tablespoons marmalade
100 g (4 oz) butter	4 small to medium bananas, sliced
175 g (6 oz) self-raising flour	150 ml (5 fl oz) double cream, lightly whipped
50 g (2 oz) flaked almonds	3 tablespoons fromage frais
	2 teaspoons caster sugar
	a few drops of vanilla essence

Pre-heat the oven to 180°C/375°F/Gas 5, 160°C fan, bottom of an Aga roasting oven. Grease a 20 cm (8 in) cake tin.

To make the shortbread base, cream the sugar and butter together until light and fluffy. Add the flour and work into a smooth paste. Flatten the mixture by hand into the tin and sprinkle with half the flaked almonds. Bake in the oven for 18–20 minutes until pale gold. Turn on to a wire rack to cool. Warm the marmalade to make it easier to spread then cover the top of the shortbread. Arrange the banana slices on top. Mix the cream, fromage frais, sugar and vanilla and mask the top of the pie. Decorate with the remaining almonds.

PRESERVES

GOOSEBERRY RELISH Ⓥ

This recipe is for a relish, half-way between a chutney and a pickle. It's a marvellous way of cooking gooseberries to keep them, and is sufficiently attractive to be eaten by certain members of my family on its own on bread and butter. But its most perfect use is with smoked fish – mackerel, eel, or any of the pâtés made from them. It has a bitter-sweet flavour and a very pretty, dark red colour when it's made.

SERVES 4

1.5 kg (3 lb) gooseberries, topped and tailed	½ teaspoon ground cloves
300 ml (10 fl oz) cider vinegar	½ teaspoon ground allspice
550 g (1¼ lb) sugar	

ut the gooseberries into a preserving pan (not aluminium), add the cider vinegar and simmer gently for 10 minutes until the gooseberries are beginning to soften. Stir in the sugar until it's thoroughly dissolved, add the spices and bring to the boil. Allow to cook until the gooseberries are fully pulped and the mixture has the consistency of jam. Put into sterilized jars and cover, sealing down tight when the mixture is cold. It should be left for a week before eating and will keep for up to a year in a cool store cupboard.

BREAD

PITTA BREAD

Pitta bread is the classic bread of the Middle East, also eaten quite often with Indian foods as an alternative to nan as it goes very well with kebabs, tandoori chicken and other similar dishes. It's very quick and easy to make. This method uses yeast, although often traditionally in Middle Eastern bakeries yoghurt and natural yeast were used in rising the bread. It's pretty flat anyway when it cooks but it does need a little help so that it separates and becomes light.

SERVES 4

450 g (1 lb) unbleached white plain flour	2 tablespoons plain yoghurt
a pinch of salt	scant 300 ml (10 fl oz) water
15 g (½ oz) yeast or half a packet of dried yeast	

ix together the flour and the salt, and the dried yeast if you're using it. If you're using fresh yeast, add a pinch of sugar and a little of the water and allow to go frothy for about 10 minutes then add that yeast mixture to the flour. Put in the yoghurt and the rest of the water. Knead by hand or in a food processor until the mixture changes texture and becomes smooth and elastic. You may need to add a little more flour or water depending upon the quality and humidity of the flour. You should have a non-sticky elastic dough at the end of it. Allow to rise for 30 minutes in a warm place in the bowl it was mixed in. You may find rolling the dough in a tablespoon of oil will help to prevent it sticking.

Knead the dough again after 30 minutes and divide into 6 balls. Flatten these on to oiled baking sheets into the shape of ovals approximately 23–30 cm (9–12 in) long and 7.5–10 cm (3–4 in) wide and very flat! Allow to prove for another 15–20 minutes in a warm place. Pre-heat the oven to 220°C/425°F/Gas 7, 190°C fan, top of an Aga roasting oven. Bake the bread in the oven for 10–12 minutes. Keep an eye on them. The pittas should rise to the thickness of about 2 cm (¾ in) and should be very lightly flecked with gold on the top. If you allow them to brown they will become crisp, hard and biscuit-like and not at all suitable for wrapping foods in. The minute they start to be flecked with brown, remove from the oven, ease gently off the baking tray and allow to cool on racks. They store well and should be re-heated if you're not going to eat them when they're still warm.

HERB

ROSEMARY

Rosemary is an aromatic herb with a strong piney smell to its needle-like leaves. For culinary use it is available both as fresh sprigs or dried. It is used throughout the Mediterranean and is a welcome reminder of sunny days, quite apt as it is also the herb of remembrance.

It can be used to season a variety of vegetables and meat dishes such as roast lamb and potatoes, or pieces of chicken and rabbit drizzled with olive oil and roasted with garlic and rosemary. Try it as a flavouring in a marinade for meat, or put directly on to the coals of a barbecue.

Make your own herb oils by infusing a sprig of fresh rosemary into a bottle of good quality olive oil. You may add other flavourings such as bay leaf, garlic and peppercorns.

Rosemary can also be sprinkled on to the top of bread before baking, such as focaccia and olive bread.

It can also be infused into milk to make custards, ice-cream and sorbets.

DRINK

MOCHA

Mocha is a marvellous European blend of coffee and chocolate often not understood at all in Britain although we sometimes use the name for a mixed coffee and chocolate flavoured ice-cream or cake. The secret is to make sure that the balance between the two ingredients is right. Good mocha ought to be coffee that is made particularly smooth and silky with the use of chocolate rather than the other way round. It began life in the coffee houses of Vienna and makes a particularly soothing late night drink for those who can't take coffee on its own before sleep.

SERVES 4

2 tablespoons drinking chocolate	**600 ml (1 pint) freshly made ground coffee**
120 ml (4 fl oz) milk	**½ teaspoon ground cinnamon**

Whisk the drinking chocolate into the milk and heat, whisking regularly, until thoroughly dissolved and foamy. Pour the coffee into the chocolate, whisk again, sprinkle with the cinnamon and serve. The coffee can be sweetened to taste but the chocolate will have some sweetness in it already.

MENU OF THE MONTH

STARTER
Asparagus with crafty hollandaise

MAIN COURSE
Roman lamb with garlic and rosemary
Spinach with orange

PUDDING
Moroccan oranges

JUNE

INTRODUCTION

June is the first of the golden months. Summer is finally with us and so too are the first of the crops that last only a moment but give great pleasure and flavour. Raspberries, asparagus, artichokes, all really come into their own this month.

June is not a great month for fish and shellfish – no 'r' in the month means oysters and mussels are not at their best – and although the weather tends to mean fishing boats can get out easily, the number of varieties on offer tend to be fewer. Dover and the other soles like lemon can be in reasonable supply. Mackerel, caught particularly off Britain's south-west coasts, is at its best at this time, and farmed salmon is in very good condition too, ideal for eating in the warmer weather outdoors. Broad beans reach their peak, and peaches and apricots arrive from the warmer climate of the Mediterranean. Towards the end of the June the first of the strawberries are with us too, but it's raspberries that really have pride of place in June. New potatoes are much cheaper and widely available in a range of varieties and so too, happily with the coincidence of long summer evenings, are the salad ingredients, particularly Webb's Wonder lettuces, radicchio, and red, green, yellow and even black sweet peppers are all suddenly in profusion.

A couple of speciality ingredients that are, in fact, incredibly economic treats are also June arrivals. Poussin – small chickens known in America as spring chickens – are in fact a fully grown bird of a variety that matures quickly and at a small size. They are often very economical, especially for two people, and are available both as whole birds or spatchcocked – split and skewered flat – ideal for grilling indoors or out. June is also a good time for British goats' milk cheeses. Goats can really only be milked after the spring and these cheeses are therefore at their freshest and newest at this time of year. They come in a variety of forms, both plain, snow-white, and flavoured with herbs and spices.

It's this profusion of ingredients and the welcome warmth of summer that combine to make our June dishes amongst the most popular of all.

PREVIOUS PAGE

1 **Crafty Peperonata with Goats' Cheese**

2 **Peach Melba**

3 **Dalmatian Moussaka**

—PRODUCE AT ITS BEST—

Artichokes ● *Broad beans* ● *Peppers* ● *Cucumbers* ● *Raspberries*
● *Peaches* ● *Apricots* ● *Poussin* ● *Salmon* ● *Scampi* ● *English goats cheese*

STARTERS

ARTICHOKES – HOT AND COLD Ⓥ

Artichokes are, in fact, the top of thistles specially grown and developed over generations to provide an edible base. The technique of eating them is almost as important as that of cooking. When they are ready, hot or cold, you peel off the outside leaves one by one, dip them in the appropriate flavouring and scrape the soft flesh off the harder casing with your teeth! You do this until you've finished all the usable leaves and then you discard the little inner bud of soft leaves and the fibrous 'choke', leaving you with the artichoke heart to be cut up and eaten with luxurious pleasure. The method of cooking is the same whether you want to eat the artichokes hot or cold; it's only the flavourings that really differ.

SERVES 4

4 large artichokes	2 teaspoons snipped fresh chives
1 tablespoon cider vinegar	salt and freshly ground black pepper
1 teaspoon salt	
2.25 litres (4 pints) water	FOR THE COLD SAUCE
	4 tablespoons olive oil
FOR THE HOT SAUCE	4 tablespoons lemon juice
100 g (4 oz) butter	50 g (2 oz) Parmesan, grated
2 hard-boiled eggs, quartered	½ teaspoon sugar

Trim the base of the artichokes flat and cut off the pointed ends of the leaves so that they sit about 5 cm (2 in) high. Put the cider vinegar and salt into the water and bring it to the boil. Put in the artichokes and simmer for 15–20 minutes until the base is tender to a skewer. Drain immediately upside-down. If eating hot, serve at once. If eating cold, allow to cool before chilling for not more than 6 hours.

Sauce for Hot Artichokes
Melt the butter until it's foaming. Pour it into a liquidizer with the eggs and chives. Season generously and process until a roughly chopped purée. This closely resembles a warm mayonnaise. Pour it into individual bowls and use as a dip for the artichokes.

Sauce for Cold Artichokes
Whisk together the olive oil and lemon juice, add the Parmesan and sugar and stir.
Serve in individual bowls as a dip for the cold artichokes.

CRAFTY PEPERONATA WITH GOATS' CHEESE Ⓥ

This is an Italian-style salad which, in its original form, required a lot of complex
grilling and peeling of the peppers to get rid of the rather waxy outside coating. The
crafty method here allows that same coating to be cooked off without too much
fiddling about. The contrast between the sweetness of the peppers and the clear-
tasting creaminess of the cheese makes this an outstanding first course or, in sufficient
quantities, a light lunch. Use at least two colours of peppers.

SERVES 4

750 g (1½ lb) sweet peppers, mixed colours	juice of 1 lemon
2 tablespoons olive oil	1 × 50–75 g (2–3 oz) 'round' of goats' cheese
1 garlic clove, finely chopped	25 g (1 oz) chopped fresh parsley
salt and freshly ground black pepper	

Halve the peppers and remove the seeds. Slice across into 5 mm (¼ in) strips. Heat
the oil in a frying-pan which will take all the peppers. Add the garlic and pepper
slices and turn over a medium to high heat for 2–3 minutes. Season and turn down
the heat and allow the peppers to cook gently for about 10 minutes until they are just
beginning to caramelize. Squeeze the lemon juice over them, turn thoroughly and
allow to cool. Cut the goats' cheese into four slices across the round and dip one side
into the chopped parsley.

To serve, place the pepper slices in an attractive dish or dishes and arrange the sliced
goats' cheese, parsley side up, on top. The peppers should be completely cool and can
be stored in the fridge for up to 12 hours before adding the goats' cheese.

BROAD BEAN SOUP WITH CHIVES Ⓥ

Broad beans are at their peak in June and it may well be you wish to do nothing but steam them and eat them with lightly herbed butter and some good brown bread. I could hardly blame you, but when you've had enough of that particular self-indulgence, try making them into this delicious light green soup.

SERVES 4

225 g (8 oz) shelled broad beans	salt and freshly ground black pepper
1 large floury potato, about 225 g (8 oz), roughly chopped	900 ml (1½ pints) water
1 medium onion, roughly chopped	2 teaspoons snipped fresh chives or 1 teaspoon freeze-dried chives
2 tablespoons cooking oil	25 g (1 oz) butter

Fry the broad beans, potato and onion gently in the oil in a large pan. Season generously and add the water. Cook, lightly covered, for about 15 minutes. The beans should still be green, not khaki. Pour the mixture into a food processor or liquidizer – you may need to do it in batches – and process until completely smooth. Add the chives and butter and stir in thoroughly before serving.

MAIN COURSES

NEW POTATO, BROAD BEAN AND MUSHROOM GRATIN Ⓥ

By happy coincidence, new potatoes and broad beans are at their best at the same time of year. This is a great gift because their flavours complement each other perfectly and make a marvellous and nutritionally balanced vegetarian gratin. This can be eaten as a course or dish on its own or served with simple grilled meats or fish if that's your inclination.

SERVES 4

350 g (12 oz) new potatoes	175 ml (6 fl oz) fromage frais, 8 per cent fat
350 g (12 oz) shelled broad beans	50 g (2 oz) Peccorino or Parmesan, grated
100 g (4 oz) chestnut or shiitaki mushrooms	100 g (4 oz) fresh white breadcrumbs

Pre-heat the oven to 200°C/400°F/Gas 6, 180°C fan, top of an Aga roasting oven.

Scrub and boil the potatoes for about 10 minutes until they're just tender. Remove from the water and drain. Use the water to boil the broad beans in for 5 minutes. Scald the mushrooms by pouring a kettle of boiling water over them in a colander in the sink and cut those into quarters. Cut the potatoes and mushrooms in half, mix together and put into a buttered gratin dish into which all the ingredients will just fit. Drain the broad beans and when completely drained, mix with the fromage frais. Spoon over the potatoes and mushrooms. Mix together the grated cheese and breadcrumbs and sprinkle over the top. Bake in the oven for 15–20 minutes until the topping is lightly golden.

SCAMPI ADRIATICA

I first ate the prototype of this dish in a café overlooking the Adriatic. The food was marvellous but the view was terrible as on the other side of the bay there was a shipbreakers' yard full of noise and rust. However, for a scampi and garlic lover, the recipe was a must. It's a luxury dish but easy to make and helped by the fact that it's bulked out quite a lot by the pasta. Made with olive oil instead of butter it can be served cold as an exotic pasta salad.

SERVES 4

225 g (8 oz) rigatoni or short fine macaroni	225 g (8 oz) fresh uncooked scampi or tiger prawns, shelled
1 bunch of thin asparagus or asparagus tips, trimmed	juice of 1 lemon
75 g (3 oz) butter	salt and freshly ground black pepper
2 garlic cloves, finely chopped	

Cook the pasta in boiling water for 4 minutes, add the asparagus, cover and set aside off the heat. Heat the butter in a heavy-based pan and add the garlic, scampi or prawns. Turn the heat down and allow to cook gently until the prawns are bright pink. Drain the asparagus and pasta mixture thoroughly; it should have been standing for 7–10 minutes. Put into a serving dish and pour the prawn, butter and garlic mixture over the top. Squeeze the juice of the lemon over, season and serve immediately.

SALMON – HOT AND COLD

This is the great time of year for salmon, even if most of it is the farmed variety. It tastes great and is so economic now that it's often cheaper than cod. Here are two recipes: one for salmon steaks to be eaten hot and one for a whole salmon to be decorated and eaten cold as a centrepiece for a buffet or big family lunch.

Hot Salmon Cutlets

HOT SALMON CUTLETS

These cutlets are cut across the fish and should be about 2.5 cm (1 in) thick and of an even size. Try to buy ones without straggly ends hanging from them.

SERVES 4

4 salmon cutlets, about 175–225 g (6–8 oz) each	salt and freshly ground black pepper
1 bay leaf	1 teaspoon chopped fresh or freeze-dried dill
6 black peppercorns	1 teaspoon snipped fresh or freeze-dried chives
1 celery stick	120 ml (4 fl oz) fromage frais, 8 per cent fat
1 sprig fresh parsley	

Wrap the salmon steaks in cling film. Place in a pan into which they will fit evenly in one layer. Cover them with water and add the bay leaf, peppercorns, celery and parsley stalks. Season with salt and bring to the boil gently. Simmer for 15 minutes. Meanwhile, mix the dill and chives into the fromage frais; this is a low-fat alternative to hollandaise sauce. When the salmon is cooked, drain it carefully, remove the cling film and the skin from around each cutlet if you wish. Serve on warm plates with a tablespoon of the sauce in the centre of each cutlet. New potatoes and a cucumber salad are the perfect accompaniments.

MOR'S CUCUMBER SALAD Ⓥ

This is a simple method for making cucumber salad that comes from Denmark. It's very simple and quite delicious and goes perfectly with hot or cold salmon.

SERVES 4

1 large cucumber	50 g (2 oz) sugar
120 ml (4 fl oz) cider vinegar	1 teaspoon salt
120 ml (4 fl oz) cooled boiled water	

Wash and trim the cucumber and slice as thinly as possible; a food processor or mandoline is ideal. Put into a china or glass bowl. In a separate bowl, mix the cider vinegar, water, sugar and salt and stir until the sugar and salt have dissolved. Pour over the cucumber and allow to marinate for at least 2 and up to 12 hours.

WHOLE SALMON WITH CUCUMBER SCALES

This is a spectacular centrepiece for a buffet or family dinner. The salmon is cooked whole, skinned and then re-scaled with cucumber slices.

SERVES 8–10

1 × 1.5–2 kg (3–4½ lb) salmon	2 lemons, thinly sliced (optional)
bouquet garni of celery, parsley and bay leaf	2 cucumbers
1 teaspoon salt	

If you have a pan or fish kettle large enough to poach the salmon, put it into cold water with the bouquet garni ingredients and salt. Bring it to the boil, simmer for just 4 minutes and then switch off and allow to cool in the cooking water. This timing will operate whatever the size of the salmon.

If you do not have a big enough pan or fish kettle, you can cook it in foil. Pre-heat the oven to 180°C/350°F/Gas 4, 160°C fan, bottom of an Aga roasting oven. Lightly butter the foil and line it with a thinly sliced lemon. Put the cleaned salmon into the foil and wrap lightly, leaving some air space in the foil itself. Bake in the oven for 10 minutes per 450 g (1 lb). Remove and allow to cool in the sealed foil before opening.

When your salmon is cooked and cooled skin it carefully. Take the cucumbers and score the skin lengthways with the tines of a strong fork. Trim and slice as thinly as possible across each cucumber – a mandoline or food processor is ideal. Place the salmon on an attractive serving dish and use the sliced cucumber to re-scale, starting at the tail end and overlapping the scales fifty per cent so that they lie in the right pattern on the fish. Garnish with watercress, dill and lemon slices. Mayonnaise or fromage frais with herbs beaten into it are also ideal accompaniments to this classic summer dish.

SPATCHCOCKED POUSSIN

These small-scale chickens are full of flavour. A test carried out by *Good Housekeeping* brought them out on top of all varieties of chicken above free-range, French black leg and traditionally reared. They're particularly suitable for grilling and in a spatchcocked or split and skewered form they have very little work left to be done to them in terms of preparation – all you add is the flavours. You can also use this recipe on a barbecue if the weather suits. The trick to remember is to cook the cut, not the skin, side first, whether you're using the grill on your cooker or a charcoal barbecue.

SERVES 4

120 ml (4 fl oz) fresh orange juice	½ teaspoon garlic salt
1 tablespoon honey	2 spatchcocked poussin
1 tablespoon sesame oil (Chinese-style)	250 ml (8 fl oz) water
1 tablespoon soy sauce	2 teaspoons cornflour mixed with a little water

ix together the orange juice, honey, sesame oil, soy sauce and garlic salt, spread over the poussin and leave to marinate for at least 2 and preferably up to 12 hours.

Remove the chickens from the marinade and grill, cut side to the heat, for 6–8 minutes and then skin side to the heat for another 5–6 minutes. Be careful they don't stick to the grill as the honey does have the capacity to caramelize. Pour the marinade juices into a non-stick pan, add the water and the slaked cornflour and bring gently to the boil, stirring. When the chicken is cooked, remove the skewers, divide in half and serve with the thickened, glossy sauce.

DALMATIAN MOUSSAKA

I discovered this recipe amongst the islands of the Dalmatian coast in the area that used to be Yugoslavia. It's an adaptation of a recipe that's common over the whole of the eastern Mediterranean. It uses potatoes as well as aubergines and I think benefits from that because it can be served just with crisp bread where the usual accompaniment for an ordinary moussaka is a doubtful decision between rice and the totally inappropriate roast potatoes.

SERVES 4

450 g (1 lb) minced lamb	1 teaspoon chopped fresh or freeze-dried oregano
225 g (8 oz) onions, finely chopped	
1 garlic clove, chopped	1 teaspoon chopped fresh or freeze-dried thyme
400 g (14 oz) tin Italian chopped tomatoes	
2 teaspoons tomato purée	1 teaspoon chopped fresh or freeze-dried basil
salt and freshly ground black pepper	
450 g (1 lb) new potatoes	85 ml (3 fl oz) olive oil
1 large aubergine	150 ml (5 fl oz) plain yoghurt
	1 egg

re-heat the oven to 190°C/375°F/Gas 5, 170°C fan, middle of an Aga roasting oven.

Fry the lamb in its own fat until browned. Add the onions and garlic. Cook with the lamb for another 3–4 minutes until the onions are translucent. Add the tomatoes, the tomato purée and salt and pepper and simmer for 10 minutes. Scrub the potatoes and cut them and the aubergine into 5 mm (¼ in) slices. Lightly oil a baking dish and place the potatoes in a layer to cover the bottom. With the remaining oil, fry the aubergine slices until gold. Mix the herbs into the meat mixture and pour half of it on to the potato. Add a second layer of potato and the rest of the meat mixture and top with the aubergine slices. Beat the yoghurt and egg together and spoon over the aubergines. Bake in the oven for 35–40 minutes. Serve in slices like a cake.

RASPBERRY BRULEE

Raspberries, like all great treats, are best eaten as simply as possible. But if you're so fortunate as to have enough raspberries to have satisfied the appetite for them sprinkled with sugar and softened with cream, then you might like to try this dish. It has essentially the same ingredients in it, but handled differently to produce what can be an extremely elegant as well as hugely popular pudding. Don't chill this once you've made it. It will keep for 3 or 4 hours out of the fridge and the crackling on the top will remain crunchy, which won't happen if it goes into cold, damp air.

SERVES 4

65 g (2½ oz) caster sugar	150 ml (5 fl oz) fromage frais
450 g (1 lb) raspberries	2 tablespoons water
150 ml (5 fl oz) double cream	

Sprinkle 1 dessertspoon of sugar on to the raspberries, stir gently and divide into 6 ramekin dishes or, if you prefer, place in a large shallow soufflé dish. Beat the double cream until it's thick then add the fromage frais, a spoonful at a time, continuing to beat till the whole mixture is thick and stiff. Spoon this on top of the raspberries and smooth down. Melt the remaining sugar in the water very carefully in a heavy, non-stick pan until it's completely dissolved. Bring it to the boil and allow it to begin to caramelize, that is, turn pale gold. Do not let it turn dark brown or it will be burnt. When it is pale gold, allow it to cool for a few moments but before it sets, pour it swiftly over the top of the cream mixture, tilting the dishes so that the surface is completely covered. It will set on contact with the cold cream, so do it with some delicacy. The caramel topping will remain crisp for 2 hours but should not be chilled.

PEACH MELBA

Peach Melba was reputedly invented by the great Escoffier in honour of Dame Nellie Melba, the turn of the century soprano diva. I'm not sure whether the combination was meant to soothe the golden tonsils or reflect its namesake's opulence and style, but either way it's certainly a delicious and rich dish, perfect to make in June when both the peaches and raspberries are available fresh.

SERVES 4

4 large ripe peaches	225 g (8 oz) real *dairy* vanilla ice-cream (look at the label)
50 g (2 oz) caster sugar	
225 g (8 oz) raspberries	

Dip the peaches into boiling water for 20 seconds (retain two cups of water) and remove the skins. Halve and remove the stones. Put the retained water into a pan, add the peach halves and the sugar and poach for 5 minutes. Drain, retaining the syrup. Boil this down until reduced to about 4 fl oz (tablespoons). Allow it to cool and then add it to the raspberries. Mix thoroughly and leave to stand for 10 minutes. Purée the raspberries either with a fork or a liquidizer and press the mixture through a sieve. Discard the pulp and keep the raspberry sauce. All this can be done up to 12 hours in advance.

To serve, put a large scoop of the vanilla ice-cream in an attractive serving dish, place a peach half on either side and pour around a quarter of the raspberry purée into each dish. Serve immediately.

APRICOT TART

In recent years, really first class apricots have become available again in Britain. There was a period when they seemed to have disappeared from the scene, but large, golden and juicy fruit once more have a four to six week season and are a rare pleasure when they're here. Eating them fresh must be the first way to react to this bounty, but they also make one of the most delicious of all tarts. Apricot tart used to be the dessert by which a French restaurant was judged in the days before nouvelle cuisine made artistic arrangement as important as flavour. It is extremely easy to make at home, especially if you use some of the excellent fresh puff pastry available in supermarkets and grocers. As with so many of these sort of sweets it's best kept out of the fridge, though if your household is anything like mine, it rarely lasts long enough to be stored.

SERVES 6

450 g (1 lb) puff pastry	1 egg, well beaten
50 g (2 oz) granulated sugar	600 ml (1 pint) water
1 teaspoon vanilla essence	750 g (1½ lb) ripe apricots
300 ml (10 fl oz) milk	50 g (2 oz) caster sugar
1 tablespoon cornflour	50 g (2 oz) apricot jam

Pre-heat the oven to 220°C/425°F/Gas 7, 190°C fan, top of an Aga roasting oven.

Roll out the pastry into a rectangle about 30 × 46 cm (12 × 18 in). Fold the outer edges in 1 cm (½ in) to make a frame for the tart. Brush the edges with a little milk. Bake in the oven for 15 minutes until risen and golden. Leave to cool.

Meanwhile, stir the granulated sugar and vanilla essence into the milk and heat until the sugar is dissolved. Slake the cornflour in a little water and stir that into the milk with the well beaten egg. Bring gently to the simmer until the sauce (which is now a custard) thickens completely. Remove from the heat and allow to cool. In a separate pan, bring the water to the boil and dip in the apricots for 30 seconds. Lift out, skin and halve them and remove the stones. Pour away all but 120 ml (4 fl oz) of the water. Put the halved, skinned apricots and the caster sugar into that and simmer gently for 5 minutes. Do not let the apricots break up. Drain and leave to cool, reserving the syrup.

To assemble the tart, pour the custard into the cool tart base. Place the cooled apricots, cut side down on the custard in neat rows or attractive patterns. Add the apricot jam to the syrup in which the apricots were cooked and stir over a gentle heat until melted. Pour over the apricot and custard mixture, glazing the tart. Allow to set for at least 1 hour, preferably 2–3 hours, before serving.

PRESERVE

HERB VINEGARS (V)

There are a variety of vinegars to choose from today including wine vinegars both white and red, cider vinegar, and the dark full flavours of sherry and balsamic vinegar. Vinegars flavoured with herbs, spices and fruit are both attractive and add unusual flavours to dressings. Making your own herb vinegar is easy and more economical. Use either white wine or cider vinegar.

Tarragon and rosemary are good flavourings, as is a peeled clove of garlic, squashed gently to release the flavours. Whole spices such as mustard seed, mace, coriander, peppercorns and chillies will also add flavour.

To flavour the vinegar, simply post the desired flavourings into a bottle of vinegar (do not be tempted to add too many flavours into one bottle) cover, and leave to mature for at least one month.

To clarify the vinegar, strain through a muslin into a clean bottle, and add a fresh sprig of the appropriate herb or spice if desired.

To make raspberry vinegar, steep 1 lb of raspberries in 1 pt of white wine vinegar for 2 hours. Strain, stir in 1 teaspoon of sugar and bottle.

BREAD

FANCY DINNER ROLLS

These rolls have a high impact value, that is, although they're easy to prepare they look as though you've taken an enormous amount of trouble over them. They're a perfect accompaniment to a dinner party but also nice for family meals as they really make an impression far beyond the effort required to make them. I think they're best made with strong unbleached white flour but it is possible to make a similar collection if you prefer it using wholemeal or wheatmeal flours as an alternative. I suggest you use fresh yeast for this which is available at all bakers and supermarkets these days, but if you prefer to use dried yeast simply add half a packet to the flour and ignore the instructions about creaming the fresh yeast.

MAKES 8 ROLLS

15 g (½ oz) fresh yeast or ½ packet dried instant yeast	1 tablespoon soy or sunflower oil
300 ml (10 fl oz) lukewarm water	½ teaspoon salt
½ teaspoon sugar	50 ml (2 fl oz) milk
450 g (1 lb) unbleached strong white bread flour	15 g (½ oz) poppy seeds
	15 g (½ oz) sesame seeds

Cream the yeast with a tablespoon of the warm water and the sugar and allow to stand for 10–15 minutes during which time it will become frothy. Mix the flour, oil and salt together. Stir in the fresh yeast when it's frothed and add the remaining water. Knead the mixture either by hand or in a food processor until elastic and resilient. Cover the bowl with a cloth and allow to stand in a warm, draught-free place for about 45 minutes – the mixture should double in bulk.

Pre-heat the oven to 220°C/425°F/Gas 7, 190°C fan, top of an Aga roasting oven.

Knead the dough and divide it into eight pieces. Roll two of these into neat balls and place on a baking tray. Roll the next two into long thin sausages and tie in a half-hitch, that is half a granny knot. Place those on the baking tray. Roll the next two into short fat sausages like miniature French loaves and place those on the baking tray. Take a pinch of dough off each of the last two and roll the larger section into two balls, place those on to the baking tray, roll the smaller bits into two marble-sized pieces and press those into the top to make miniature cottage loaves. Brush all the rolls with the milk and sprinkle the knotted bread with the poppy seeds and the round rolls with the sesame seeds. Cut a couple of little slashes in the French loaves diagonally and bake the collection in the oven for 20 minutes until golden and cooked through.

To test, lift one of the round rolls and tap on the base. It should sound hollow. If not, turn the heat down and allow to cook for another 5 minutes or so. They should be allowed to cool thoroughly on a wire rack before serving. If you want to serve them hot, re-heat them rather than serve them straight out of the oven.

HERB

CHIVES

There are two varieties of chive, the fine grass-like strands that have the taste of mild onions, and the fatter Chinese variety that taste like mild garlic.

Both are good cut into salads and salad dressings, into cottage cheese, mayonnaise, scrambled eggs, omelettes and sandwich fillings. Try enlivening mashed potatoes by adding a generous amount of finely snipped chives. They are also a good addition to soup, stews and stir-fries.

Chives are excellent freeze-dried but should be added with sufficient liquid to rehydrate them thoroughly. When cut they can be used as a garnish, and are often used in nouvelle cuisine to tie up 'bundles' of vegetables such as string beans.

DRINK

PEACH NECTAR

With peaches beginning their happily extended season in June, one of the most delicious of all fruit-based drinks is suddenly possible. You will need a liquidizer and some over-ripe peaches. These may be ones left over from your bowl or ones you can buy really cheaply in a market or greengrocers. The peach nectar itself can be drunk as it is, diluted with plain or fizzy water, or mixed with milk and a little ice-cream as the basis of a milk shake. Mixed with Champagne, as it is in Italy sometimes, it's known as a Bellini.

SERVES 4

8 very ripe peaches	25 g (1 oz) caster sugar
½ teaspoon ground cinnamon	600 ml (1 pint) water

ip the peaches into a bowl or pan of boiling water for 30 seconds then remove the skins – they will slip off easily. Cut the peaches in half, remove the stones and cut each half into quarters. Place them in a liquidizer or food processor with the cinnamon, sugar and water. You may need to do this in more than one batch. Process until completely smooth. You may want to pass the purée through a nylon, not a metal, sieve, just to make sure. Stir the resultant purée and store it in a sealed bottle in the fridge. You can dilute it in any of the ways described above to make wonderful summer drinks. It also is nice with a sprig of mint added.

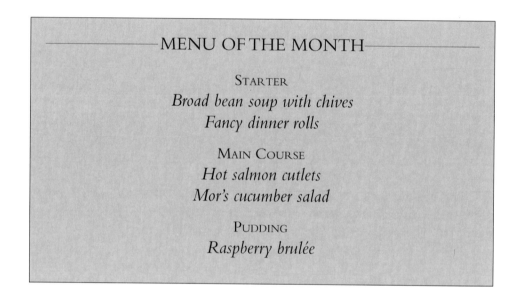

MENU OF THE MONTH

STARTER
Broad bean soup with chives
Fancy dinner rolls

MAIN COURSE
Hot salmon cutlets
Mor's cucumber salad

PUDDING
Raspberry brulée

CRAFTY TIPS FROM THE CRAFTY COOK

● This is simply the best method for cooking perfect pasta. I discovered it on the back of a pasta packet in Clapham in 1974 and have used it ever since. Put a large saucepan of water on to boil and add a pinch of salt and a little olive oil. When it is boiling, put the pasta in and leave it to boil for three minutes. Take it off the heat, put the lid on and leave for a further seven minutes. At the end of this time, the pasta will be cooked, not sticky but perfectly *al dente*.

● For a fresher salad, tear the leaves into pieces about half the size of a postcard. Don't cut lettuce – this allows the liquid to drain out and you are left with a floppy salad. Wash the pieces thoroughly and place on a clean tea towel to drip dry. Half an hour in the fridge at this stage before dressing will make your salad even crisper.

● Always use fresh Parmesan, not the bought grated kind. A lump will keep in the fridge for weeks – grate it just before serving. The difference is well worth it!

● To remove the skins from soft fruits like peaches or tomatoes, dip them in boiling water for thirty seconds, drain and the skins slip effortlessly off.

● Topping and tailing green beans can seem like a lifetime's work – unless you do it the crafty way! Take a handful of beans, hold them vertically over a chopping board and shake them gently until the tip of each bean just touches the surface of the board. Now that they are level, lay them flat and cut all the ends off at once. Turn the beans around and repeat the process with the other end.

● Avoid burnt fingers when you barbecue – and keep the food in one piece when you turn it over – by buying a fish-shaped or square grid with a long handle. These are freely available from your local barbecue stockist and really do save time and energy.

● Use Spanish onions when possible – they are much quicker ot peel and easier to deal with.

● To stop avocados going brown when you cut them, leave the stone in the middle and cover tightly with cling film. This also works with avocado puree and *guacamole*.

● To coat meat with flour easily and with little mess, put both the meat and flour into a large plastic bag and hold it so it is tightly closed. Then shake the bag about – whirl it round your head if you like! – until each piece of meat is well covered.

● If you are making mayonnaise or any similar sauce in a food processor and it separates, add a tablespoon of iced water, whizz briefly and the sauce should amalgamate.

● The crafty way to remove fat from soups or stocks is to put the cooled liquid in a bowl in the fridge and chill it for a few hours. The fat will form a hard layer on the surface and can now easily be lifted off.

● How to cook cream, fromage frais, yoghurt, etc, without it curdling, separating or other horrors:
– Double cream will not curdle, separate ot do anything nasty when it is heated. You can safely boil it.
– For single cream and the low-fat alternatives, a teaspoon of cornflour added to a small pot and beaten means you can simmer without problems. Do not be tempted to fast boil.

JULY

INTRODUCTION

July – Wimbledon, strawberries, salads and hot-weather foods – sunshine permitting – the whole of the month seems to lead towards what the French call *'déjeuner sur l'herbe'*. Literally translated that means lunch on the grass. What it doesn't mean, emphatically, is barbecues, but eating proper meals on proper plates out of doors. What could be nicer on a sun-dappled terrace than a tomato salad, then a butterfly roast leg of lamb with the first of the English broccoli and a bowl piled high with strawberries and thick whipped cream to follow.

Apart from strawberries, July is also the month for currants – red, black and even white. Mangetout, those marvellous peas you can eat the whole of, make their welcome appearance, as do the first of that great British delicacy, runner beans. New potatoes are still at their peak and at their cheapest, and cauliflowers are at their creamiest and curdiest. All kind of salad greens abound – round and Webb's lettuces, icebergs, oak leaf, frisée, lollo rosso and biondo; the first of the red chicories, the radicchio de verona puts in its early appearance, and home-grown cucumbers, tomatoes and watercress enrich salads.

July is truly a month of plenty with lots of fish, both round and flat, available. A good time, too, for sea trout and particularly that Welsh delicacy, sewin, just a little paler and more delicate than its larger cousin the salmon. Altogether a month to enjoy summer's generous plenty and with the blessings of autumn still to come.

July

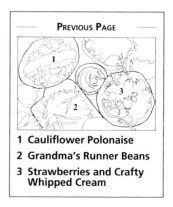

PREVIOUS PAGE

1 **Cauliflower Polonaise**
2 **Grandma's Runner Beans**
3 **Strawberries and Crafty Whipped Cream**

─────────────── Produce at its Best ───────────────

Runner beans ● *Mangetout* ● *Broccoli* ● *Cauliflowers* ● *Chicory*
● *Salads* ● *Tomatoes* ● *Strawberries* ● *Currants* ● *Cherries* ● *Beef*
● *Sardines* ● *Brill* ● *Plaice*

STARTERS

SOUPE AU PISTOU Ⓥ

This is a vegetable soup made with fresh beans and flavoured with a marvellous basil and cheese concoction known in southern France as pistou. It's a close relative of the Italian pesto but simpler and a little more direct. This makes a lovely first course in small quantities, or, eaten generously, a meal on its own with some cheese and perhaps a little salad to follow.

SERVES 4

225 g (8 oz) shelled broad beans	2 tablespoons olive oil
100 g (4 oz) onions, chopped	salt and freshly ground black pepper
100 g (4 oz) carrots	900 ml (1½ pints) water or stock
100 g (4 oz) shelled fresh peas	25 g (1 oz) fresh basil leaves
100 g (4 oz) celery	1 garlic clove
100 g (4 oz) tomatoes	50 g (2 oz) Gruyère cheese

Peel and dice all the vegetables, you can substitute or add to the mixture if it suits you – courgettes, potatoes and 1 cm (½ in) lengths of French beans are all acceptable. Gently fry all the vegetables except the tomatoes in half the olive oil. Season generously with salt and pepper and add the water or stock. Bring to the boil and simmer for 12 minutes. Meanwhile, put the remaining oil, the basil leaves and garlic into a food processor and purée until smooth. You may need to add a little more oil or a tablespoon of water to make the mixture work smoothly. Add the grated Gruyère and process again until thoroughly blended. Add the chopped tomatoes to the soup, allow to simmer for a further 1 minute and serve with a separate bowl of the pistou mixture. Guests stir a spoonful of the pistou into their soup before eating.

TOMATO AND BASIL SALAD Ⓥ

At this time of year, sun-ripened tomatoes become a reality. Unless it's been a very fine summer they're probably from across the Channel, but at last varieties chosen and grown for their flavour and not just their uniformity of shape are available. Try and find the large Marmande-type tomatoes for this particular salad as their texture as well as their flavour makes it more interesting. An alternative is to use the cherry-type, marble-sized tomatoes which also have an intensity of flavour.

SERVES 4

450 g (1 lb) tomatoes, large or small	1 tablespoon red wine vinegar
25 g (1 oz) fresh basil	splash of lemon juice
3 spring onions	½ teaspoon sugar
1 tablespoon olive oil	½ teaspoon salt
3 tablespoons salad oil	

Wash and slice the tomatoes, if large, into 5 mm (¼ in) thick slices and lay them in an attractive pattern in a shallow china dish. If using cherry tomatoes, halve these and place in the same sort of container. Rinse the basil leaves and trim the spring onions and cut into 1 cm (½ in) lengths. Put these into a liquidizer or food processor with the oils, wine vinegar, lemon juice, sugar and salt. Process until a smooth, thick, green purée. Pour this over the tomatoes and leave to marinate for at least 30 minutes or up to 2–3 hours in the fridge. Decorate if you wish with a few reserved basil leaves and eat with lots of crusty French bread.

GRANDMA'S RUNNER BEANS Ⓥ

This is a recipe from my childhood and comes via my mother from her mother in turn. It used to be a family treat in the Welsh valley they and I were born in, and is from a time when work and money were scarce and the kitchen garden was the great supplier of nutrition as well as flavour. It's extremely simple and extraordinarily delicious eaten with granary or wholemeal bread and that marvellous bright gold, Welsh farmhouse butter. In the old days runner beans used to be quite a chore, needing both stringing and careful cutting. Nowadays, however, they tend to come fairly stringless unless you buy the mammoth kind used for exhibitions, and there are a number of terrific devices on the market which help you slice them almost effortlessly. You can serve this in small portions as a starter for a family meal or, as in my family, as a main course in its own right, on what often turned out to be special occasions.

SERVES 4

450 g (1 lb) runner beans	salt and freshly ground black pepper
40 g (1½ oz) butter	

rim, string if necessary, and slice the beans into fine 5 mm (¼ in) thick slices. Bring a pan of salted water to the boil, drop in the beans and allow to cook for 5 minutes until bright green but still crunchy. Drain. Put half the butter back into the dried pan, add the beans, cover with a lid and shake thoroughly, off the heat, then leave for 1 minute. In the pan, add a generous seasoning of fresh black pepper and a good pinch of salt. Shake once more and serve into individual-sized bowls. Add the rest of the butter, dotted on top of the beans, to allow it to melt and run down. Serve hot with plenty of good brown bread.

GRILLED SARDINES

It must be because of the effect of holidays on the Mediterranean and, in particular, in Portugal, but fresh sardines are suddenly available these days in most of our fishmongers and fish counters. They are the size of small herrings but taste very different – the darker the flesh the more intense the flavour. They're not a delicate fish and respond well to grilling, even on an outdoor barbecue, which is how they are so often eaten in Portugal. If you're grilling at home and indoors, it's as well to remember the trick of lining the grill pan with foil before you cook fish. This not only makes cleaning a great deal more pleasant and easy but also reflects heat up on to the fish so that they cook more quickly and with less time and smell. Sardines cooked like this make a terrific course with little more than some good salt and half a lemon to squeeze over them. If you want something a little more sophisticated, use a good tartare sauce or mayonnaise mixed with some chopped gherkin, spring onion and parsley.

SERVES 4

8 medium-sized sardines, trimmed and gutted	**2 tablespoons olive oil**
25 g (1 oz) sea salt	**1 large lemon**

ub the sardines with the salt and leave for 10 minutes. Wash off the salt thoroughly, allow them to dry on kitchen paper and rub lightly with the olive oil. Heat your grill to maximum temperature for at least 10 minutes. Lightly oil the grid so that the fish doesn't stick and place the sardines on it. Grill 4–5 cm (1½–2 in) away from the grill for 2–3 minutes on one side, turn and grill for another 2 minutes on the other side. The skin may char slightly but the flesh should be firm and not burnt. Remove from the grill and squeeze the lemon over them immediately. Serve while they're hot.

COLD CREAM OF ALMOND SOUP ⓥ

This is an unusual soup with a delicate, light flavour which makes it a wonderful starter on a hot day. Unexpectedly, its origins are in the Mediterranean, particularly in Spain where cold soups have a wide popularity. You can make this soup starting with whole almonds, taking them out of the shell and taking the brown skin off, but frankly that's not a very crafty way to cook and these days it's much easier to buy the new season's almonds freshly prepared for you.

SERVES 4

1 medium-sized onion, finely chopped	1 garlic clove, chopped
100 g (4 oz) potatoes, peeled and finely diced	900 ml (1½ pints) water
1 tablespoon salad oil (not olive)	150 ml (5 fl oz) single cream
225 g (8 oz) peeled almonds	TO GARNISH
salt and freshly ground black pepper	fresh fennel leaves or chopped fresh parsley

Fry the onion and potato gently in the oil till the onion is translucent but do not allow them to brown. Add the almonds, season generously, add the garlic and water. Simmer the whole mixture for 35 minutes until the potatoes and almonds are thoroughly soft. Place in a food processor or liquidizer and purée until completely smooth. You may need to scrape the sides down a couple of times to achieve this effect. Add the cream and season again. Leave to cool and chill for at least 2 hours before serving. Garnish with the fennel leaves or parsley. You may also add a couple of ice cubes to each bowl.

MAIN COURSES AND VEGETABLES

SESAME CHICKEN SALAD

Chicken salads come in many different guises. We often forget that in parts of Asia, particularly in the south-east of Asia, the Chinese rules about never eating cold food don't apply, and salads have a slightly different flavour and texture to those we're used to. This is one which reflects that, with the use of sesame bringing a hint of the exotic to one of our more common ingredients.

SERVES 6

6 boned chicken breasts	FOR THE DRESSING
100 g (4 oz) mangetout peas	5 tablespoons sesame oil (roasted)
25 g (1 oz) sesame seeds	2 tablespoons white wine vinegar
½ Chinese leaf or iceberg lettuce, shredded	½ teaspoon Dijon mustard
1 small red pepper, thinly sliced	½ teaspoon sugar
1 small yellow pepper, thinly sliced	1 small garlic clove, crushed
2 celery sticks, thinly sliced	a good pinch of salt
100 g (4 oz) seedless black grapes, halved	freshly ground black pepper
100 g (4 oz) firm white mushrooms, thinly sliced	

Cook the chicken breasts by poaching in water or stock in a covered pan for 20–25 minutes until thoroughly cooked. Drain and cut into dice. Cook the mangetout in boiling water for 3 minutes then drain and run under cold water. (This will keep their bright green colour.) Toast the sesame seeds in a dry frying-pan over a moderate heat, shaking the pan until they are pale gold. Arrange the shredded lettuce on to a serving plate or bowl. Arrange the fruit and vegetables in an attractive pattern on the lettuce. Pile the chicken in the middle and sprinkle over the sesame seeds. Whisk the dressing ingredients together, pour over the salad and serve.

THAI-STYLE BEEF AND BASIL SAUTE

This is one of the basic dishes of Thai cooking, adapted for easily accessible ingredients and delicious eaten with rice and a stir-fried vegetable dish. In Thailand, of course, it would be part of a much larger group of dishes eaten as part of a collective on the buffet table, and you can, if you like, try it that way as well, with other Chinese or Thai-style dishes included. It's very simple to cook and very quick in addition, so it makes for a really fresh convenience dish.

SERVES 4

1 tablespoon cooking oil (not olive)	1 teaspoon ginger paste
450 g (1 lb) lean minced beef or steak	½ teaspoon chilli paste or sauce
2 tablespoons soy sauce	12 fresh basil leaves, shredded
1 teaspoon garlic paste	grated rind and juice of 1 lime

Heat the oil in a heavy-based frying-pan and brown the meat in it thoroughly. Add the soy sauce and the garlic, ginger and chilli and turn over a low heat until the flavours are blended and the mixture is almost dry. Add the basil leaves and lime rind and mix together thoroughly. Sprinkle with the lime juice. Check for seasoning and serve with plenty of boiled rice and a stir-fry vegetable.

PLAICE MEUNIERE

You can make this dish with any of the small flat fish that are available throughout the summer, especially at seaside locations. The fish should be 23–30 cm (9–12 in) long and weigh about 175–225 g (6–8 oz), that is a one person portion. Sometimes they're baby sole, often plaice, sometimes one of the other flat fish like brill or lemon sole, but they all need to be treated in very much the same way. This is the simplest and perhaps one of the nicest ways of cooking fresh fish, straight from the sea or the beach into the pan.

SERVES 4

½ teaspoon celery salt or plain salt	50 g (2 oz) cooking oil
25 g (1 oz) plain flour	50 g (2 oz) butter
4 flat fish, about 175–225 g (6–8 oz) each, cleaned and trimmed	juice of 1 large lemon

Mix the celery salt or salt and flour in a paper or plastic bag, dip the cleaned, trimmed fish in that and shake it so that they are covered. In a large pan or pans into which all the fish will fit flat, put the oil and then half the butter and bring to a heat so that the butter melts and finishes sizzling. Add the fish immediately and fry over a moderate heat for 3–4 minutes on each side. When the fish is done enough to flake when tested with a fork on the thick part of the flesh, take them out of the pan and place on a warm plate. Discard the fat in the pan, add the remaining butter and when that melts, pour it over the fish. Add the lemon juice to the pan, swirl it round and pour that over in turn and serve still sizzling hot. This is easy to eat provided you start in the middle of the fish along the backbone line and lift the fillets off from the centre. It is nicest eaten with bread and butter with a vegetable or salad course to follow.

CAULIFLOWER POLONAISE Ⓥ

With cauliflowers at their best at this time of year it's nice to make a dish that can either be eaten with other foods or as a course on its own, whether you're of vegetarian inclination or not. Not only does this method of cooking cauliflower taste delicious, it also looks very attractive. The name Polonaise is simply because the French believed that anything sprinkled with hard-boiled, finely chopped egg had a Polish origin. I know of no evidence that supports this view but it's a pretty name anyway. This makes a lovely light lunch or, in small quantities, a very good vegetable to go with a juicy meat or fish dish.

SERVES 4

1 large cauliflower, trimmed	40 g (1½ oz) butter
2 slices white bread	1 teaspoon garlic salt
2 eggs	1 tablespoon chopped fresh parsley

reak the cauliflower into about eight florets and place in cold water. Bring to the boil and cook for 5 minutes until the cauliflower is cooked but still firm and crisp. Drain thoroughly. Cut the bread slices into cubes and, using a food processor or liquidizer, turn into fine breadcrumbs. Boil the eggs until they are hard-boiled (this can be done in the same water as the cauliflower is cooking if you wash the shells first). They should be cooked for 8–10 minutes. Cool immediately in cold water and shell. Split the eggs and chop the whites and yolks separately. Heat the butter in a frying-pan into which all the cauliflower will fit. Put in the breadcrumbs and fry until golden. Add the garlic salt and parsley and turn thoroughly. Add the drained cauliflower and turn with the breadcrumbs for a minute or so until heated through thoroughly. Put the cauliflower and breadcrumbs into a serving dish and sprinkle the whites over and lay a trail of the yolk down the centre of the dish as a decoration and flavour.

BUTTERFLY ROAST LEG OF LAMB

This is a modern way of cooking lamb which is very quick and efficient but produces lamb of an excellent flavour and considerable moistness. You will need to get your butcher to bone the leg of lamb so that it comes out in what is known as a butterfly. You can do this yourself if you wish, the trick being to cut the lamb lengthways along the bone and then peel it off so that it remains in one piece an inch or so thick. This allows it to cook very fast while retaining its succulence and juiciness. It makes an excellent alternative to old-fashioned roast lamb and can be served with the same sort of vegetables and accompaniments.

SERVES 4

1 × 1.25–1.5 kg (2½–3½ lb) leg of lamb, butterfly boned	1 garlic clove, crushed
	1 teaspoon salt
2 sprigs of fresh rosemary	

re-heat the oven to 230°C/450°F/Gas 8, 200°C fan, top of an Aga roasting oven. Line a roasting pan with foil.

Trim any excess fat off the leg of lamb. Place the rosemary sprigs on the foil and lay the leg of lamb open, skin side down, on the rosemary. Crush the garlic with the salt and spread that over the cut side of the lamb. Roast in the oven for 15 minutes. Turn, baste with the juices and cook for another 10 minutes for rare, 15 for medium and 20 minutes for brown all the way through. Check for the level of doneness; it will relate to the accuracy of your oven. Take the meat out and allow it to rest for 5 minutes before carving across the grain in thick slices.

SALADE NIÇOISE

Salade Niçoise has a very chequered history. Purists believe it has to contain nothing except tuna fish, olives, onions and hard-boiled eggs, but it's come to contain a much more balanced group of ingredients as it's made and eaten these days all over France, and by its fans in the rest of the world. There is a vegetarian version which can leave out the tuna fish and anchovies, though they are undoubtedly traditional. It's marvellous made in a big glass bowl and eaten outdoors in the sunshine. It has a freshness and crispness which belies its capacity to be quite a filling dish in its own right. It's a main course, not an accompanying salad, and should be followed by cheese and a pudding or fruit.

SERVES 4

1 large crisp lettuce	**FOR THE DRESSING**
225 g (8 oz) new potatoes	100 g (4 oz) olive oil
4 eggs, scrubbed	1 tablespoon white wine vinegar
100 g (4 oz) stringless French beans, topped and tailed	1 tablespoon lemon juice
100 g (4 oz) cherry tomatoes, halved	½ teaspoon sugar
175 g (6 oz) tin tuna in oil or brine, drained	½ teaspoon salt
50 g (2 oz) tin anchovies, drained and oil reserved	
8 black olives	

Wash the lettuce, dry thoroughly, break it into postcard-sized pieces and use these to line a large glass bowl. Scrub the new potatoes, cut into even-sized pieces and bring to the boil in a pan of water with the eggs. Once the water boils, boil the eggs for 8 minutes then remove them and run them under cold water. Shell and halve the eggs. Continue to cook the potatoes for another 4–5 minutes until they are done but still firm. Remove them from the water. Add the beans and boil for just 5 minutes then drain thoroughly. Mix the dressing by whisking the oil, wine vinegar, lemon juice, sugar and salt together.

To build the salad, put a ring of cooled potatoes around the edge of the lettuce, follow with a ring of the cooled beans, then the halved hard-boiled eggs, then the cherry tomatoes, and pile the tuna in the middle. Decorate with the olives and the strips of anchovies. You can add the oil from the anchovies to the dressing which should be poured over the salad not more than 5 minutes before you eat it.

CHERRY CLAFOUTIS

Clafoutis is like a sweet Yorkshire pudding stuffed with fruit and spices. It can be made all the year round with different fruits but the most classic clafoutis of all is made in the south-west of France in the brief period when the great big, black, sweet cherries are available. At this time of year they are available in Britain too, though very few of them are grown here, and it's a brief fortnight or so in the second half of July that you can find them. When you can, and when you've had enough of them just eaten from a bowl of iced water, this makes a lovely dish that does their juiciness and flavour justice. You can stone the cherries if you have the patience but I prefer to cook them whole and warn guests to eat them slowly to preserve their teeth. You can also use pitted tinned cherries. Rinse them before using.

SERVES 4

450 g (1 lb) large dark cherries	150 ml (5 fl oz) milk
150 g (5 oz) self-raising flour	1 tablespoon cooking oil (not olive)
3 eggs	100 g (4 oz) icing sugar

Preheat the oven to Gas Mark 5, 375°F, 190°C, 170° fan, middle of the roasting oven in the Aga.

Wash, stalk and, if you wish, stone the cherries. Whisk the flour, eggs and milk together into a batter, add the oil and beat in the icing sugar a spoonful at a time. Pour the mixture into a lightly buttered gratin or baking dish and add the cherries. One option is to sprinkle the mixture now with about half a teaspoon of ground cinnamon but some prefer it without the spice. Either way, bake it in a moderately hot oven for about 45 to 50 minutes until risen and golden and firm. Eat it hot – it will sink as it cools. Single cream rather than double is nicest with this.

SUMMER PUDDING

Summer pudding is one of the great puddings on which the British culinary reputation rests. There are all kinds of myths and legends attached to it but, in fact, it is extremely simple: a mixture of the summer fruits cooked gently together until their juice runs, then packed into a casing of crustless white bread with enough juice to soak the whole confection to a luscious dark red. You can use a mixture of fruit though the combination of the three I suggest is the traditional one. You can also make it in individual-sized portions or, as I've suggested here, in one large pudding basin-sized confection. Either way, make sure there's enough juice to soak the bread completely, and leave the puddings to stand for at least 3 to 4 hours before eating them.

SERVES 4

225 g (8 oz) raspberries	**75–100 g (3–4 oz) caster sugar, according to taste**
225 g (8 oz) blackcurrants	**½ loaf medium-sliced white bread**
225 g (8 oz) redcurrants (alternatives include strawberries and cherries, stoned)	

Trim and de-stalk the fruit and place it in a bowl with the sugar. Crush slightly with a stainless steel or silver fork until the juices run. Tip into a pan and cook gently for about 5–10 minutes until thoroughly hot through but not jammy. Allow to cool. Trim the crusts from 8–10 slices of white bread and use these to line a 1.2-litre (2-pint) pudding basin, leaving no gaps but avoiding overlap as much as possible. Pour the slightly cooled fruit into the lined basin, making sure there's enough juice to saturate the bread completely. Put another layer of crustless bread across the top of the basin, sealing it. Tap a couple of times on a wooden surface to settle the mixture then chill for at least 6 hours, preferably overnight. Invert a plate over the basin, tip it upside-down, remove the basin and serve the summer pudding in slices like a cake with double cream or custard to eat with it.

STRAWBERRIES

Strawberries are the queen of summer fruits. Traditionally their season was quite short, although we now import strawberries from all over the world to provide us with them from January to December. The four weeks that stretch from the end of June to the end of July are still the high point, when British strawberries are at their most delicious. As with many fruits these days, varieties grown for their flavour as well as their shape, colour and handling quality are becoming increasingly available. It's worth looking and asking to taste both in shops and in the pick-your-own farms and stalls that are springing up all over the place. Once you've got your strawberries, what to do with them can provide a wealth of different opinions. There are many different versions of what enhances the flavour, from black pepper to a variety of marinades. At the peak of the season little improves on a sprinkling of caster sugar over freshly picked and lightly washed strawberries when they're being topped with cream. To avoid the over-richness of old-fashioned double cream, however, you might want to try my crafty whipped cream.

Cherry Clafoutis

CRAFTY WHIPPED CREAM

SERVES 4

150 ml (5 fl oz) double cream	150 ml (5 fl oz) plain yoghurt
1 scant teaspoon caster sugar	

Whip the double cream with the caster sugar until it's thick but not grainy. Add the yoghurt a spoonful at a time, whipping as you go, and you will find that the mixture retains its thickness and airiness while only having half the fat for the same amount of double cream. Continue until all the yoghurt is incorporated. This mixture will thicken even more if left in the fridge for up to 6 hours.

FLAVOUR ENHANCERS FOR STRAWBERRIES

Of all the ways of improving the flavour of strawberries, only two really recommend themselves. One is a small sprinkling of freshly ground black pepper with the strawberries eaten with no cream but a little caster sugar. The pepper flavour doesn't appear hot or spicy but does seem to intensify the strawberryness.

The other alternative is the only satisfactory marinade I've ever found. Alcohol destroys both the flavour and the texture of strawberries, but a small quantity of freshly pressed orange juice heightens the flavours and softens the texture, particularly useful if you're using large or slightly bruised strawberries in your mixture.

CRUSHED STRAWBERRY CREAM

In Germany they make a marvellous mixture of crushed strawberries mixed with sour cream with whole strawberries mixed in. I first ate it on a farm in Westphalia as a student and have never forgotten the intense pleasure it gave.

SERVES 4

450 g (1 lb) strawberries	475 ml (16 fl oz) fromage frais or quark, 8 per cent fat
50 g (2 oz) caster sugar	

Crush half of the hulled strawberries with the caster sugar and allow to stand for 15 minutes until the juice runs. Beat the fromage frais or quark until it's smooth and add the crushed strawberries, mixing thoroughly. Trim the remaining strawberries and hull them. If they're very large, slice them in half, then add them to the strawberry and cream mixture. Stir till they're thoroughly incorporated and allow to chill in the fridge for an hour or up to 6 hours before serving.

PRESERVE

STRAWBERRY CONSERVE Ⓥ

Strawberry conserve differs from strawberry jam really only in that it uses less sugar per weight of fruit and the fruit itself is kept whole if possible. In order to make any jam successfully it's important to start with the best natural ingredients but, where strawberries are concerned, it's absolutely essential that every fruit be ripe, unbruised and undamaged. This recipe uses 1.75 kg (4 lb) of strawberries to make about 2.25–2.75 kg (5–6 lb) of jam. The great rule with jam-making normally is to soften the fruit slowly before adding the sugar and then to boil it fast. This uses a rather different technique, designed to keep the fruit whole.

MAKES ABOUT 2.25 kg (5 lb)

1.75 kg (4 lb) strawberries	juice of ½ lemon
1.5 kg (3 lb) preserving sugar (with extra pectin)	

Wipe the strawberries thoroughly and hull them. Place them in a glass or china bowl and sprinkle the sugar over them. Leave for 6 hours. Tip the resulting mixture into a preserving pan (preferably stainless steel, copper or non-stick). Add the lemon juice and bring gently to the boil. As soon as all the sugar is dissolved, this should take no more than 5 minutes or so, boil rapidly for about 6–7 minutes and test for setting by dropping some of the juice on to a chilled saucer. It should set firmly enough not to run off the saucer. If not, cook for a little bit longer. The intention is to cook it enough to provide a good set but for the fruit to remain whole. Bottle immediately in sterilized jars and seal tightly. It may be slightly runnier than conventional jams but the flavour and the texture of the whole strawberries will be wonderful.

BREAD

CORN BREAD

Corn bread, or bread made from cornmeal, is common all over America, the country of the grain's origin. It's made in all sorts of styles from a spoon bread, really a kind of heavy soufflé that's literally spooned out of the dish it's baked in, to this pale gold and slightly crumbly bread which is eaten very much like an ordinary loaf. It can be sliced and even toasted. It has a slightly sweet flavour and is particularly nice at breakfast time or eaten with American-style dishes like fried chicken. It does not make good sandwiches.

MAKES 1 × 900 g (2 lb) LOAF

175 g (6 oz) fine cornmeal (not cornflour!)	1 teaspoon caster sugar
150 g (5 oz) strong white bread flour	2 eggs
3 heaped teaspoons baking powder	300 ml (10 fl oz) milk
1 teaspoon salt	50 ml (2 fl oz) oil (not olive)

Pre-heat the oven to 200°C/400°F/Gas 6, 180°C fan, middle of an Aga roasting oven. Grease and line a 900 g (2 lb) loaf tin.

Mix together the flours, baking powder, salt and sugar. Beat the eggs with the milk. Add the oil and mix into the dry ingredients until you have made a fairly coherent batter. Pour the mixture into the prepared tin and cook in the oven for about 40–45 minutes. Test with a skewer which should go in and come out clean. If it's still smeary, turn the heat down and allow the bread to cook for another 5–10 minutes. It should be allowed to stand for 5 minutes before turning out. You may find some non-stick parchment lining the tin helps this considerably. Allow to cool a little before eating but unlike ordinary yeast bread it can be eaten before it's completely cooled.

HERB

BASIL

Basil is one of the great culinary herbs, most popular in Mediterranean style cooking but also used widely in Thai dishes. Sweet basil is the variety best known to us, although holy basil with purplish leaves and lemon basil are grown in Thailand.

Basil is good eaten raw and cooked. The leaves should be torn rather than chopped and added to salads, eggs, cheese and, last but not least, sliced tomatoes. It finds a perfect marriage in the well-known Italian salad of tomatoes, avocado and Mozzarella cheese. It can be added to salad dressings to flavour a whole salad.

Try it cooked on pizza, rice dishes, eggs and pasta. It is the staple ingredient for pesto sauce, traditionally made in a mortar and pestle to bruise the oil from the leaves.

PESTO SAUCE (V)

SERVES 4

50 g (2 oz) fresh basil leaves	3 garlic cloves, peeled
75 g (3 oz) pine nuts	85–120 ml (3–4 fl oz) olive oil
75 g (3 oz) Parmesan, freshly grated	freshly ground black pepper

Blend all the ingredients together, put into a clean jar and keep chilled. It will keep for up to 3 weeks. To make pesto effortlessly use a blender.

TOMATO JUICE COCKTAIL

A great starter for an evening's entertaining outdoors. Bright, strong tastes and a substantial texture make this an adults' favourite.

SERVES 4

600 ml (1 pint) tomato juice	a dash of Worcestershire sauce
4–5 fresh basil leaves	salt to taste
1 tablespoon freshly squeezed lemon juice	4 small celery sticks with leaves
a few drops of tabasco sauce	ice

Put all the ingredients into a liquidizer and blend. Pour into glasses, cool with ice and garnish each with a stick of celery.

MENU OF THE MONTH

STARTER
Cold cream of almond soup

MAIN COURSE
Salad Niçoise
Corn bread

PUDDING
Summer pudding

AUGUST

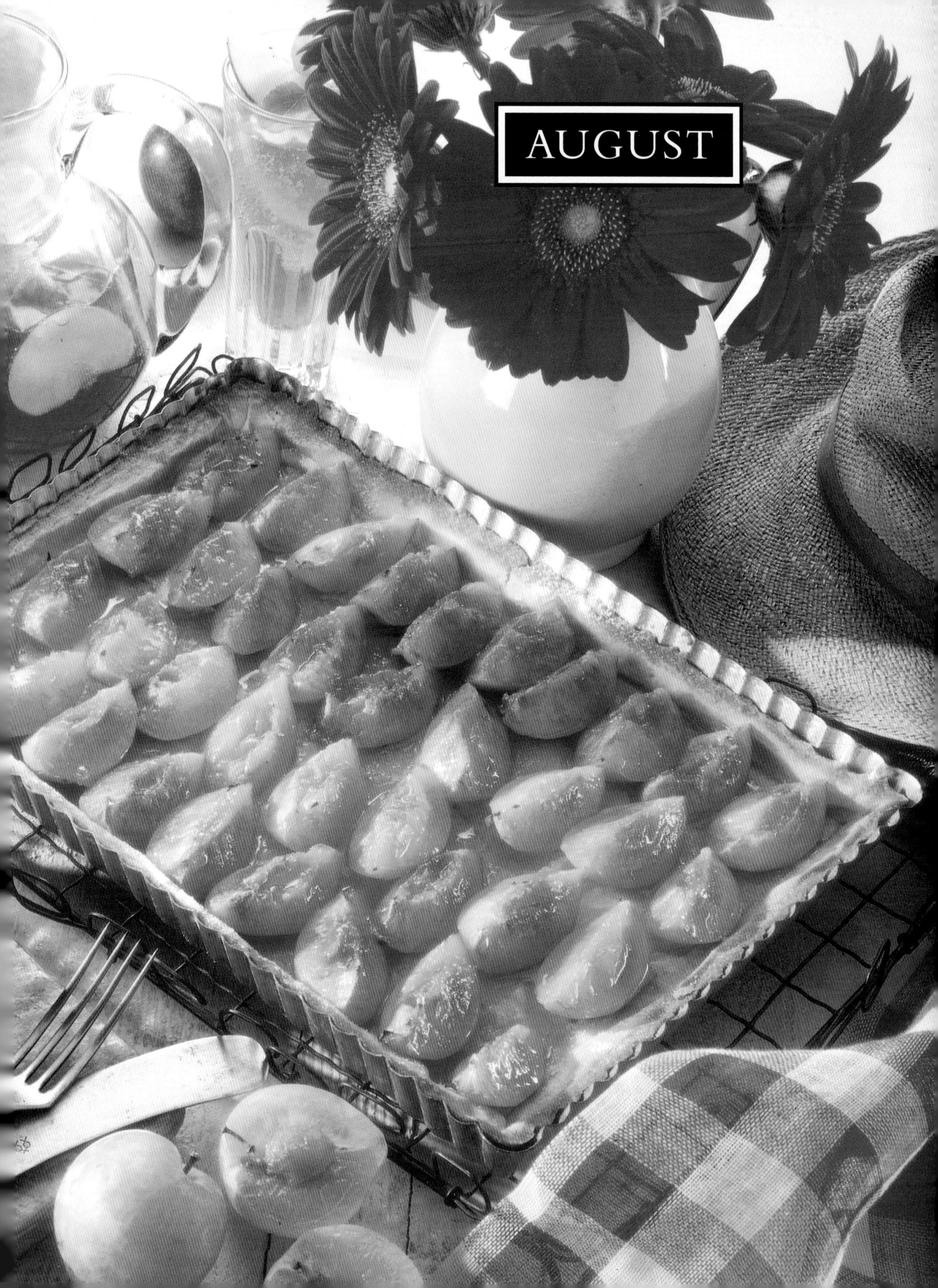

INTRODUCTION

W here food is concerned, August isn't a wicked month at all, it's another of the months of summer's richness. The Mediterranean vegetables like aubergines, courgettes and peppers are at their peak, salad greens abound and it's even possible, on rare occasions, to get really ripe tomatoes – the kind that have a rich flavour and a natural sweetness. Very often these are still imported from warmer climes but if you grow your own, towards the end of August you should be reaping the benefit. August is also the month for holidays, particularly if you have children at school, and during a fine summer, a month for outdoor eating as well. In recent years barbecues have become part of that habit, an ideal time for British lamb flavoured with the mint that is at its best in this month of high summer.

On the fruit front it's the brief time when British plums are available. We seem to grow and enjoy more varieties than most other countries; our pleasures range from greengages and Victorias and the purple Czars through to the tart, bitter-sweet damsons that make such wonderful jam, flavoured yoghurts and ice-cream.

If you're at the seaside during August, crabs are at their plump and succulent best. And if you're further inland on the moors, the glorious twelfth brings the beginning of the grouse season, for many the most special, delicious and certainly the most idiosyncratic of all British birds. But above all, August is a time for light eating, for food that doesn't sit too heavily but is still bursting with flavour, and the excitement of enjoying the great outdoors.

August

PREVIOUS PAGE

1 **Aubergine and Courgette Fritters**

2 **Sole Monte Carlo**

3 **Greengage Tart**

STARTERS

CUCUMBER AND MINT YOGHURT SOUP ⓥ

The combination of cucumber, mint and yoghurt has its roots in the Middle East and there it comes in many forms, from a light refreshing whipped drink served in Persia called 'Aryan' right the way through to very substantial sauces for roast lamb and spiced rice dishes from Turkey and Arabia. This soup treads a middle course being both very rich in flavour but having the lightness and delicacy that makes it perfect for what should be a hot weather dish. It can be made up to six hours in advance and keeps well in the fridge. It makes a splendid starter to a spicy meal or one with quite a dry main course.

SERVES 4

1 large cucumber	300 ml (10 fl oz) plain unsweetened yoghurt
1 garlic clove	300 ml (10 fl oz) water
1 teaspoon salt	bunch of mint 50 g (2 oz)

Top and tail the cucumber and cut in half lengthways. Using a strong teaspoon, scoop out the soft centre which contains the seeds and discard this. Grate the remaining cucumber reasonably finely or chop it in a food processor. Peel and crush the garlic with the salt so that it forms a smooth purée. Beat the yoghurt and water together and add the cucumber and salt and garlic mixture. Stir well. If the yoghurt is extremely thick it may need a little more water to turn it into a soup-like consistency, but the cucumber will give off liquid when it comes into contact with the salt so don't dilute the soup for 10 to 15 minutes after you've made it. Wash the mint, strip the leaves off the stalks and chop them finely. Ten minutes before serving, stir the chopped mint into the soup, reserving a little for a garnish. Chill the soup before serving. You can, in extremely hot weather, add an ice cube or two but don't overdo it as that dilutes the soup even further.

CRAB SALAD

Crabs are at their best at this time of year and around the coast of Britain they are readily available. Cleaning one is quite a simple, if slow, process. Once the crab has been split open from the rear, remove the 'dead man's fingers', or spongy feathery gills that are on the top of the inside of the crab and remove the sac and its contents from immediately behind the mouth end. After that, everything else in the crab is edible, though getting some of the meat out of the claws, legs and the complicated bony centre may take a while. Whether you clean the crab yourself or buy one ready-dressed, here is a salad that makes the delicious meat go a little further. Although smart restaurants serve salads like this in mounds on the centre of flat plates, I think it's nicest served in a lettuce leaf cup in a soup bowl. Thinly sliced brown bread and butter is absolutely the best thing of all with this.

SERVES 4

1 eating apple	225 g (8 oz) white crab meat (use the brown to make potted crab (page 63)
2 teaspoons lemon juice	
4 celery stalks	1 teaspoon French mustard
100 g (4 oz) radishes	4 tablespoons mayonnaise

Halve the apple, remove the core and grate it on a medium grater. Mix immediately with the lemon juice to prevent it going brown. Wash and trim the celery and shred it finely across the grain into ⅓ mm (⅛ in) slices. Trim the radishes and cut those in half and then across into wafer thin slices. Mix the apple, celery and radish together with half the crab. Mix the mustard into the mayonnaise and add half of that to the crab and apple mixture. Mix the remaining mayonnaise into the crab that you have left. Divide the crab and apple mixture into four and use it to fill the bottom of soup bowls lined with lettuce leaves. Whip the plain crab and mayonnaise mixture together lightly with a fork and spoon as a topping over the main salad. A sprig of parsley enhances the look of this. It should be chilled for about half an hour before serving.

AUBERGINE AND COURGETTE FRITTERS Ⓥ

Aubergines and courgettes are at their peak at this time of year and many of them are now home grown. In both cases choose vegetables whose skin is firm and glossy, of medium size, neither too small nor too large and watery. The method of cooking them in fritters like this has connections all over the world, as far apart as South-east Asia, Turkey and California. It's extremely simple and most delicious, though it's worth pointing out that where the aubergines are concerned, the amount of oil that gets absorbed can be quite surprising.

SERVES 4

225 g (8 oz) aubergines	1 teaspoon garlic salt
225 g (8 oz) courgettes	½ teaspoon paprika
4 tablespoons plain flour	6 tablespoons olive oil for frying

Trim the aubergines and courgettes and slice across on the diagonal into 5 mm (¼ in) slices. Mix the flour, garlic salt and paprika together. Heat the oil in a frying-pan to a medium to high heat. Dip the slices in the flour mixture and fry immediately in the hot oil for 2–3 minutes, turn and fry for a minute or so longer. The fritters should be served as rapidly as possible. They can be drained on kitchen paper while you fry a second batch but they should not be kept waiting more than 2–3 minutes after cooking or the crisp coating will suffer. The vegetables should be hot and cooked right through but not soggy and the flour will have provided a crisp shell for them. This can be served with a fresh tomato sauce made by puréeing 100 g (4 oz) of tomatoes, a couple of spring onions and a pinch of salt and cayenne pepper together to make a simple salsa. This dish is also excellent as part of a larger vegetarian buffet.

MAIN COURSES

INDIAN MARINATED TROUT

The nice thing about this recipe is you can either cook it indoors under a grill or outdoors on a barbecue. Trout is one of the fish that has a surprising amount of oil in its flesh, unexpected when you consider how delicate it is. It nevertheless makes it ideal for grilling and also helps prevent sticking and other unpleasant habits on the barbecue. The marinade is an adaptation of an Indian tandoori-type marinade often used with trout or similar fish in the sub-continent. It's quite a delicate set of flavours to balance the delicacy of the flesh itself. You can do this either with rainbow or brown trout but it's particularly useful for livening up the rather flat flavour of otherwise excellent farmed fish.

SERVES 4

4 trout, about 225 g (8 oz) each	4 large sprigs of fresh mint
150 ml (5 fl oz) natural yoghurt	1 teaspoon paprika
2 teaspoons garam masala	2 tablespoons sunflower or soya oil
1 large onion, sliced	1 teaspoon coarsely ground black pepper
2 garlic cloves, sliced	

Put all the ingredients together, except for the trout, into a liquidizer or food processor and mix thoroughly until it forms a purée. Put the trout into a glass or ceramic bowl and pour over the yoghurt mixture. Allow to marinate for at least 1 hour, up to 12 hours is fine.

To cook, take the trout out of the marinade and discard the remaining yoghurt mixture. Grill the trout on an oiled grid, either under a hot grill or over a medium barbecue, for about 5 minutes per side. You may wish to brush the uncooked side of the trout with a little oil before turning it on to the grill base. Serve with a lemony salad and crisp bread, either European or Indian.

SOLE MONTE CARLO

At this time of the year, although the weather suggests light eating, many fish are not at their best. This is not, however, true of Dover sole which is excellent, although regrettably, seriously expensive. It's not only in Britain that it's highly valued, and indeed this recipe comes from the shores of the Mediterranean; from one of the more expensive parts of those shores at that, from Monte Carlo, in the nineteenth and early parts of the twentieth century the high point for luxurious living. It's not an everyday dish but it is great fun to cook and also goes surprisingly far so a large well-filled sole will feed two people easily; the flesh is firm and filling as well as delicious. The combinations may seem a little exotic but work surprisingly well as hot weather food.

SERVES 4

½ teaspoon paprika	40 g (1½ oz) butter
½ teaspoon ground bay leaves	2 large slightly under-ripe bananas
1 tablespoon plain flour	juice of 1 lemon
4 generous fillets of sole	120 ml (4 fl oz) water
3 tablespoons olive oil	4 tablespoons mango and ginger chutney (plain mango is okay)

Mix the paprika and bay leaves into the flour and lightly flour the sole. Heat the oil and butter in a large frying-pan into which all the fillets will go at once (you can use two pans) and fry the sole for 1½–2 minutes on each side over a moderate heat. Remove from the pan and keep warm. Peel the bananas and split lengthways. Use the remaining flour to coat them and fry briskly in the remaining butter and oil for a minute or so until lightly browned. Place the fillets of sole on individual warm plates and arrange the slivered banana along the centre of each fillet of sole. De-glaze the pan with the lemon juice and water, bring to the boil, add the mango chutney and stir until thoroughly mixed. Pour the sauce carefully over the banana down the centre line of the sole. Serve with sautéed or mashed potatoes and spinach or another green vegetable.

TIAN OF CHARD AND LEEKS Ⓥ

A tian is the name for an earthenware pot used to make a gratin of vegetables originally from Provence in the south of France. It's one of the legendary dishes that has twenty-five authentic versions and as many non-authentic ones as there are cooks to create them. It is, however, a very fine dish for high summer, being capable of being eaten hot or cold and also being vegetarian. It can be eaten as a substantial main course on its own or with grilled or roasted meats or fish. Salt cod and grilled sardines are particularly associated with a tian on the Mediterranean, but it's extremely tasty made without, and eaten in an English summer, in the open air in dappled sunlight. The chard that is its central ingredient is the vegetable that looks like spinach with a white ruler up the middle of the leaf. It's easily grown in your own garden as it's a variation on perpetual spinach but it's also increasingly common in greengrocers and super-markets these days.

SERVES 4

900 g (2 lb) chard	50 g (2 oz) fresh breadcrumbs
450 g (1 lb) leeks	4 eggs, whisked
175 ml (6 fl oz) olive oil	salt and freshly ground black pepper
2 garlic cloves, chopped	

Pre-heat the oven to 180°C/350°F/Gas 4, 160°C fan, bottom of an Aga roasting oven.

Strip the green leaves from the white central stalk of the chard and wash them thoroughly. Trim the base of the stalk and cut it across the grain into 1 cm (½ in) slices. Trim and wash the leeks and cut those into 5 mm (¼ in) slices across the grain and mix with the chard stalk. Heat 2 tablespoons of oil and fry the leek and stalk mixture gently until it's well softened. Put aside into a bowl. Add another 2 tablespoons of the oil to the pan with the garlic. Add the green leaves of the chard, washed thoroughly, with the water still on them, and allow them to soften and break down into a rough purée. Heat the remaining oil in a separate pan and fry the breadcrumbs until lightly browned. In a deep ovenproof earthenware dish, put a layer of the green leaves, then a layer of the stalk and leek mixture, pour over half the egg, another layer of green leaves and another layer of stalk, then the remaining egg, mixing gently to make sure the egg penetrates into the vegetables. Put the lightly browned breadcrumbs over the top and bake in the oven for 45–50 minutes until the whole of the dish is bubbling and set. This can be eaten either hot as it comes from the oven or allowed to cool and served, as it is in Provence, as the centrepiece of a picnic.

TWO GREAT BARBECUE DISHES

Considering the time of year and our penchant for outdoor eating, here are two delicious barbecue dishes which can, given foul weather or a loss of nerve, be excellent cooked and eaten indoors. They are both quite quick to cook and go well with a variety of accompaniments including rice salads, hot breads and baked potatoes.

TEXAS BARBECUED LAMB

Although Texas is rather more famous for its beef than its lamb there has always been a tradition, particularly in those parts of the huge state where beef cattle don't flourish, for rearing sheep. Indeed, at the end of the nineteenth century there were the most vicious range wars fought between sheep and cattle farmers for the use of grazing and water. There's no violence involved in this dish, however, just the slightly spicy sour and sweet flavours that are associated with the outdoor cooking of this part of America that's closest to Mexico.

SERVES 4

1 large onion, finely chopped	1 teaspoon salt
1 garlic clove, finely chopped	1 tablespoon soft brown sugar
50 ml (2 fl oz) oil (not olive)	1 tablespoon cider vinegar
1 teaspoon freeze-dried thyme	500 ml (17 fl oz) passata (sieved Italian tomato purée)
1 teaspoon freeze-dried sage	
½ teaspoon mustard powder	900 g (2 lb) boneless lamb, fillet, shoulder or leg, cut into 2.5 cm (1 inch) cubes
½ teaspoon cayenne pepper	

Fry the onion and garlic gently in a non-stick pan in the oil until translucent but not brown. Add the herbs and spices and stir for 1–2 minutes. Stir in the salt, sugar, cider vinegar and passata and simmer gently for 5 minutes. Partially cover and simmer at the lowest possible heat for another 15 minutes, making sure that the mixture doesn't burn or stick. Allow to cool. Marinate the lamb cubes in the barbecue mixture for at least an hour and up to 24 hours.

Pre-heat the grill or barbecue. Thread the meat on to 8 skewers and grill over a high heat or under a pre-heated grill for 4–5 minutes, turning to grill for another 3–4 minutes and then turning one last time for a last 3–4 minutes. The lamb should be crisp on the outside but still succulent on the inside. Meanwhile, re-heat the marinade, bring it to the boil again, allow to simmer for 5 minutes and serve with the barbecued kebabs.

CHICKEN WITH A SATE PEANUT SAUCE

This sauce is a crafty adaptation of a sauce that's enormously popular all over south-east Asia – Malaysia, Indonesia, Thailand all have their own versions. This is a simple one made using peanut butter rather than starting with whole peanuts but it's none the worse for that. It's delicious with chicken, but I have to say goes well with almost all grilled meats.

SERVES 4

4 tablespoons soy sauce	12 chicken drumsticks
50 g (2 oz) soft brown sugar	100 g (4 oz) crunchy peanut butter
juice of 1½ limes	150 ml (5 fl oz) water
1 tablespoon cooking oil (not olive)	1 generous teaspoon chilli sauce
1 garlic clove, crushed with 1 teaspoon salt	

Mix the soy sauce, sugar, lime juice, oil and garlic together and use to marinate the chicken drumsticks in a glass or china bowl. They can be marinated for as little as 30 minutes and as long as 12 hours without any deterioration.

Pre-heat the grill or barbecue. Remove the chicken from the marinade and grill for 5–6 minutes a side on a hot barbecue or under a pre-heated grill. Meanwhile, pour the marinade mixture into a non-stick pan with the peanut butter and the water. Bring to the boil and stir gently. It will look extremely unpromising at first but as it starts to boil it will blend together into a smooth golden sauce. Add the chilli flavouring (you can adjust this to taste) and allow to simmer until the drumsticks are ready. To serve, pour a little sauce over the drumsticks and serve extra on the side to be eaten with the chicken and the rice or potatoes that you should serve with it.

PUDDINGS

GREENGAGE TART

This is the season for perhaps the most delectable plums of all – greengages. They are ripe even when bright green – if they're yellow they're probably over-ripe – but for the purposes of this tart green and firm is the standard to look for. It's a simple summertime recipe with a dry crumbly pastry to contrast with the richness of the fruit. All open tarts like this based on the French model are meant to be, and are best, eaten cold. Chilling is not necessarily a good idea as it does tend to make the pastry a bit on the soggy side.

SERVES 4

450 g (1 lb) greengages	175 g (6 oz) plain flour
100 g (4 oz) caster sugar	a pinch of salt
	75 g (3 oz) sugar
FOR THE PASTRY	1 egg
100 g (4 oz) butter	1–2 teaspoons cold water (optional)

To make the pastry, rub the butter into the flour and salt. Add the sugar and rub it together until it resembles coarse breadcrumbs. You can do this by hand or in a food processor. Add the egg and process or blend until the pastry forms a working texture and forms a ball. If it remains too dry to cohere properly you may need to add 1–2 teaspoons of cold water but be careful not to add too much. Knead the pastry together, wrap in a piece of cling film and leave in the fridge to chill for 30 minutes.

Pre-heat the oven to 200°C/400°F/Gas 6, 180°C fan, top of an Aga roasting oven. Roll out the pastry and use to line a Swiss roll tin, leaving a little raised rim around the edge. Prick it all over and bake it in the oven for about 10 minutes until the pastry is just set but not golden. Split the greengages and remove the stones or, if you prefer it, cut the 'cheeks' off the greengages and discard the remaining bits. Lay them, cut side up, in neat overlapping rows on the pastry. Sprinkle with the sugar and return to the oven for 15–18 minutes. The pastry should be golden brown and the sugar and fruit should have melted together but not dissolved into pulp. Remove from the oven, place on a rack and allow to cool thoroughly before cutting and eating.

PLUM FOOL

This can be made with almost any plums, though you will have to adjust the amounts of sugar to match the sharpness or sweetness of the fruit. It's perhaps at its most delicious made with damsons, the dark purple-coloured tiny plums with an intense flavour. Originally, as their name suggests, these came from the Middle East from the vicinity of Damascus, brought back so theory has it, by the Crusaders. Because of their colour and flavour they make wonderful confections but they do have a lot of stone to the weight of fruit so if you're going to make this fool with damsons you have to have the patience to get the stones out of the mixture. Served in tall wine glasses this has a lovely colour as well as a delicious and delicate flavour.

SERVES 4

750 g (1½ lb) damsons or 450 g (1 lb) other plums	150 ml (5 fl oz) double cream
175 g (6 oz) sugar	150 ml (5 fl oz) fromage frais
½ teaspoon allspice	

ash the damsons and cook them gently with the sugar in a non-stick pan until the juice runs and the fruit begins to cook. Cook for 15–20 minutes until the fruit has become a textured purée and the stones have become loose. You may need to add a little water. Allow to cool and remove the stones completely. Check for sweetness at this point; you may need a little more sugar. Stir in the allspice. Whip the double cream until thick then add the fromage frais a spoonful at a time and continue to whip. It will take up the fromage frais and produce a lower fat, high volume, whipped cream mixture. Fold the cold damson purée into the cream mixture and stir until blended but not thoroughly homogenized. Pour into tall wine glasses and put in the fridge to set for at least 1 hour before using.

MINT TEA ICE-CREAM

I first had this kind of ice-cream in, of all places, a Japanese restaurant in New York City, but it's a technique that translates very well to the British summer and taste. It's quite easy to make using a technique that creates what the French know as a parfait: a smooth crystal-less ice-cream mixture that doesn't need a special machine to make it. For the mint tea you can either make your own (see page 145) or you can buy ready-prepared herb teas with mint flavouring or even made from pure mint leaves themselves. Any are perfectly acceptable as they create a variety of flavours, all of which taste delicious in the ice-cream.

SERVES 4

4 eggs, separated	250 ml (8 fl oz) double cream, whipped until thick but not stiff
100 g (4 oz) icing sugar	120 ml (4 fl oz) strong mint tea, cooled

eat the egg yolks with the icing sugar until fluffy and light. Mix in the tea. Beat the whites until stiff and fold together carefully. Chill for four hours in the freezer.

PRESERVES

PRESERVED PLUMS Ⓥ

This is a recipe similar to that used all over Europe and rather different from the traditional British boiled bottled plums which were simply used as the ingredients for a dessert. This is a preserve that can be served with cold meats or puréed to serve with Chinese-style duck. They can be used where you might otherwise serve chutney. They're a pleasure to the eye preserved in their jars as well as for the palate when they're opened. Don't use anything except white wine vinegar for this recipe.

SERVES 4

2.75 kg (6 lb) ripe but not squidgy plums	**6 cloves**
900 ml (1½ pints) white wine vinegar	**½ nutmeg, grated**
675 g (1½ lb) caster sugar	

Wipe the plums and prick each of them with a needle. Make a syrup by mixing the wine vinegar, sugar, and spices and bringing to the boil, simmering for 5 minutes. Put the plums into the boiling syrup and take each one out with a slotted spoon as soon as its skin begins to split. Put each of them into a colander over a basin. When you have all the plums cooked like that, place them carefully into sterilized bottles (the chemical sterilizer used for babies' bottles is probably the best in this connection). Pour the liquid in the bowl under the colander into the syrup in which you've cooked the plums, bring it to the boil for 5 minutes then pour it over the fruit. Make sure the plums are covered. Seal down the lids and allow to cool and stand for at least 1 month before using.

BREAD

PIZZA BASE

Pizza bases are widely available ready-made in supermarkets and shops but none of them have the same flavour or texture as a properly made pizza base on to which the ingredients can be placed raw. You can, of course, make the same bread mixture and bake it on its own, in which case it becomes a kind of focaccio, one of the legendary breads of Italian rustic cooking. It's very easy to make this and very quick, not more than about 15 minutes from a standing start until it goes into the oven. The method uses a technique involving fresh yeast, and a pinch, no more, of vitamin C powder which speeds up the rising process remarkably. If you use dried yeast the whole process takes much longer.

MAKES 2 × 30 cm (12 in) PIZZAS

15 g (½ oz) fresh yeast	**1 teaspoon salt**
½ teaspoon sugar	**¼ teaspoon vitamin C powder (ascorbic acid)**
scant 300 ml (10 fl oz) finger-warm water	
450 g (1 lb) strong bread flour	**120 ml (4 fl oz) olive oil**

Plum Fool

ream the yeast with the sugar and a couple of spoonfuls of the warm water and allow to stand for about 5–10 minutes until it becomes frothy. Mix the flour, salt, vitamin C and olive oil, add the yeast mixture and the remaining water, and knead thoroughly for 2–3 minutes until the dough feels firm and elastic. Put in a warm place with a cloth over the bowl and leave for 10–12 minutes. It should rise and double in bulk.

Pre-heat the oven to 220°C/425°F/Gas 7, 190°C fan, top of an Aga roasting oven. Divide the dough in half and, using your hands, not a rolling pin, stretch it out into the shape of the pizzas, making sure there is a ridge around the edge. Cover with your favourite fillings and bake in the oven for 20–25 minutes.

To make focaccio, spread out the bread as before and sprinkle with a little sea salt and some rosemary or other fresh Italian-style herb. Allow to rise and then bake at the same temperature as the pizzas but for 15–20 minutes until golden and risen.

HERB

MINT

Mint has a wonderfully clean, fresh taste and is one of the most frequently used herbs in Britain. Many types are grown both in Europe and Asia, the most common culinary varieties being spearmint, peppermint, bergamot and apple mint.

It is available fresh, frozen, freeze-dried and dried, or as peppermint essence. It lends itself to a whole range of foods both sweet and savoury.

Peppermint essence is wonderful added to chocolate mousse, ice-creams and sweets, otherwise for most other dishes I would say that fresh is usually best.

Try adding a sprig of fresh mint to the cooking water for peas, new potatoes and carrots. It is good cut into salads, even in fruit salads. A refreshing salad can be made by mixing sliced cucumber, natural yoghurt and finely chopped mint. Mint and yoghurt marry well and in India yoghurt and mint are blended together with ice and water, then garnished with toasted cumin seeds to make a drink called 'lassi'; very soothing with a hot curry.

As well as culinary uses mint has been grown for its medicinal qualities, and is regarded as an aid to good digestion. The mint tea recipe below is very refreshing.

MINT SAUCE Ⓥ

Mint sauce is a traditional accompaniment to roast lamb and very easy to make.

SERVES 4

a large handful of fresh mint leaves	2 tablespoons boiling water
2 tablespoons caster sugar	2 tablespoons cider vinegar

ash the mint leaves and pat dry, then chop finely. Put the mint, sugar and water into a bowl and stir until the sugar has dissolved, then add the cider vinegar. Chill before serving.

ICED MINT TEA

Even in high summer the weather in Britain doesn't always lend itself to a wide range of cooling drinks but here's one that was enjoyed in Victorian times but we appear to have lost our taste for, while it's been maintained by our cousins in America. Iced tea is so much a part of life in the United States that it's available alongside Coca-Cola and orange juice in McDonalds' burger bars. It's very easy to make though and most refreshing. If you like your tea sweetened, it's as well to make up a little sugar syrup to stir into it, or use one of the artificial sweeteners that dissolve in cold as well as hot liquids.

SERVES 4

900 ml (1½ pints) boiling water	sugar or honey to sweeten
2 teaspoons Ceylon tea	sprigs of fresh mint to garnish
4–5 tablespoons dried peppermint or spearmint leaves	

our the boiling water on to the tea and mint leaves and leave to infuse for at least 10 minutes. Strain into a jug, sweeten to taste and leave to cool. Cover and leave in the fridge to chill.

To serve, fill a tall glass with ice and wedge a few mint leaves between the cubes, then pour in the tea.

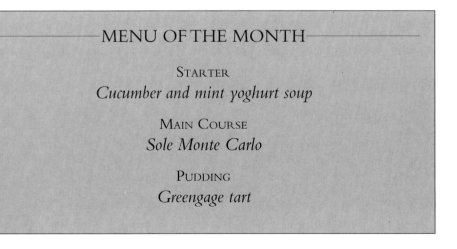

MENU OF THE MONTH

STARTER
Cucumber and mint yoghurt soup

MAIN COURSE
Sole Monte Carlo

PUDDING
Greengage tart

SEPTEMBER

INTRODUCTION

September is the cornucopia month when produce of all sorts reaches its peak. It's the time of harvest and harvest festival, of orchards bright with apples and pears, the last of the summer's plenty and the beginnings of autumn's richness. As well as cultivated fruits reaching their peak so, too, do the wild produce which still exist even in this overcrowded island – blackberries for pies and jellies; sloes (the forerunner of our dessert plums) for preserves and flavoured drinks and the first of the autumn mushrooms can be found wild in the woods, though it's important with these to make sure you know what you're picking before you eat them.

All of these add to the plenty of September. Peppers, courgettes and tomatoes are still in supply as well as home-grown tomatoes, often at their brief peak of natural ripeness. The wonderful variety of English apples and pears are to be found so that as well as the great classic Cox, Discoveries and Worcesters, James Grieves and Jonathans, Elstars and John O'Golds all offer their individual tastes and a variety of tartness to the table. They make a good match for the first of the summer milk cheeses which come into the shops around now. The profusion of British cheese-makers on farms in the last ten years is one of the great developments and improvements in the ingredients we have to hand. Almost all those cheeses are at their best in September, having been produced from milk benefiting from the early summer's rich pastures. Cheese from Devon and the Dales of Yorkshire, from Ireland and from the West of Wales, Scotland and the Lake District, are all to be found now in speciality shops and market stalls and even some supermarket cheese counters. Beef, also benefiting from summer's rich pasture, is starting to come into its best at this time.

September leaves you spoilt for choice, but in the recipes for this month I've harked back to one or two of the more traditional splendours of harvest time, including a wonderful way to use the great marrows that still adorn the competitions of vegetable shows and old-fashioned greengrocers' shelves. I include ideas, too, for old-fashioned bramble jelly and a fruit loaf. Altogether a month to be savoured and enjoyed before plunging into the more solid tastes that the colder weather brings.

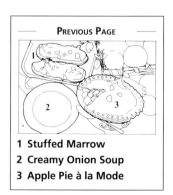

PREVIOUS PAGE

1 **Stuffed Marrow**
2 **Creamy Onion Soup**
3 **Apple Pie à la Mode**

September

PRODUCE AT ITS BEST

Corn • Beetroot • Marrow • Onions • Apples • Pears • Blackberries
• Beef • Partridge • Red mullet • Haddock

STARTERS

SPICED CORN ON THE COB Ⓥ

Corn on the cob is still a slightly exotic vegetable in Britain, although it's common-place in America and the other lands where it's grown more widely than it is here. Recent years have produced marvellous 'sweet' varieties that are even more delicious than their predecessors when boiled and eaten with butter. This recipe is an adaptation of that basic technique, adding a little spicing to balance the rich sweetness of the new kinds of corn. You can adjust the hotness of the mixture to suit your palate and whether or not it's adults, children or both that the dish is destined for.

SERVES 4

4 heads of corn, still in their husks	¼ teaspoon allspice
50 g (2 oz) butter	¼ teaspoon chilli powder
½ teaspoon garlic salt	¼ teaspoon cayenne pepper
½ teaspoon paprika	juice of ½ lemon

Snap the base off the corn and remove the papery husk and all the string. Trim the pointed end if it's at all immature. Bring a large pan of water to the boil and put in the corn without adding any salt – half a teaspoon of sugar is a much better idea as it doesn't toughen the kernels. Simmer for 10–12 minutes. Meanwhile, mash the butter with the garlic salt and spices until thoroughly blended, add the lemon juice and mash again. Roll the butter into a cylinder and divide into four. When the corn is cooked, drain it thoroughly, put on to warm plates and top with a portion of the spiced butter. Make sure the corn has a chance to be coated and absorb the butter before you begin to eat it. This will also save you from a burnt mouth.

CREAMY ONION SOUP Ⓥ

If you're lucky enough to grow your own onions or to have a supplier who can provide the fresh milky variety, this soup is a true gourmet delicacy. But even if all you can find is new season's English onions in your shop or supermarket, it's still outstandingly delicious. It's very different from the kind of French onion soup that we're so used to with bread and cheese floating on the top of it. It's a pale, almost white soup of great delicacy but surprising richness of flavour. I find it particularly pleasant in the evenings in September when the sting of autumn can be felt in the air. It's quite substantial and a fairly light meal to follow is probably a good idea, not least as you usually get asked for seconds of the soup anyway.

SERVES 4

1 tablespoon cooking oil	600 ml (1 pint) water
50 g (2 oz) butter	600 ml (1 pint) milk
900 g (2 lb) new season's English onions, halved and thinly sliced	1 tablespoon cornflour
salt and freshly ground black pepper	1 tablespoon chopped fresh parsley to garnish

Heat the oil and butter in a heavy pan and fry the onions gently over a very low heat for 25–30 minutes until they are almost dissolved and melted away but *not* browned. They will need stirring from time to time as you do this. When they are cooked, season them generously and add the water and the milk. Bring to the boil and simmer gently for 10 minutes. Remove from the heat and blend the cornflour with a little of the liquid from the pan. Stir back into the pan and whisk until the cornflour has thickened and the soup has come back to the boil. Season and allow to stand for 2–3 minutes to allow the flavours to blend completely. Serve with a sprinkling of parsley over each bowl.

HADDOCK CEVICHE

Ceviche is a method of 'cooking' fish using not heat but citrus juices. It comes from South America and Mexico where it is a very popular method of dealing with fish and it's ideal for our white fish. The close grain and rich but delicate flavour of haddock quite matches the favourite black bass of Central American ceviche, and the citrus tang makes it a delicious first course for a spicy or slightly exotic meal. It's important to give the fish time to mature in the marinade in order to lose any look or feeling of rawness.

SERVES 4

450 g (1 lb) filleted and skinned haddock or sea bass	1 medium-sized cos lettuce
2 spring onions	1 large sweet orange
juice of 1 lemon	3 tablespoons salad oil (not olive)
juice of 2 limes	a few sprigs of fresh coriander or parsley

Cut the fish lengthways into 1 cm (½ in) wide strips. Trim and very finely chop the spring onion and mix it with the juices of the lemon and lime. In a china or glass bowl, pour this over the haddock strips and leave to marinate for at least 6 hours until the strips are completely opaque and flake.

To serve, shred the lettuce finely across the grain to make a bed on four individual plates and arrange the strips of haddock, cut to a suitable length, neatly on the lettuce. Mix the juice of the sweet orange into half the marinade and add the salad oil. Blend the dressing until thoroughly mixed and pour over the salad and fish. Decorate with a sprig or two of fresh coriander or parsley and serve with thinly sliced brown bread and butter.

PIPERADE ⓥ

Piperade is one of those dishes that began as a peasant recipe using local ingredients and has become an international favourite. It started life in the south-west of France and the north-west of Spain in the Basque country. At this time of year it's the perfect dish to make because it's when red peppers are fully and naturally ripe and at their cheapest. It's a dish that can be enhanced and turned into a main course by the addition of fish or cooked meats, but this is the simple basic recipe that I love best. It's not, by the way, as some chef-based books suggest, a kind of omelette. It's meant to be a kind of grand vegetable scrambled egg and it's best served in small bowls accordingly. Hot French bread goes wonderfully with it but it's also very good, I discovered many years ago in France, served cold as an hors d'oeuvre.

SERVES 4

2 tablespoons olive oil	1 garlic clove, finely chopped
2 large red peppers, de-seeded and thinly sliced	25 g (1 oz) butter
1 large green pepper, de-seeded and thinly sliced	6 eggs
	salt and freshly ground black pepper
225 g (8 oz) Spanish onions, thinly sliced	juice of ½ lemon
225 g (8 oz) large tomatoes	

Heat the olive oil in a non-stick or well seasoned heavy-based pan and fry the peppers and onions gently for 5–7 minutes until softened but not browned. Halve the tomatoes, scoop out and discard any seeds and slice them thinly. Add to the pan with the garlic and butter. Break the eggs into a bowl and beat them until they are mixed but not frothy. Season the vegetables generously and add the eggs to the mixture, scrambling them continuously over a medium heat until they are creamy but not set hard. Add the lemon juice, stir one last time and serve before the eggs become totally firm.

MAIN COURSES

BRETON FISH CASSEROLE

Brittany is famous for its fish casseroles or '*cotriades*' as they are called. Depending on where they're made and the available fish, they vary considerably. They do, however, have one or two common points. They all contain a lot of potato, a generous flavouring of onion, plenty of herbs and at least three kinds of fish. If this sounds daunting it's really not, and with an 'r' back in the month again it's possible to use all kinds of shellfish. This casserole is a close relation of the American chowders. It's a one dish meal and perfect for warming and nourishing at the end of a cool autumn evening. Make sure that someone else does the work of preparing the fish. Although in Brittany they put it in bones and all, I'm a great believer in using fillets for dishes like this where the sharp bits can sneak up on you unexpectedly. It's traditionally eaten as two courses, first the soup and secondly the fish and vegetables in a slightly drier version in the same dish with plenty of French bread and butter.

SERVES 4

900 g (2 lb) potatoes	1.2 litres (2 pints) water
450 g (1 lb) onions	2 bay leaves
2 celery sticks	1 teaspoon fresh or freeze-dried thyme
3 tablespoons oil	1 teaspoon fresh or freeze-dried chives
900 g (2 lb) assorted fish, choose three from: whiting, coley, cod, conger eel, mackerel or pollack. Shellfish could include prawns, mussels or cockles	40 g (1½ oz) fresh parsley, chopped
	1 lemon, cut into wedges

Clean, peel and trim the vegetables and cut into 1 cm (½ in) slices. Fry them gently in the oil until lightly browned. If using uncooked shellfish, add these, the water and bay leaves, bring to the boil and simmer gently for 10 minutes until the potatoes are cooked through and the shellfish is cooked. If using cooked shellfish or none at all, cook the vegetables gently in the water until the potatoes are almost done. Cut the fish into 2.5 cm (1 inch) pieces and, whichever method you're using, add the fish to the pan and simmer over a medium heat for 4–5 minutes. If using cooked shellfish, add this at the end. Season generously. Decant the liquid into a soup tureen, add the chopped herbs and serve as a first course. Keep the potatoes and fish warm and serve that as a dry stew immediately following. Serve with lemon wedges or possibly some garlic mayonnaise. Don't forget the French bread and butter.

LIVER VENETIAN STYLE

Although the ingredients are the same, this way of cooking liver couldn't be further from our liver and onions in gravy if it tried. The liver itself cooks for barely a couple of minutes and is still delicate and slightly pink in the middle when you eat it. In Venice, where the dish comes from, this is eaten with Risi e Bisi, or rice and peas, not the Caribbean rice and peas some of us are familiar with but risotto rice cooked with fresh green peas. Long grain rice works perfectly well, too, and probably the best way to do it is to add a handful of frozen peas to the cooking just 2 minutes before the rice is ready. A knob of butter stirred in at the end gives you the proper foil for this unexpected way of serving liver and onions.

SERVES 4

450 g (1 lb) sweet onions	2 tablespoons balsamic vinegar
2 tablespoons olive oil	2 tablespoons water
25 g (1 oz) butter	salt and freshly ground black pepper
750 g (1½ lb) calves or lambs liver, cut into very thin slices	

Peel and very thinly slice the onions. Heat the oil in a large frying pan and cook them, very gently, for 20–25 minutes without allowing the onions to brown significantly but just to turn pale gold. They should just have begun to caramelize when they are ready. Season and remove the onions from the pan and place on 4 warmed plates. Heat the pan very hot, add the ounce of butter and fry the liver very rapidly for 45 seconds to a minute on each side and then place onto the onions. Deglaze the pan by pouring in the balsamic vinegar and water, swilling it around and pouring it immediately over the liver. Season and serve without hesitation as the dish is best eaten when really hot.

STUFFED MARROW Ⓥ

The great big marrows that adorn Harvest Festival arrangements are often ignored in culinary terms these days in favour of their much smaller brother, the courgette, but they make excellent eating and are delicious when filled with an appropriate stuffing. This is a totally vegetarian version which nevertheless manages a combination of savouriness and contrasting textures to go with the marrow itself.

SERVES 4

1 large 30–35 cm (12–14 in) marrow	225 g (8 oz) fresh white breadcrumbs
225 g (8 oz) onions, finely chopped	½ teaspoon fresh or freeze-dried marjoram
3 tablespoons cooking oil	½ teaspoon fresh or freeze-dried thyme
4 celery sticks, thinly sliced	salt and freshly ground black pepper
225 g (8 oz) ripe tomatoes, diced	4 tablespoons fromage frais
100 g (4 oz) shelled cob nuts or hazelnuts, roughly chopped	300 ml (10 fl oz) water

Pre-heat the oven to 180°C/350°F/Gas 4, 160°C fan, bottom of an Aga roasting oven.

Split the marrow lengthways, scoop out all the seeds and soft filling and discard. Fry the onions in the oil for a couple of minutes. Add the celery. In a bowl, mix the fried onions, celery, tomatoes, nuts, breadcrumbs and herbs and season generously. Add the fromage frais and use the mixture to stuff the halved marrow. Place the halves in a baking dish into which they will both fit comfortably without too much movement, add the water to the dish and bake in the oven for 40 minutes until the marrow flesh is soft and the filling well baked. You may need to cover them for the last 5 or 10 minutes with a piece of butter paper or buttered greaseproof paper. To serve, cut them in half across the middle to provide four portions. This is nice with a fresh tomato sauce but other vegetables should be left for a separate course.

BEEF WELLINGTON

This is perhaps the grandest beef dish of all – a fillet of beef with pâté and mushrooms inside a puff pastry case. It's certainly special occasion food as fillet of beef is the most expensive cut, but it's also very rich so a little goes quite a long way. In fact a whole fillet is enough to feed eight people. Half a fillet, and you can usually buy the thin end at a slightly lower price, will feed four very adequately. You'll need to go to a real butcher for it, though, because it's not the kind of meat or cut that most supermarkets sell. Because of the impressive appearance it's nice to slice this at table into serving portions. Serve it with suitable vegetables like small new potatoes buttered and minted and one of the delicate green vegetables like string beans or mangetout peas.

SERVES 8

1–1.25 kg (2–2½ lb) piece of fillet of beef	100 g (4 oz) chicken liver pâté
2 tablespoons cooking oil	salt and freshly ground black pepper
350 g (12 oz) puff pastry (shop bought is fine)	1 egg, beaten
100 g (4 oz) button mushrooms, thinly sliced	

P re-heat the oven to 230°C/450°F/Gas 8, 200°C fan, top of an Aga roasting oven.

If you're using the thin end or tail of the fillet, fold it in half so that it is an even thickness all the way along and either lightly skewer or tie. Heat the oil in a heavy-based pan and brown the fillet all over for a couple of minutes. Roll the pastry out into an oval that will allow you to enclose the fillet completely. Put a layer of half the mushrooms along the middle of the pastry. Put the fillet on that, removing any skewer or string you may have used, spread the liver pâté on top, add the remaining mushrooms, season generously and fold the puff pastry around the fillet, brushing the edges with the egg to help them stick. You may want to turn it upside-down to have a perfect finish and use any scraps from the puff pastry to decorate it as leaves or other appropriate patterns. Brush the pastry all over with beaten egg a couple of times so that it's golden and coated before putting it into the oven. If you like your beef pink it should take approximately 10 minutes per 450 g (1 lb), thus about 20–25 minutes. If you like it not too rare, add another 1–2 minutes per 450 g (1 lb). It's not worth cooking this dish if you wish to cook if for more than 30 minutes. Remove from the oven and allow to stand for 5 minutes before carving and serving.

CHICKEN WITH SAUTEED APPLE SLICES

Chicken, apples and cream are a classic tradition from both sides of the Channel, in Normandy and in Kent. This is a modern adaptation of those rather more substantial and casserole-style dishes as it doesn't use a cream sauce. It still, however, benefits from the ability of chicken to carry a variety of flavours and to appreciate the slightly sweet and sour combination that the apples give it. It also brings the smells and flavours of the September orchards indoors and on to the plate. Mashed potatoes and the last of the summer's courgettes go particularly well with this.

SERVES 4

4 chicken breasts	1 tablespoon fresh or 1 teaspoon freeze-dried tarragon
1 tablespoon cooking oil (not olive)	
100 g (4 oz) shallots or small onions, very finely chopped	2 English eating apples
	50 g (2 oz) butter
salt and freshly ground black pepper	2 teaspoons arrowroot
1 tablespoon cider vinegar	1–2 tablespoons water
250 ml (8 fl oz) freshly pressed apple juice	

F ry the chicken breasts gently in the oil until they are golden on both sides. Add the shallots or onions and cook for another 2–3 minutes. Season generously and pour on the cider vinegar. Allow that to bubble almost dry and then add the apple juice. Turn the heat to low, add the tarragon, cover the pan and allow to simmer for 20 minutes until the chicken breasts are cooked through.

Meanwhile, core but don't peel the apples and divide into 12 sections per apple. An apple cutting device is ideal for doing this effortlessly. In a separate pan, heat the butter till it foams, add the apples and, over a medium heat, turn until they're golden but not breaking up. To serve, transfer the chicken pieces to a serving dish. Blend the arrowroot and water then stir into the sauce. Stir over a medium heat for about 2 minutes until the sauce thickens and clears. Arrange the apple slices around the chicken and pour the sauce over or around depending on whether you prefer old-fashioned or nouvelle presentation.

PUDDINGS

PEARS WITH GINGER AND CINNAMON

Pears cooked in this way are absolutely delicious eaten just on their own but they also make a marvellous accompaniment to ice-cream or a basis for that famous French dish Pears Belle Hélène, which is vanilla ice-cream with a poached pear half on top coated in hot chocolate sauce. However you use them, the preparation is effortless and just right for this time of year. Choose not-too-ripe pears, big English Conference are ideal, so too are Comice. Williams pears tend to be a bit soft for this dish but if you get them before they're ripe they're perfectly satisfactory. It will keep with improvement in the fridge for up to 24 hours if covered lightly in cling film.

SERVES 4

4 pears, about 550–750 g (1¼–1½ lb)	300 ml (10 fl oz) ginger ale
lemon juice	2 cinnamon sticks
100 g (4 oz) sugar	50 g (2 oz) preserved ginger in syrup

Peel the pears, split them and remove the cores, leaving them in halves. You may need to put a little lemon juice on them to prevent them discolouring. Put the sugar in a pan and add the ginger ale. Bring to the boil and stir until the sugar is completely dissolved. Add the cinnamon sticks and 2 tablespoons of syrup from the preserved ginger. Put in the pears and simmer for 5 minutes. Meanwhile, cut the pieces of ginger into matchstick-sized shreds. Add those to the cooking pears and allow to simmer for another 5–10 minutes until the pears are cooked through but not soggy. This will depend on the ripeness and the size of the pears. Transfer the pears to a serving dish or bowl and boil the liquid for 5 minutes at a vigorous boil. Pour over the pears and allow to chill for at least 4–6 hours before serving.

TWO VARIATIONS ON TRADITIONAL APPLE DISHES

Here are two slightly different ways with traditional British apple recipes. They are both just small differences but I think they make a great improvement to what is often rather a casual use of one of our great ingredients.

BAKED 'MERINGUE' APPLES

Baked apples have a much loved place in British cooking but they tend to be nursery type food. Not so when made with eating apples and topped with this effortless Italian style meringue studded with almonds. It sounds incredibly grand but is really quite effortless to make. The important thing is not to cook the apples for too long as even eating apples disintegrate after 45 to 50 minutes of cooking, and the appearance is very important in this as well.

SERVES 4

4 large ripe English eating apples (Coxes, Jonathans or Russets are preferable)	½ teaspoon cinnamon
75 g (3 oz) soft brown sugar	2 egg whites
75 g (3 oz) raisins	1 teaspoon wine vinegar
75 g (3 oz) sultanas	50 g (2 oz) caster sugar
grated rind of 1 lemon	25 g (1 oz) slivered almonds

Pre-heat the oven to 180°C/350°F/Gas 4, 160°C fan, bottom of an Aga roasting oven.

Core the apples carefully leaving a little bit of base in the bottom of the hole if possible. Cut round the equator of the apple with a very sharp knife just splitting the skin but not cutting into the apple very far. This prevents the peel tearing and bursting as the apple cooks. Mix the brown sugar, raisins, sultanas, lemon rind and cinnamon together and use it to stuff the core space of the apples. Whip the egg whites until stiff, add the vinegar and whip again. Whip in a tablespoon of the caster sugar and then fold in the remaining caster sugar. When the meringue is complete, stir in most of the slivered almonds. Place tablespoons of the meringue mixture on top of the apples and decorate the very top with a few almond slivers. Bake in baking dish for 35 to 40 minutes until the apples are tender and the meringue has set on the outside. It will still be deliciously chewy in the middle. If you wish, you can add half a pint of water or apple juice to the dish to provide a sauce to serve with the apples.

APPLE PIE A LA MODE

American apple pie is different from ours in that it has a crust top and bottom and also a solid filling that doesn't collapse when you cut it either hot or cold. To me this seems a great benefit and it also allows for the pie to be used in that most American of pudding traditions, pie à la mode, that is served hot with a large scoop of real vanilla ice cream. The best of American cooking may seem occasionally indulgent but it does manage to combine extraordinarily combinations of tastes and textures.

SERVES 4

450 g (1 lb) shortcrust pastry, home-made or shop bought	1 teaspoon ground cinnamon
	1 pinch of ground cloves (optional)
675 g (1½ lb) cooking apples	25 g (1 oz) butter
1 tablespoon cornflour	225 g (8 oz) vanilla ice-cream
100–175 g (4–6 oz) caster sugar (according to taste)	

Preheat the oven to 225–230°C/450°F/Gas 8, 210°C fan, top of an Aga roasting oven.

Divide the pastry into two-thirds and one-third and use the larger amount, rolled out, to line a deep pie dish at least 2.5–4 cm (1–1½ in) deep. Peel, core and cut the apples into pieces the size of half a walnut. Place these in a bowl, sprinkle over the cornflour, the sugar (according to the sweetness of your tooth) and the cinnamon. You may, if you like, add a pinch of ground cloves. Stir until thoroughly mixed and pile into the pie dish leaving a peak in the middle. Dot with the butter and cover with the remaining pastry rolled out. Cut a couple of slots in the top and brush with milk if you like a glazed surface on your pie or sprinkle with a little sugar if you prefer that effect. Bake for 15 minutes and then lower the heat to 180°C/350°F/Gas 4, 160°C fan, bottom of an Aga roasting oven, with the separator shelf put in above it, for another 25 to 30 minutes until the top is completely golden. You can eat this pie hot or cold with vanilla ice-cream.

BREAD AND BUTTER PUDDING

It turns out that bread and butter pudding is now the most popular restaurant pudding in Britain (even overturning Black Forest Gâteau). This extraordinary transformation has largely come about thanks to Anton Mossiman and the *Food & Drink* programme. More than ten years ago it showed his amazing light confection developed from the classic bread and butter pudding – more of a soufflé than a pudding really. I've developed a crafty version of it which is slightly more substantial but still has the most delicate lightness to it.

Bread and Butter Pudding

SERVES 4

4 × 2.5 cm (1 in) thick slices fresh white bread	**50 g (2 oz) caster sugar**
50 g (2 oz) butter, softened	**2 eggs**
25 g (1 oz) raisins	**300 ml (10 fl oz) full cream milk**
25 g (1 oz) sultanas	**½ teaspoon freshly grated nutmeg**
25 g (1 oz) chopped candied peel	

Pre-heat the oven to 180°C/350°F/Gas 4, 160°C fan, bottom of an Aga roasting oven. Lightly butter a soufflé or baking dish about 15 cm (6 in) across and at least 5–7.5 cm (2–3 in) deep.

Butter the bread, cutting off any hard crusts. Cut it into four fingers per slice. Put a layer of bread into the prepared dish, sprinkle on some raisins, sultanas, candied peel and sugar, another layer of bread and so on, making three to four layers altogether. Beat the eggs and milk together and pour over the mixture through a sieve. The liquid should just come to below the very top of the bread. Gently press the bread under the liquid with a spoon. If you need to, add a little more milk to bring it up to this level. Sprinkle with the nutmeg and place in a bain-marie, that is a baking dish filled with 2.5 cm (1 in) of water. Place in the oven and bake for 35–40 minutes until the custard is set and the top is golden brown but not in any way burnt. This can be eaten hot or cold. I prefer it warm with just a little pouring cream to add a touch of moisture and richness.

PRESERVE

BRAMBLE JELLY Ⓥ

You can make this with garden blackberries or, best of all, with the wild ones which have a more intense flavour though they are smaller and more fiddly to deal with. I've suggested adding a couple of cooking apples for their additional volume and also for the pectin that their inclusion brings, helping the jelly to set better. This is lovely eaten on bread and butter or melted as a sauce for steamed puddings or included, perhaps best of all, in a hot rice pudding. The flavour is the very essence of autumn.

MAKES ABOUT 1.75 kg (4 lb)

1.5 kg (3 lb) blackberries	**juice of 1 lemon**
450 g (1 lb) cooking apples	**about 1.5 kg (3 lb) preserving sugar**
175 ml (6 fl oz) water	

ick over and rinse the blackberries. Peel, core and finely chop the apples. Put the apples, water and lemon juice into a large, preferably non-aluminium pan and cook gently until they begin to purée. Add the blackberries and cook those gently in the mixture until they are thoroughly soft and puréed and the juice has fully emerged. This will take from 30 to 45 minutes. Stir the mixture thoroughly and allow to cool.

Pour into a jelly-bag or a muslin-lined sieve and allow the juices to run through under their own weight into a glass or china bowl below. This may take up to 12 hours before all the liquid has come through. Do not be tempted to hurry the process by squeezing or you will get a cloudy jelly. (Jelly bags are available at most cook shops and by mail order.) Measure the liquid, and for every 600 ml (1 pint) of liquid add 450 g (1 lb) of preserving sugar. Pour this back into the pan and simmer gently until the mixture thickens. This will take between 35–40 minutes. To test to see if the jelly is setting, drop a teaspoonful on to a cold saucer. It should immediately form a blob which will not run off when the saucer is tipped. If it's still runny it needs to cook a little bit longer though be careful not to allow it to burn on the bottom. When it's set adequately, pour it into clean sterilized jars (the method of sterilizing babies bottles is ideal for preparing jam jars) and seal. Allow to mature for at least a week before using. It will keep for a year in a cool, dark cupboard.

BREAD

SPECKLED BREAD

Speckled Bread is one of the great teatime favourites especially in the Celtic area of Britain. Properly made it's not a cake of any sort but real bread with an enrichment of fruit and flavouring. It can be eaten on its own, with butter and cheese or toasted, buttered and sprinkled with a little cinnamon to make that old-fashioned and oft-forgotten treat – cinnamon toast. You can make this while making other bread, as you can take a portion from your standard white bread dough and enrich it using the method below.

MAKES ONE LARGE LOAF

15 g (½ oz) fresh yeast or 1 packet dried yeast	**100 g (4 oz) mixed fruit (as for fruit cakes)**
½ teaspoon soft brown sugar	**25 g (1 oz) caster sugar**
300 ml (10 fl oz) warm water	**½ teaspoon ground cinnamon**
450 g (1 lb) strong white bread flour	**½ teaspoon ground allspice**
½ teaspoon salt	**1 tablespoon milk**
50 g (2 oz) butter	

re-heat the oven to 220°C/425°F/Gas 7, 200°C fan, top of an Aga roasting oven.

If using fresh yeast, cream it with the brown sugar and a quarter of the warm water. Mix the flour and salt together (if using dried yeast add it at this point). When the fresh yeast has foamed, add it and the remaining water to the flour and knead to a firm dough. You can do this by hand or using a kitchen machine. Smear the bowl with a little oil, turn the dough ball in the oil and leave to rise, covered in a warm place, for approximately 45 minutes to an hour. When it has doubled in size, knock it down with your hand and add the softened butter, the fruit and most of the caster sugar and the spices. Knead thoroughly until they're blended into the dough. Place in a greased loaf tin and leave again to rise in a warm place. When the dough has risen over the top of the tin, brush with the milk and sprinkle with the remaining caster sugar. Bake for 45 minutes. Tip out of the tin and knock the bottom to see if it sounds hollow. If it is hollow, it's done. If it still has a slightly thick sound, put the loaf back in, out of the tin, on its side into the turned off oven for another 10 minutes before removing and cooling on a rack. Let the bread cool completely before you eat it.

SPICE

CINNAMON

Cinnamon, once more valuable than gold, was used for embalming, religious ceremonies and witchcraft. It is the prepared bark of the evergreen cinnamon tree. Peels of millimetre-thin bark are rolled into thin sticks up to a metre in length. It is easily breakable and has an exotic, warm, spicy aroma.

Cinnamon is available in various forms. The sticks are usually sold in cigarette lengths. They are best used for infusions, casseroles or curries, or as a muddler for stirring a drink. Try using one to stir coffee or hot chocolate.

Ground cinnamon best lends itself to baking, cakes, biscuits, breads, pies, pastries. But it is also good sprinkled on to sliced oranges, bananas and pineapples. Try it with rice pudding, baked custard and milky drinks. Cinnamon is a perfect spice to add to apple dishes of all sorts. In the Middle East it is even used in savoury dishes using chicken and minced meat.

Oil is distilled from fragments of bark for use in food, perfumes and liqueurs.

FRESH APPLE DRINK

This refreshing apple juice is very easy to make, and would be a good way of using up windfall apples.

SERVES 4

450 g (1 lb) eating apples	2 tablespoons caster sugar
juice of ½ lemon	600 ml (1 pint) boiling water

Wash the apples well and cut away any bruises. Slice the apples finely and put into a glass or china bowl. Stir in the lemon juice and sugar and pour on the water. Leave to soak for at least 4 hours, preferably overnight. Strain into a jug and serve either at room temperature or over ice.

MENU OF THE MONTH

STARTER
Spiced corn on the cob

MAIN COURSE
Stuffed marrow

PUDDING
Bread and butter pudding

OCTOBER

INTRODUCTION

October is the high point of autumn; there's a bite in the air and even on fine mornings that slight smell and taste of smoke that seems sometimes to precede rather than follow the bonfires. It's a time for the rich, warming foods of autumn too – pumpkins and mushrooms and casseroles, with pheasant joining partridge and venison on the menu. Game has become almost an everyday food, certainly in terms of its availability with farmed animals supplying meat that's often cheaper than its domestic counterparts. Pheasant and venison, widely on sale in supermarkets, are not only at the same sort of price as chicken and beef but also offer game's advantages of low cholesterol and fat.

On the fruit front, too, October is a rich period. British orchards are still supplying some of the more exciting varieties of British apples – Blenheim Orange and Elstars – as well as still seasonal Cox. Comice pears and the early Conference pears have replaced Williams and, from abroad, the last of the wonderful muscat-flavoured Italia grapes are at their peak – grapes to eat on their own or with cheese or even as part of a delicious sauce with savoury food like chicken. All Hallows Eve finishes the month and so the shops and greengrocers are full of pumpkins from about half-way through. Like many Halloween activities, pumpkins have arrived from the United States, and so too have the best recipes for their use – pumpkin pie and marvellous golden pumpkin soups. You can still use the shell for making funny faces or putting a candle in.

On the fishmonger's slab, October is usually a good month because the weather isn't too bad and the fish, with an 'r' firmly back in the month, are coming into their best again. Beef, too, reaches its peak around this period, having benefited from the rich pastures of the summer, and has had a chance to be hung properly to give it full maturity. It's worth looking out for beef that has one of the quality marks associated with good husbandry, humane killing and proper treatment of the meat afterwards. The Scots and the Irish have both moved into a system of quality checking and identifying beef that has been handled in this way, as have some major supermarkets.

Also from abroad now come those marvellous strings of garlic tied up into ropes that look

PREVIOUS PAGE

1 **Halloween Pie**
2 **Fennel and Ricotta Gratin**
3 **Belgian Orange Salad**

as much designed for decoration as for cooking. Look for the purple-tinged garlic if you can find it. It comes from a part of France which is famous for growing the best flavoured and, in some ways, the mildest garlic of all.

And last but not least, October is chutney time, traditionally the last of the great groups of preserves that were put aside all through the summer and autumn against winter shortages. There's no need for any of that now, but home-made chutney still has a quality, flavour and an appeal all its own — in sandwiches, with a piece of cheese, with cold meats or the salads of next summer. What could be nicer than a jar of apple chutney carrying within it October's golden glow?

PRODUCE AT ITS BEST

Pumpkin • *Brussels sprouts* • *Mushrooms* • *Fennel* • *Chicory* • *Apples*
• *Goose* • *Mallard duck* • *Lamb* • *Beef*

STARTERS

CARROT AND PUMPKIN SOUP

Pumpkins come in a lot of different sizes and shapes but the ones we are most able to buy these days are designed for the Halloween celebrations, being bright-golden-coloured and usually about the size of a football. Whether you're buying it for a lantern or simply to make a couple of dishes, you'll find there's plenty of flesh in it. Use half to make this golden glowing soup that has a marvellous warming sense of the sun, helped by the colour of the carrots, about it. It is surprisingly light because the texture of pumpkin when it's cooked is not as heavy as its density when it's raw would lead you to believe.

SERVES 4

225 g (8 oz) onions	1 garlic clove
450 g (1 lb) trimmed pumpkin (seeds and rind removed)	salt and freshly ground black pepper
225 g (8 oz) carrots, diced	900 ml (1½ pints) chicken stock (a cube will do)
2 large ripe tomatoes	Croûtons to garnish
2 tablespoons cooking oil	1 tablespoon fresh chives, chopped

eel and cut the onion up into small dice. Cut the pumpkin and carrots into half-inch pieces and cut the tomatoes into eight pieces. Fry the onions, carrots and pumpkin in the oil in a large pan for 3 to 4 minutes until the onion softens. Peel and chop the garlic and add that and then the tomatoes. Season generously and cook together for another 2 minutes. Add the stock, bring to the boil and simmer gently for 15 minutes until the pumpkin is completely cooked through. Put into a liquidizer or food processor or, if you prefer, push through a sieve. The resulting purée should be the texture of double cream. Serve it hot with half-inch wholemeal croûtons and a sprinkling of freshly chopped chives.

BELGIAN ORANGE SALAD (V)

October brings with it the pleasures and unexpected textures of winter salads. It's now possible to buy a range of lettuces all year, with supplies coming from as far afield as Kenya, but the weather and appetite dictate salads that have got a little more substance to them and a wider variety of flavours. This is an unusual and unexpected combination using the bullet shaped chicons of chicory grown in the Low Countries. It makes a good first course or an interesting addition to a larger salad buffet. You can, for an alternative interest, sprinkle the finished salad with a handful of crushed walnuts.

SERVES 4

4 medium sized pieces of chicory	½ teaspoon sugar
2 large navel type oranges	½ teaspoon salt
100 g (4 oz) salad oil (not olive)	Pinch of English mustard
50 g (2 oz) lemon juice	

inse and wipe dry the chicory. Trim off the base and slice it across the grain into 5 mm (¼ in) rounds. Put these into a salad bowl, breaking them up slightly with your fingers as you do to separate the rings. Peel the oranges, removing as much as possible of the white pith, and slice them across the grain into 5 mm (¼ in) slices as well. You may find it easier to cut them in half lengthways first. Remove any pips and add the oranges to the chicory and turn gently together. Put all the dressing ingredients into a jar and shake, or whisk in a bowl, until thoroughly blended. Pour over the salad, toss and allow to stand for 15 minutes before serving.

Chicken Livers with Mushrooms and Grapes

CHICKEN LIVERS WITH MUSHROOMS AND GRAPES

Chicken livers are available, usually frozen but increasingly often fresh, all the year round. They are very economical, light and delicious to eat even for people who normally 'don't like' liver. Here they are combined into a quickly cooked first course with the generously flavoured muscat Italia-style grapes and oyster mushrooms. As with so much produce these days, the supermarkets have led the way in bringing the more exotic mushrooms within the reach of all of us, both in terms of distribution and price. Oyster mushrooms are a fascinating alternative to the Paris mushrooms we're used to. Slightly more meaty in texture but still delicate in flavour, they make this dish both earthy and exotic.

SERVES 4

225 g (8 oz) chicken livers	50 g (2 oz) butter
100 g (4 oz) oyster mushrooms	salt and freshly ground black pepper
2 teaspoons arrowroot	50 g (2 oz) Italia white grapes, split and seeded
150 ml (5 fl oz) water	4 slices of toast

Wash and trim the chicken livers, cutting into pieces about the size of half a walnut. Trim and rinse the oyster mushrooms and cut those into pieces about the same size. Stir the arrowroot into the water. Melt the butter in a sauté or deep-sided frying-pan and fry the chicken livers gently for about 2–3 minutes until golden on all sides. Season lightly, add the grapes and the oyster mushrooms and continue to cook over a high heat for another 1½–2 minutes. Using a large glass or cup as a template, cut rounds from each of the slices of toast, butter the rounds and place each one on a serving dish. Spoon the mushrooms, grapes and chicken livers on to the pieces of toast and tip the water and arrowroot mixture into the pan. Stir round, scraping up all the bits, and bring rapidly to the boil when it will thicken and clear. Check for seasoning, pour over the rounds of toast and serve immediately.

MAIN COURSES

SEA BREAM WITH GREMOLATA

Sea bream is one of those fish we seem not to have noticed. It's particularly good and widely available in fishmongers at this time of year. It's a round not a flat fish with solid flesh and a good flavour, but if you can't find it, any firm-fleshed fish like haddock, halibut or monkfish will act as a good alternative and all are now available. Gremolata is an Italian seasoning mixture that's normally used in the area around Milan to season veal dishes, particularly Osso Bucco, but as it's a mixture of garlic, lemon and parsley, it happens to suit fish particularly well, though it has a somewhat vigorous flavour and needs substantial fish. This is nice with potatoes or rice cooked as a risotto or pilau, preferably flavoured with a little saffron. A green vegetable dish or salad is best as a separate course as the flavours are pretty strong already.

SERVES 4

4 × 175 g (6 oz) fillets of sea bream or equivalent firm white fish	2 tablespoons finely chopped fresh parsley
3 tablespoons olive oil	2 garlic cloves, finely chopped
salt and freshly ground black pepper	25 g (1 oz) butter
juice and grated rind of 1 lemon	

Fry the fish fillets in the olive oil gently for 3 minutes each side. Season and add the lemon juice. Turn the heat right down, cover and simmer for 3 minutes while you make the gremolata.

To make this, mix the parsley with the grated lemon rind and garlic. To serve, place the fillets on individual warmed plates. Add the butter to the pan and allow to melt without browning, mixing with the cooking juices. Pour this over the fish, sprinkle a tablespoon of gremolata mixture on top and serve immediately.

FENNEL AND RICOTTA GRATIN Ⓥ

This is a pretty and unusual vegetarian dish and one of the ingredients is also the container for the food. You should find Ricotta in most supermarkets, speciality cheese counters and grocers, but if you can't, buy cottage cheese and beat until it's smooth.

SERVES 4

2 large heads of fennel	225 g (8 oz) Ricotta
1 bunch spring onions, chopped	1 teaspoon freeze-dried basil
1 tablespoon olive oil	salt and freshly ground black pepper
50 g (2 oz) pine nuts	

Pre-heat the oven to 180°C/350°F/Gas 4, 160°C fan, bottom of an Aga roasting oven. Lightly oil a baking tray.

Cut the base off the fennel and pull the stalks away gently. You should wind up with four large spoon-shaped stalks and a central section of the bulb from each head of fennel. Chop the centres of the fennel. Fry the chopped fennel and spring onions gently in the oil until softened. Add the pine nuts and cook for another 1–1½ minutes until the pine nuts turn pale gold. Put the Ricotta into a bowl and stir in the slightly cooled fennel and pine nut mixture. Add the basil and season generously. Place the fennel 'spoons' in the baking tray and spoon the cheese mixture into the centre of the 'spoons', distributing it evenly. You can, as an option, drizzle a little more olive oil on to each spoon. Bake in the oven for 25–30 minutes until the fennel spoons are softened but not disintegrated and the cheese centre is lightly browned. Serve with brown rice pilau and a tomato salad for colour as well as texture and flavour balance.

CHICKEN PAPRIKASH

This is a crafty adaptation of a favourite chicken recipe from Hungary. It features the spice and colouring that is most associated with Hungarian food – paprika – which although it looks fiercely hot, is actually quite mild but vividly flavoured nonetheless. This makes a warming and substantial stew for this time of year, quick to cook but enormously comforting on a night when the first chill of the coming winter might be felt.

SERVES 4

1 tablespoon plain flour	2 garlic cloves, finely chopped
½ teaspoon ground bay leaves	225 g (8 oz) onions, finely chopped
1 tablespoon paprika	450 g (1 lb) firm new or waxy potatoes, cut into walnut-sized pieces
8 chicken pieces	salt and freshly ground black pepper
1 tablespoon cooking oil	150 ml (5 fl oz) soured cream

Mix the flour, ground bay leaves and a teaspoon of the paprika in a paper or plastic bag and use this to coat the chicken pieces. Fry these in the oil in a large frying-pan for 7–10 minutes until golden. Add the garlic and onions and fry gently for another 2–3 minutes. Add enough water to come up just below the top of the chicken then add the potatoes. Season the mixture generously and add the remaining paprika, stirring so that it's smoothly distributed. Simmer the mixture for 15–20 minutes until the chicken is cooked right through and the potatoes are tender. Transfer the chicken pieces and the potatoes to a serving dish and stir the soured cream into the sauce, bringing it quickly to the boil and pouring it over the chicken pieces before serving. It's traditional in Hungary to eat this with flat noodles very similar to Italian tagliatelle.

BRAISED SHOULDER OF LAMB WITH WHOLE GARLIC

The ideal cut for this dish is a boned shoulder of lamb. If that's daunting, just ask your butcher or butchery counter at the supermarket. It's actually not too difficult to do at home – you work along the line of the bone, on the cut side of the shoulder, opening it out as you go. But I'm a great believer in having the tradesmen do the work for you, so give your expert 24 hours notice and ask for a boned shoulder. Make sure you also ask them to cut off any surplus fat as the shoulder can be quite a fatty joint. The other ingredients – whole cloves of garlic – may sound outlandish but in fact are cooked to a very mild and delicate flavour indeed, less damaging to the social graces than a smaller amount less thoroughly cooked. This is delicious with roast potatoes and a substantial green vegetable like early sprouts or autumn cabbage.

SERVES 4

1 × 1.5 kg (3 lb) boned shoulder of lamb	½ teaspoon freeze-dried marjoram
12 garlic cloves	½ teaspoon freeze-dried thyme
120 ml (4 fl oz) white wine or cider vinegar	salt and freshly ground black pepper

Pre-heat the oven to 190°C/375°F/Gas 5, 170°C fan, middle of an Aga roasting oven.

The lamb should be tied in a sausage shape, skin side out. Brown it in a heavy casserole or frying-pan in its own fat for about 7–8 minutes. Rinse but don't peel the garlic and place it in the bottom of a casserole into which the lamb will just fit (it can be the casserole you've been browning the lamb in). Pour the wine or cider vinegar into the pan you've been frying the lamb in and stir to extract any of the brown flavoursome bits then pour those over the garlic. If you're using the same pan, just stir in with the garlic. Place the lamb on top of the garlic, sprinkle over the herbs and season generously. Pour in enough water to come 2.5 cm (1 in) up the lamb; the quantity will depend for volume on the size of the pan and how well the lamb fits. Place in the oven for about 20 minutes per 450 g (1 lb) plus 20 minutes. If you like your meat exceptionally well done, you may want to make this 25 minutes per 450 g (1 lb). To serve, remove the lamb, place on a carving board and cut across in slices like a loaf. Serve the lamb with the garlic cloves, which will now be completely cooked through, and the strained juices from the pan as gravy. To eat it, squeeze the garlic gently with a fork and spread the remaining purée on the pieces of lamb and then eat the delicious combination.

SAUTE OF BEEF WITH OYSTER MUSHROOMS

Beef is at its best at this time of year, and lately arrived on the scene should be the new season's oyster mushrooms. They're flat, heavily ribbed mushrooms with a slightly meatier flavour than the ones we're used to. There are also to be found in greengrocers and supermarkets recently a variety of wild, or bred from the wild mushrooms, in vivid and exciting colours and often with unusual names like shiitake (a Japanese mushroom which top chefs and foodies have rather taken to). Any of these slightly exotic mushrooms will do for this dish, but oyster mushrooms are certainly the most widely available and cheapest. The beef should be of good quality. Look for one of the quality marks or for beef being sold as traditional or matured beef. It should not be bright red but rather maroon coloured and well marbled with fat. Although the cut's expensive, a little goes quite a long way with this dish and its slightly exotic flavourings. Mashed potatoes or rice seem to make the best accompaniment although new potatoes, which are now available all through the year, are also delicious.

SERVES 6

750 g (1½ lb) rump or sirloin steak, trimmed of fat and gristle	100 g (4 oz) onions, finely chopped
225 g (8 oz) oyster or similar mushrooms	3 tablespoons soy sauce
3 tablespoons cooking oil (not olive)	juice of ½ lemon
1 garlic clove, finely chopped	

Cut the beef across the grain into 1 cm (½ in) strips. Rinse the oyster or other mushrooms in a colander with hot or boiling water. If they're excessively large, cut the mushrooms into 1 cm (½ in) strips as well. Heat the cooking oil in a large frying pan or wok. Just before it smokes add the beef strips and turn them rapidly for 2 minutes. Add the garlic and onions and turn that for another minute. Add the mushrooms and turn over maximum heat for 1–1½ minutes until they're cooked but not shrivelled. Pile on to a warm serving plate, add the soy sauce and lemon juice to the pan, swirl round, bring to the boil and pour over the beef. If you wish, you can thicken this sauce by using a teaspoon of cornflour slaked with a little water added at the same time as the soy sauce and lemon juice.

PUDDINGS

HALLOWEEN PIE

Though we've heard of Pumpkin Pie in Britain we've very rarely eaten it, at least not since the eighteenth century when it was a popular item of diet. It's recently come back to us from across the Atlantic especially to be eaten on All Hallows' Eve, the 31st October, and very welcome it is too. It's a kind of treacle tart's cousin, being rich and dark and quite sticky. It should be eaten warm, neither hot nor too cold, and certainly not refrigerated if you can avoid it. It's nicest, I think, made with shortcrust pastry. The Americans make this with a little more fat than we do, but a good old-fashioned English shortcrust, either home-made or bought, will do very well.

SERVES 4

225 g (8 oz) shortcrust pastry	100 g (4 oz) soft brown sugar
450 g (1 lb) pumpkin	½ teaspoon ground cinnamon
50 g (2 oz) softened butter	½ teaspoon ground allspice
2 eggs	

re-heat the oven to 200°C/400°F/Gas 6, 180°C fan, top of an Aga roasting oven.

Use the pastry to line a 20-cm (8-inch) flan or pie dish with a depth of at least 2.5 cm (1 in). Peel and remove the seeds from the pumpkin and cut into 2.5 cm (1 in) cubes. Boil these in a cupful of water for about 20 minutes until they're tender. Drain and mash them with a fork. Beat in the butter and the eggs and sugar and stir until thoroughly mixed. Add the spices and pour into the tart case, making sure it doesn't come within more than 5 mm (¼ in) of the top to allow for the filling to rise. Bake for 30–35 minutes until the pastry is golden and the centre is risen and firm. Allow to cool slightly but eat warm. If you allow it to cool completely, while it will still taste delicious, the centre will sink right down into a thick and gooey confection.

ST CLEMENTS MOUSSE

Like the children's nursery rhyme says, oranges and lemons make up the flavours of St Clements. This is a refreshing citrus fruit fool, ideal at this time of the year with the last of the Mediterranean lemons in the shops and the first of the Christmas oranges beginning to put in their appearance. You can make it with all cream but I much prefer to do it with a mixture of double cream and fromage frais or Greek yoghurt, which produces a delicious and creamy result but is much less high in fat. This is a perfect ending to rich autumnal meals and is nicest served in pretty wine glasses although it still tastes delicious from a large soufflé dish served into ordinary pudding plates.

SERVES 4

2 large sweet oranges	250 ml (8 fl oz) double cream
2 lemons	250 ml (8 fl oz) fromage frais (low fat) or Greek yoghurt
25 g (1 oz) caster sugar	

rate the rind from one of the oranges and one of the lemons and cut slivers of peel from the others and put on one side. Halve and squeeze both for their juice. Mix the rind and juice together with the caster sugar and check for the level of sweetness you would prefer. This depends to a certain extent on the fruit themselves but you may need to add a little more sugar to balance the tartness. Whip the double cream until thick. Add the fromage frais or yoghurt a spoonful at a time, whipping between times until the whole mixture is thick. Add the lemon and orange juices and stir thoroughly. Pour into wine glasses or a suitable dish or dishes. Chill for at least 2 hours before eating, then decorate with the slivers of peel.

APPLE CAKE

There are apple cake recipes from all over the world and they vary enormously from region to region. This is very much more a cake than a pudding but a moist and fruity cake for high tea rather than for delicate slices and china plates. It uses English cooking apples which have that wonderful capacity for cooking to a fairly smooth pulp. It *can* be made with eating apples though it takes on a rather different texture then as they remain quite chewy in the mixture.

SERVES 4

100 g (4 oz) butter	120 ml (4 fl oz) milk
175 g (6 oz) caster sugar	750 g (1½ lb) cooking apples, peeled and cored
2 eggs	
225 g (8 oz) self-raising flour	2 teaspoons water
1 teaspoon baking powder	1 teaspoon ground cinnamon

Pre-heat the oven to 160°C/325°F/Gas 3, 140°C fan, bottom of an Aga roasting oven. Grease and line an 18–20 cm (7–8 in) cake tin at least 4 cm (1½ in) deep.

Cream together the butter and sugar. Beat in the eggs and then sift on the flour and baking powder and mix together thoroughly. Add the milk. The mixture should be quite thick but not completely stiff. Until now you can do it with a food processor. Finely chop 225 g (8 oz) of the apples and stir them into the cake mixture. Cut the rest of the apples into cubes and put them into a non-stick pan with the water and cook gently until softened. Add the cinnamon and taste. If you have a sweet tooth you may wish to add another 25 g (1 oz) or so of sugar at this stage. Put half the cake mixture into the cake tin, then spoon in the apple purée, being careful not to allow it to reach the sides, then put on the remaining layer of cake mixture. Smooth down and bake in the oven for 1–1¼ hours, testing in the last sequence with a skewer, putting the skewer into the cake section not through into the apple layer. The skewer should come out unsmeared. If it's still streaky, turn the heat down a little and allow to cook for another 5–10 minutes. When the cake is cooked, remove and place on a cooling rack and allow to cool completely before removing from the tin.

PRESERVE

PEAR CHUTNEY Ⓥ

This is a simple country chutney to which you can add other exotic ingredients if you choose. Pear and ginger is made by adding some chopped preserved ginger and its syrup, and half a teaspoon of dried ginger to the vinegar mixture. A mixture of apple and pears makes an interesting chutney. Dried fruit, particularly in the form of sultanas and raisins goes well, and green tomatoes and marrow are also good possible additions.

You can use under-ripe fruit particularly if you've got windfalls in the orchard and they make an interesting addition in terms of texture as well as flavour.

MAKES ABOUT 2.25 kg (5 lb)

1 kg (2 lb) onions	25 g (1 oz) pickling spice, wrapped in a piece of muslin
1 garlic clove	
2 kg (4½ lb) firm pears, peeled and cored and roughly chopped	350 g (12 oz) preserving or caster sugar (for a dark chutney, use soft brown sugar)
600 ml (1 pint) cider vinegar	2 teaspoons turmeric
	50 g (2 oz) cornflour

Peel and finely chop the onions and garlic and put them and the pears into a preserving pan with the vinegar and the pickling spice sachet. Cook over a low heat, making sure that nothing catches or burns, until the pears are dissolved into a rough purée and the onion is cooked through. Stir in the sugar until dissolved and check for balance of sweetness and sharpness. This can depend on the pears – you may need to add a little more sugar. Bring to the boil and simmer for 5 minutes. Remove the pickling spice and discard. Assess the thickness of the mixture. If it is quite thick, stir the turmeric and half the cornflour together with a little water and add to the chutney, putting the rest of the cornflour back in the packet. If it is runny, use all the cornflour and turmeric and mix it into the chutney, stirring until it's smooth. Bring to the boil and allow to thicken. The turmeric will give it a golden colour. Bottle immediately in sterilized jars (I use a baby bottle sterilizing tablet to achieve this) and screw the lids down while the chutney is still hot. It should be kept for at least a week before using and will improve for 3 months or more in a cool store-cupboard.

BREAD

COB LOAVES

Cob loaves are baked without tins in the shape of cauliflower. Do find unbleached white flour if you can, it makes a far more attractive loaf to look at as well as a more tasty one to eat. This recipe makes two large loaves which will keep for up to 3 days in a cool place. By the way, despite the wonderful smell that the bread gives off, don't be tempted to try and eat it until it's cooled thoroughly, otherwise it may well be soggy on the inside as well as giving you a severe case of indigestion.

25g (1 oz) fresh yeast	1½ teaspoons salt
½ teaspoon caster sugar	50 ml (2 fl oz) cooking oil (sunflower or soya)
1½ pints warm water	
1.5 kg (3 lb) unbleached white bread flour	

P re-heat the oven to 210°C/425°F/Gas 8, 190°C fan, top of an Aga roasting oven.

Put the yeast into a basin, add the sugar and a couple of tablespoons of the warm water. Mash with a fork until smooth and leave for 10 minutes until completely frothy. Meanwhile in a large bowl, sift the flour and add the salt and half the oil. Stir round until mixed. Add the yeast mixture and the remaining warm water and knead thoroughly. This will take about 2 minutes if you're using a kitchen machine and about 4 to 5 minutes if doing it by hand. You will notice or feel the texture of the dough change from being sticky to being firm and elastic. Stop kneading, make sure all the dough is gathered together into one ball, pour over the rest of the oil and turn quickly in the bowl so that it doesn't stick. Cover with a clean tea towel and leave in a warm place for about 45 minutes to 1 hour until it has doubled in bulk.

Knead again for a minute or so, divide in two and shape into two balls. Cover these again, return to the warm place and allow to rise for about 40 minutes until the bread is quite proud. With a very sharp knife cut a pattern of 3 crossed lines into the dough, cutting no more than 1 cm (½ in) into it. Sprinkle with a little extra flour and bake for 45 to 50 minutes. If you're using an Aga, you may want to move them down to the bottom of the roasting oven after 20 minutes.

At the end of this time take one of the loaves, and tap the bottom. If it sounds hollow it is completely cooked. If not, put it and its companion loaf back into the oven for another 5 minutes or so with the heat turned off if possible. When they sound hollow, take out and cool on a bread rack for at least 2 hours before consuming.

HERB

GARLIC

Grown in much the same way as an onion, garlic is in fact a member of the lily family. It is native to Asia and is therefore essential to much oriental cooking. It has been highly regarded throughout history, believed to cure many ailments and improve general health. Today garlic capsules are sold to aid digestion and purify the blood. Indeed, garlic does have antiseptic properties.

The bulb is made up of several cloves, each encased in its own skin. The easiest way to peel a clove is by gently squashing it under the flat side of a knife, or the heel of your hand. Once the skin has split the clove is easily removed. The clove can either be chopped, grated, put through a crusher or worked into a paste with salt.

It can also be bought in a variety of ways; as a purée in a tube, as powder, salt, or ready chopped in oil. Once cooked its pungent aroma turns into a subtle flavouring that enhances most savoury dishes; try the recipe for braised shoulder of lamb with whole garlic.

It is wonderful added to butter to make garlic bread, or to mayonnaise. Try it rubbed into meat before cooking, or added to sautés, stir-fries, curries and casseroles. A lightly crushed clove popped into a jar of salad dressing will give off a mild garlic flavour.

For those who find garlic too powerful it is worth remembering that chewing parsley will help to neutralize garlic breath.

DRINK

HOT CHOCOLATE

There is something almost naughty about a mug of real hot chocolate topped with Chantilly cream. But what better way to warm one after a brisk walk on a clear cold October day? This is guaranteed to change the way you think about a cup of cocoa.

MAKES 2 LARGE MUGS OR 4 CUPS

50 g (2 oz) good quality plain chocolate (at least 50 per cent cocoa solids)	**600 ml (1 pint) milk**
3 tablespoons water	

Gently melt the chocolate and water together in a pan. In another pan, heat the milk until scalding; do not let it boil. Pour the milk into the chocolate, whisking as you do so to incorporate air and make the drink foamy. Pour into warmed cups or mugs and serve.

If you are feeling extravagant, add a spoon of sweetened whipped cream, flavoured with vanilla. You could also sprinkle the surface with ground cinnamon or use a cinnamon stick to stir the drink. A marshmallow floating on the top is a good treat.

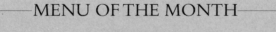

MENU OF THE MONTH

STARTER
Carrot and pumpkin soup

MAIN COURSE
Sauté of beef with oyster mushrooms

PUDDING
Apple cake

NOVEMBER

INTRODUCTION

With the advent of November, cold weather cooking is properly upon us. It can provide some of the greatest pleasures of all food when the direct relationship between warmth, nourishment and well-being is most apparent. November's also a smoky month – Guy Fawkes Night, the first of the winter's log fires, and the bonfires burning all those fallen leaves seem to leave a tang in the air and in the appetite. There's a need for solid, filling, warming food and the range of produce available in November makes this no problem at all. Goose and duck are plentiful and the 'green' geese, because they were fed on grass, begin to be available. So, too, are the early turkeys, possibly in response to the presence of Thanksgiving Day in November, although that is one of the American celebratory traditions that may never completely cross the Pond. But all poultry comes into its mature best at this time of year.

There are plentiful supplies of most fish – shellfish and white fish in particular – and it's a good time for considering the pleasures of smoked fish again with kippers at their succulent best. Pears and apples continue to be in excellent supply with the best of the English Conference pears often reaching their peak in November if the season's been a bit late. Green-grocers' stalls and supermarkets are beginning to glow with gold – the gold of satsumas, clementines and tangerines and those marvellous late Valencia oranges, all building up to the climax of citrus varieties available at Christmas time.

With the first of the frosts, some of the winter vegetables are at their best too, particularly parsnips and Brussels sprouts. Both are, according to legend, much improved by frost; they seem in reality, sweeter and more flavoursome after it. It's a good time for other winter favourites like leeks and swedes, which make wonderful soups and gratins and vegetable dishes in their own right. On the baking front, the new walnuts are in from France and California and make a flavoursome addition to a rich, slightly sweet bread that's the most perfect thing to eat with cheese. It's also a great time for real puddings, baked and steamed, and being a popular season for dinner parties gives us a chance for a little showing off as with the

PREVIOUS PAGE

1 **Autumn Fruit Salad with Thyme and Ginger**

2 **Parsnip Soup with Pine Nuts**

3 **Vegetarian Baked Beans**

November

Chocolate Roulade you'll find in this chapter. Chocolate is not seasonal, but the chance to enjoy it without too many feelings of guilt certainly is.

November may be the autumn of the year but it's certainly one of the seasonal high points from the kitchen viewpoint. It's also a time, as almost an afterthought, to start getting ready for Christmas, and to that end you'll find the most delicious and outrageously lavish Christmas chutney to lay down ready for the cold meats and pies of the festive season.

PRODUCE AT ITS BEST

Cabbages ● Salsify ● Parsnips ● Turnips ● Clementines ● Satsumas
● Cranberries ● Pears ● Pomegranates ● Beef ● Pheasant ● Halibut

---

STARTERS

PARSNIP SOUP WITH PINE NUTS Ⓥ

Parsnips are just coming into their own and are delicious eaten in a wide variety of ways – roasted, puréed, poached and buttered – but one of my favourite ways is as a soup where their combination of substance and slight sweetness is highlighted. The pine nuts in this are quite an exotic ingredient but you'll find them easily today in supermarkets and speciality grocers. You don't need a lot, but they replace croûtons in this recipe to add a tremendous crunch and an appealing appearance as well as flavour.

SERVES 4

750 g (1½ lb) parsnips	salt and freshly ground black pepper
225 g (8 oz) onions	900 ml (1½ pints) water or light chicken stock
225 g (8 oz) potatoes	
2 tablespoons cooking oil	2 celery sticks with leaves
25 g (1 oz) butter	50 g (2 oz) pine nuts

Peel and cut the parsnips, onions and potatoes into 1 cm (½ in) pieces. Fry these gently in the oil and butter in a large pan for about 5 minutes until the onion has just taken on a slightly translucent appearance. Season generously and add the water or stock. Bring to the boil and simmer for 5 minutes. Trim and finely chop the celery, reserving a couple of leaves. Add this to the soup and continue to simmer for another

10–12 minutes until all the vegetables are soft. Purée the soup in a liquidizer, food processor or, if you wish, push it through a sieve, although this is quite hard work. In a small frying-pan, with just a smear of oil, toast or fry the pine nuts until they are golden. Chop the reserved celery leaves. Pour the soup into bowls, decorate with the chopped leaves and, at the last moment, add the hot pine nuts which will sizzle and snap as they go into the soup. Serve immediately.

NEW YORK COLESLAW Ⓥ

Coleslaw literally translated means 'cabbage salad', and America, which is its great home, has a vast number of recipes. Food from New York tended to combine the influences of Jewish and Italian immigrants in particular and this version of coleslaw reflects the first group's liking for sweet and sour flavours and the second's for bright colours and vivid tastes. It makes an excellent first course, particularly for a New World-style meal.

SERVES 4

	FOR THE DRESSING
450 g (1 lb) coleslaw cabbage (hard, white, close-leaved and often known as Dutch)	100 g (4 oz) Dolcelatta or similar blue cheese
1 large cooking apple	4 tablespoons milk
a little lemon juice	1 tablespoon white wine vinegar
2 large dill pickles (pickled cucumbers), about 10 cm (4 in) long	½ teaspoon salt
1 bunch of spring onions	½ teaspoon sugar
1 red pepper, diced	2 tablespoons olive oil

Trim the cabbage, cut it into quarters and remove the solid core. Shred across the grain into fine strips and place in a large bowl. Core but don't peel the apple, grate that coarsely, toss with a little lemon juice to prevent it discolouring and add that to the coleslaw. Split the dill pickles into four lengthways and cut finely across the grain into paper thin slices Cut the spring onions equally finely and add to the bowl with the diced red pepper. Toss to mix thoroughly.

To make the dressing, put the blue cheese and milk into a liquidizer and blend. Add the wine vinegar, salt and sugar and blend again then gradually pour in the oil. The dressing will thicken like mayonnaise. Add to the salad immediately and toss and turn until thoroughly coated. You may keep this with advantage for up to 4 hours and if necessary up to 12 hours in the fridge. Serve on lettuce leaf cups.

TURKEY LIVER PATE

At this time of year you will find, particularly in supermarket freezer compartments, packets of turkey livers, and of course chicken livers which are there all the year round. Either, or a mixture of these, make the most marvellous pâté for a first course. It's also an excellent sandwich filling or part of a cold buffet. It's very easy to make this and you can use either a liquidizer or food processor, one of the old-fashioned mouli-legumes or, if you're feeling strong, a solid fork and plenty of elbow grease. How finely textured you want the pâté is a matter of taste and the different methods produce very different levels of smoothness. This is delicious eaten with lots of brown toast, French mustard and those little gherkins known as cornichons.

SERVES 4

450 g (1 lb) turkey and/or chicken livers	1 small wine glass of apple or orange juice
100 g (4 oz) butter (no substitutes)	good pinch of chopped fresh thyme
1 garlic clove, chopped	salt and freshly ground black pepper

Put the livers into a colander and wash them carefully under cold water. Remove any discoloured parts or any stringy bits. Put three-quarters of the butter into a solid, preferably non-stick, pan and melt until the hissing noise stops. Add the drained livers and the garlic and fry gently for 4–5 minutes until the livers are well cooked on the outside but still have a tinge of pink in the middle. Add the fruit juice and thyme and season very generously. While warm, purée the livers either in a liquidizer or food processor, through a food mill or, if you prefer, in a large basin by hand using a fork. Make sure that all the livers achieve the texture you prefer. Check the mixture for seasoning, pack into a soufflé dish or mould and smooth down the top. Melt the remaining butter and pour the clear part of that over the pâté, leaving any white residues in the pan, making sure the butter covers the pâté completely. Chill the whole dish for at least 4 hours. If the pâté is completely covered with butter it will keep under a piece of cling film for a week in the fridge with no harm at all and a slight enhancement of the garlic flavour. This is probably a pâté to serve with a spoon rather than to try to cut into slices.

MAIN COURSES

SALSIFY MORNAY ⓥ

Salsify is a vegetable that really comes into its own in November. Highly regarded by the Victorians who described it as a vegetable oyster, it resembles a very long carrot in shape with a slightly furry brown skin. It's delicate in flavour and makes an interesting vegetable course or indeed main dish. The light cheese sauce complements both flavour and texture perfectly. You can prepare it the day before, keep it cool in the fridge then bake it in the oven when you wish to serve it. Don't try freezing it, though; the texture of the salsify deteriorates rather radically.

SERVES 4

750 g (1½ lb) salsify	¼ teaspoon freshly grated nutmeg
squeeze of lemon juice	30 g (1½ oz) butter
150 ml (5 fl oz) milk	salt and freshly ground black pepper
150 ml (5 fl oz) single cream	50 g (2 oz) grated Parmesan
1½ tablespoons plain flour	1 tablespoon snipped fresh or freeze-dried chives

Pre-heat the oven to 200°C/400°F/Gas 6, 180°C fan, top of an Aga roasting oven.

Peel the salsify into a bowl of water with a good squeeze of lemon juice or a dash of cider vinegar. Cut it into 10 cm (4 in) lengths and simmer these in boiling water for 5 minutes. Drain and place in a gratin or baking dish. Mix the milk and cream and whisk in the flour and nutmeg. Add the butter and heat the mixture gently, stirring and whisking occasionally until the mixture comes to the boil and forms a smooth sauce. Season the salsify generously and the sauce mildly. Stir in most of the Parmesan and the chives and pour the mixture over the salsify, making sure that it's all coated. Spread the remaining Parmesan over the top. When ready to eat, bake this in the oven for 20 minutes until the sauce is bubbling and golden.

VEGETARIAN BAKED BEANS Ⓥ

This is a simple adaptation of the Boston baked beans that are the ancestor of our own tinned varieties. Don't be put off, however. Their original form is one of the great dishes of the world and this vegetarian version makes an extraordinarily delicious meal in its own right. You can, if you're not a vegetarian, add sausages or other grilled meats either into the casserole for the last half hour or on the side. One other small adaptation to the original is the reduction in the level of sweetness. Boston baked beans in the form they're eaten in New England have a substantial amount of brown sugar and molasses in them and while I've kept a hint of the flavour, I've reduced that level of sweetness quite considerably, as it enhances neither our health nor the taste of the dish.

SERVES 4

450 g (1 lb) dried haricot or pinto beans, soaked for 6 hours in fresh water	50 g (2 oz) sun dried tomatoes, roughly chopped
6 cloves	15 g (½ oz) Barbados sugar
1 medium-sized onion	1 tablespoon olive oil (optional)
½ head of celery, finely chopped	salt and freshly ground black pepper
100 g (4 oz) tomato purée	

I f you are going to cook the beans in the oven, pre-heat it to 180°C/350°F/Gas 4, 160°C fan, middle of an Aga roasting oven.

Bring the beans, which have been thoroughly soaked, to the boil in their soaking water. Boil for 10 minutes, strain, discard the water and cover again with fresh water to a depth of 1 cm (½ in) above the surface of the beans. Stick the cloves into the onion and bury it and the chopped celery in the beans. Add the tomato purée, the sun-dried tomatoes and the soft brown sugar. You can also at this stage, although it isn't authentic in Massachusetts, add a tablespoon of olive oil. Bring gently to the boil, cover the pot and either simmer on top of the stove or in the oven for 1½–2 hours until the beans are completely cooked and have absorbed all the liquid. Check half-way through to make sure that all the liquid has not gone and it isn't drying out too much. On the other hand, as beans differ, if there is still a lot of liquid left at the end of the cooking time, remove the lid and boil rapidly, stirring continuously until the sauce is thickened. When the beans are completely cooked, stir the mixture and remove the onion. You may remove the cloves, chop the onion and put that back if you choose – it's an optional extra. Salt the dish at this point using about a teaspoon of salt and check for the balance of sweet and sour and adjust if necessary. Serve with plenty of moist wholemeal bread and butter and a salad to follow.

FINNAN HADDIE WITH EGG AND PARSLEY SAUCE

For me the ultimate of British smoked fish is Finnan haddie, salmon and Arbroath smokies notwithstanding. The proper Finnan haddie isn't bright gold but a pale, almost silvery, colour, with the fish undyed after it's been split and salted and hung up to smoke over oak chippings. A little one weighs about 750 g (1½ lb), big ones coming up to 1.5 kg (3 lb), and may need dividing before you can cook them. Either way they're a tremendous treat and don't be put off by the line of bone down one side which can be lifted off completely and cleanly as soon as the fish is cooked. The sauce is an adaptation of one that's been popular in one form or another in Britain for over 500 years and which was originally made much of in the first of Mrs Beeton's subsequently much misquoted book. It makes quite a rich dish and a substantial main course eaten with mashed potatoes. Any vegetables need to be eaten separately as the flavours are quite vivid. You can also serve it in small ramekins as a grand first course without the potatoes.

SERVES 4

1.5 kg (3 lb) Finnan haddie (1 large or 2 small)	white pepper
600 ml (1 pint) milk	50 g (2 oz) fresh parsley, finely chopped
25 g (1 oz) butter	1 hard-boiled egg
40 g (1½ oz) plain flour	

Pre-heat the oven to 180°C/350°F/Gas 4, 160°C fan, middle of an Aga roasting oven.

Poach the haddock in the milk in a roasting pan in the oven, covered with a bit of foil, or if you have a large sauté pan in that on top of the stove. Watch it carefully so that the milk doesn't boil over. It will take from 5–15 minutes depending on the thickness of the haddock. The flesh should flake easily and the bones lift off when it is cooked. Put the fish to keep warm while you strain the milk through a sieve into a non-stick pan. Allow it to cool for a moment then stir in the butter and flour. Bring back to the boil, whisking continuously until the sauce is thick and pale gold. Check for seasoning. It shouldn't need any salt but might benefit from a little white pepper. Add the finely chopped parsley and stir. Cut the hard-boiled egg in half, finely chop the whites and add. Take the bones off the fish as neatly as possible, divide into four portions and put on to warm plates. Pour the parsley sauce over the fish and decorate with the sieved hard-boiled egg yolk. Serve immediately.

Finnan Haddie with Egg and Parsley Sauce

KIDNEYS IN CURRY CREAM SAUCE

In a perfect world this would be made with veal kidneys (from humanely raised calves) but that particular commodity is almost impossible to come by and lamb's kidneys make a very satisfactory substitute. Make sure you buy them very fresh, preferably still in their envelope of fat which needs to be peeled off and discarded. The sauce is quite pungent to balance the strong flavour of the kidney. This is delicious eaten with plenty of freshly cooked spinach and sautéed potatoes, but it's also nice as a centre to a herbed rice mould. (Press cooked rice into a buttered mould liberally sprinkled with parsley. Put over it a warm plate, turn over, and shake gently before removing the mould leaving the rice in a ring. Put the kidney mixture in the middle to serve.)

SERVES 4

8 lamb's kidneys	2 teaspoons mild curry powder
flour (optional)	seasoning
25 g (1 oz) cooking oil	250 ml (8 fl oz) double cream
25 g (1 oz) butter	

Split the kidneys, remove the thin membrane and cut out the white core using a V-shaped cut. You can, if you wish, lightly flour the kidneys at this stage with plain flour. Heat the oil and butter together in a sauté pan. Add the curry powder and cook gently for two minutes. Put in the kidneys and sauté them over a high heat for 2–3 minutes until thoroughly browned on all sides. Season generously, pour in the cream and stir the mixture, making sure it's thoroughly blended and allow the sauce to bubble and boil for one minute – it will not separate. Serve immediately onto warm plates, scraping the sauce out over the kidneys.

ROAST RIB OF BEEF WITH HERBED PUDDING AND QUICK COOKED GREENS

This dish is an adaptation of an early way of serving the roast beef of Old England. Yorkshire pudding used to be quite a regional dish and in other parts of the country a suet pudding generously flavoured with herbs was widely used. It makes real substantial rib-sticking food for the cold end of November and if you've got a hungry family to feed it is really worth knowing about. The pudding makes a pleasant change from the batter mixture from the north-east of England, and the herbs also add something unusual to a well-known dish. The greens are not a medieval speciality. They would have been both frowned upon and, if eaten at all, cooked a great deal longer, but they do make a wonderful brightly coloured and flavoured addition. A few roast potatoes would complete the ensemble. It's not worth making this with a small piece of beef or one of the more expensive roasting joints like sirloin. Rib of beef is both the cheapest and the most flavourful of the roasting cuts, and is perfect for this combination. You can buy it on or off the bone.

SERVES 8

2.25 kg (5 lb) rib of beef on bone (1.75–2 kg (4–4½ lb) rolled)	1 teaspoon freeze-dried thyme
salt and freshly ground black pepper	1 teaspoon freeze-dried marjoram
2 teaspoons English mustard powder	1 small leek
	1 egg
FOR THE PUDDING	**FOR THE GREENS**
175 g (6 oz) self-raising flour	750 g (1½ lb) green cabbage (hispi, primo, etc.)
100 g (4 oz) shredded suet	
25 g (1 oz) fresh parsley, chopped	15 g (½ oz) butter

Pre-heat the oven to 200°C/400°F/Gas 6, 180°C fan, top of an Aga roasting oven.

Rub the beef with the salt, pepper and mustard powder and put it to roast in the oven for 12 minutes per 450 g (1 lb) plus 12 minutes for rare; 15 minutes per 450 g (1 lb) plus 15 minutes for medium; and 17 minutes per 450 g (1 lb) plus 17 minutes for overdone. Mix together the flour, suet and chopped herbs. Season very generously. Split the leek, rinse it thoroughly, chop it finely and add to the mixture. Add the egg and knead together. Add an egg shell of water and knead again until the mixture becomes firm and binds together. The amount of water will depend on the flour and the moisture in the herbs but shouldn't amount to more than 3 egg shells. Put into a pudding basin, cover with a lid of foil with a fold in it and put to steam in a pan with 5 cm (2 in) of boiling water for 1 hour. Cover the pan and check and top up the water occasionally if necessary.

Wash and slice the cabbage across the grain into 1 cm (½ in) ribbons. Remove the beef from the oven when it's roasted and put in a warm place to rest for at least 10 minutes. Switch off the pudding and allow that to rest equally. Five minutes before you're ready to eat, bring 2.5 cm (1 in) of water to boil in a pan into which all the cabbage will fit. Season with plenty of salt and add the butter. Add the cabbage all in one go, put on the lid and shake vigorously. Leave over a high heat for 45 seconds to 1 minute. Shake vigorously again, cook for another 45 seconds and decant the cabbage into a hot serving dish. Use the liquid remaining to make gravy with the drippings from the roasting pan. Cut the pudding into slices and slice the beef. Serve with roast potatoes and a little extra mustard or horseradish sauce if you fancy them.

PUDDINGS

AUTUMN FRUIT SALAD
IN THYME AND GINGER

We tend to think of fruit salad as consisting only of fresh fruit but in fact the idea of a cooked fruit salad or compote goes back far in culinary history. This is a simple autumn compote flavoured with ginger and thyme, unexpected as a combination for fruit but marvellously effective nonetheless. You can chill this compote before you eat it, but it is best eaten while still slightly warm.

SERVES 4

25 g (1 oz) ginger in syrup	2 eating apples
50 g (2 oz) caster sugar	2 slightly under-ripe pears
150 ml (5 fl oz) water	100 g (4 oz) white grapes
1 large orange	1 large sprig of fresh or 1 teaspoon freeze-dried thyme

Drain the syrup from the ginger, add it to the sugar and water in a pan. Stir and heat gently to make a clear syrup. Peel the orange and slice across the grain into rounds 5 mm (¼ in) thick, removing any pips. Cut each apple in half horizontally, remove the core and quarter. Cut the pears in half lengthways, remove the core and quarter each half. Remove the grapes from the stalks and, if they have seeds, halve and de-pip them. Put the apples and pears into the syrup and simmer for 5 minutes. Add the thyme (if it's dried thyme, not a stalk, put it in a muslin bag so you can retrieve it without it coating all the fruit). Add the orange slices and continue to simmer for another 5 minutes. Slice the pieces of ginger as thinly as you can, add those and the grapes and simmer for 5 more minutes. Pour into a shallow china or glass gratin dish or similar container, remove the thyme and allow the whole mixture to cool before eating.

SPOTTED DICK WITH REAL CUSTARD

This good, old-fashioned steamed pudding harps back to British traditions of nursery food. It is a warming golden sponge studded with currants, best served with lots of piping hot custard.

SERVES 4

FOR THE SPOTTED DICK	FOR THE CUSTARD
150 g (5 oz) butter, softened	600 ml (1 pint) full cream milk
100 g (4 oz) caster sugar	1 teaspoon vanilla essence
juice and grated rind of ½ lemon	4 tablespoons caster sugar
grated rind of ½ orange	1 teaspoon cornflour
150 g (5 oz) self-raising flour	2 eggs, beaten
3 large eggs, beaten	1 egg yolk, beaten
75 g (3 oz) currants	
1 tablespoon plain flour	

Generously butter a 1-litre (1¾-pint) pudding basin.

To make the spotted dick, cream the butter and sugar together until smooth. Add the grated lemon and orange rind and the lemon juice. Stir in a little of the flour at a time, alternating with a little egg until you have a smooth batter. You could do this in a food processor. Coat the currants in the tablespoon of flour and stir into the mixture. Pour into the pudding basin and cover with a sheet of pleated greaseproof paper and foil, secured by the rubber band. Set into a pan with 4 cm (1½ in) of simmering water in the bottom, cover and steam for 1½ hours (in a pressure cooker it will take 45 minutes). When cooked, run a sharp knife around the pudding before inverting on to a plate.

To make the custard, heat the milk in a pan. Add the vanilla and sugar. Slake the cornflour with a little water and add, stirring until the sugar has dissolved. Strain the eggs and egg yolk through a sieve into the milk mixture, stirring continuously until thickened. Do not let the mixture boil. You can keep the custard warm for up to an hour by putting it over a pan of hot water with a piece of cling film placed directly on to the surface of the custard to prevent a skin forming.

CHOCOLATE ROULADE

This all-time favourite dessert makes a sophisticated and festive end to a dinner party. Here I have suggested a chestnut cream filling, but once the technique of making a roulade has been mastered you could make all kinds of variations. Chopped fresh fruit, candied peel, chocolate shavings, all manner of flavourings can be added to the cream filling. Do buy good quality chocolate. Look for a brand with at least 50 per cent cocoa solids; it makes all the difference.

SERVES 4

175 g (6 oz) plain dark chocolate, not cake covering	
2 tablespoons water	
5 eggs, separated	
175 g (6 oz) caster sugar	

FOR THE FILLING

175 ml (6 fl oz) whipping cream

75–100 g (3–4 oz) chestnut purée

2 teaspoons caster sugar or to taste

2 marron glacé, chopped (optional)

icing sugar to dust

re-heat the oven to 190°C/375°F/Gas 5, 170°C fan, middle of an Aga roasting oven. Line the bottom and sides of a 33 × 23 cm (13 × 9 in) Swiss roll tin with baking parchment.

Melt the chocolate and water together over a gentle heat. Whisk the egg yolks and sugar together until thick, pale and mousse-like. Gently fold in the chocolate. With a clean, dry whisk, beat the egg whites until stiff, then fold into the chocolate mixture. Pour into the prepared tin and smooth to the edges. Bake in the oven for 15–20 minutes. The surface will have risen and have a crust, gently press the centre to make sure it is cooked.

Remove from the oven, cover with a sheet of baking parchment and a tea towel and leave to cool in the tin for at least 8 hours. Uncover the roulade, lay the baking parchment on to the tea towel and carefully invert the roulade on to this and peel away the lining paper. Trim the edges using a sharp knife.

To make the filling, whip the cream until thick. Mash the chestnut purée with the sugar. Fold into the cream. Stir in the marron glacé, if using, and taste for sweetness.

Spread the roulade with the cream. Roll the roulade lengthways, using the parchment to help you. It is the nature of a roulade to crack. Carefully lift on to a plate and dust with sifted icing sugar. You can decorate with whipped cream or chocolate flakes if you wish. This dessert can also be frozen quite successfully.

CHRISTMAS PRESERVE Ⓥ

This festive preserve is packed with seasonal goodies: pine nuts, crystallized ginger, figs, sultanas. It keeps well and the flavours mature with time. This would make an ideal Christmas gift.

MAKES 2 LITRES (3½ PINTS)

3 navel oranges	100 g (4 oz) pine nuts
1 lemon	225 g (8 oz) sultanas
3 litres (5¼ pints) water	225 g (8 oz) dried figs, chopped
2.25 kg (5 lb) preserving sugar	100 g (4 oz) crystallized ginger, chopped

Cut the oranges into quarters, remove the pips and slice thinly. Halve the lemon, removing the pips, slice thinly and put into a large pan with the oranges and water and bring to the boil. Simmer, uncovered, for about 1 hour until the peels are soft. Warm the sugar in the oven, then add to the fruit, stirring until dissolved. Toast the pine nuts in a dry frying-pan for 2–3 minutes until golden and add to the pan with the remaining ingredients. Boil rapidly, uncovered, until setting point is reached. This will take about 40 minutes. Remove the pan from the heat and leave to stand for 10 minutes. Stir to distribute the fruit and pour into warm sterilized jars. You may need to stir the preserve again in the jars to stop the fruit sinking. When cool, cover and seal.

WALNUT BREAD

One of the most interesting aspects in the resurgence of good food in Britain in recent years has been the extraordinary array of new breads. Many of these have been Italian-inspired like ciabatta, others from the Middle East like pittas, but one of my favourites has been from the south-west of France, *pain aux noix*, or walnut bread. Small loaves often with a dark brown crust, studded with nuts and with a slight sweet and chewy texture, they go perfectly with cheese or are a pleasure to eat on their own with just a little butter. This recipe makes two medium-sized loaves which will keep very well for four or five days, particularly if once they're completely cooled they are kept loosely wrapped in a plastic bag.

MAKES 2 × 450 g (1 lb) LOAVES

1 tablespoon soft dark brown sugar	350 g (12 oz) wholemeal bread flour
25 g (1 oz) fresh yeast	½ teaspoon salt
450 ml (15 fl oz) warm water	3 tablespoons walnut oil
350 g (12 oz) unbleached strong white bread flour	100 g (4 oz) shelled walnuts

Take a pinch of the sugar and mix it with the yeast and 120 ml (4 fl oz) warm water. Stir until thoroughly blended and leave for 10 minutes until frothy. Mix the flours together and add the salt and walnut oil. When the yeast has frothed, add it to the flour with most of the remaining warm water and knead together until you have a resilient elastic dough. Don't add all the water, keep a little bit back, and see how much water the flours will absorb. Put the dough aside to rise in a warm place under a cloth for about 45–50 minutes. It should comfortably double in size.

Knock it down with the back of your hand and knead it again briefly, adding the sugar and three-quarters of the walnuts, which you can crush lightly in your hand as you knead. Divide the dough into two, and form into two cushion shapes or large rolls or into two 450 g (1 lb) loaf tins. Stud these with the remaining walnuts and put to rise on a baking tray in the warm place covered with a cloth for 30–40 minutes until fully risen.

Pre-heat the oven to 220°C/425°F/Gas 7, 190°C fan, top of an Aga roasting oven. Bake the loaves in the oven for 25 minutes. Reduce the oven temperature to 180°C/350°F/Gas 4, 160°C fan, bottom of an Aga roasting oven and bake for another 20–25 minutes until the bottom sounds hollow when you tap it with your knuckle. Remove to a baking tray and allow to cool completely before slicing and eating.

SPICE

THYME

Thyme is a low-growing, small-leafed shrub native to southern Europe where it still grows wild. The most common varieties are garden thyme, lemon thyme and caraway thyme. In the ancient temples of Greece it was burnt as incense, and it is from the same land that bees make wild thyme honey, delectable on yoghurt.

Rub fresh thyme leaves between your fingers before adding to food to release the pungent, fresh aroma fully. It can also be bought dried and freeze-dried. If using dried herbs you will not need to add as much as the flavours are more concentrated.

Thyme is a wonderful addition to so many dishes: it is good rubbed into all red meat and poultry; turkey stuffing would not be the same without it. It is good with fish, herb butter, sauces and soups. It is used to flavour sausages and pies, and most casseroles and stews. Think of Mediterranean cooking and one thinks of thyme: on aubergines, tomato sauces, pasta and pizza. It can be added to scrambled eggs, omelettes, baked eggs and soufflés, stirred into cottage and cream cheese or sprinkled on to salads, even on to fruit salads as in the recipe for Autumn Fruit Salad in Thyme and Ginger (see p. 192). It is also an essential addition to a bouquet garni of fresh herbs.

DRINK

MULLED CRANBERRY JUICE

This non–alcoholic drink is a spicy winter warmer perfect for bonfire night and good for adults and children alike. Cranberries are packed with vitamin C, just the thing to keep away chills. This drink can also be strained and served cold, possibly fizzed up with a squirt of soda water.

MAKES 6–8 GLASSES

500 ml (17 fl oz) cranberry juice	4 allspice berries
300 ml (10 fl oz) freshly squeezed orange juice	4 whole cloves
	1 cinnamon stick
300 ml (10 fl oz) water	a few slices of lemon and orange
juice of ½ lemon	

Add all the ingredients to a pan and slowly bring to the boil. Simmer for 10 minutes to infuse the flavours. Using a slotted spoon, remove the spices. Serve with a slice of fruit in each glass.

MENU OF THE MONTH

STARTER
New York coleslaw

MAIN COURSE
Kidneys in Curry cream sauce
Quick cooked greens

PUDDING
Spotted dick with real custard

DECEMBER

INTRODUCTION

December

Christmas dominates the month of December but we shouldn't let it overwhelm us. The traditional foods that we really begin to eat on the 25th of the month – turkey and tongue, goose and puddings, smoked salmon and mince pies – are all wonderful in their own way and greatly to be enjoyed, but there are another three weeks of December before the real jollifications begin. No one wants those days to be lean and mean, and there are plenty of other dishes and pleasures to be had in this month.

Turkeys themselves are particularly interesting in that almost all turkey in Britain is raised and matured so that it reaches its peak at the end of November and December. In fact some experts go so far as to say that you're much better off buying a frozen turkey if you wish to eat turkey at any other time of the year because it's all been matured for the Christmas market. I'm not sure I'd go as far as that but there's no doubt that the range of turkeys available nowadays at Christmas, including the bronze and traditionally reared varieties, add greatly to the pleasures of the Christmas feast, and to the cold cuts that follow it. Geese, too, are making a comeback for those with the opportunity to indulge adult tastes at Christmas.

Luxury goods all hit their peak at this time of year: smoked salmon and gravad lax, brandy butters and Turkish delight, exotic dried fruits and, these days, exotic tropical fruits in tiptop fresh condition, suddenly appear on our shelves and market stalls. Paw paws, lychees and mangoes have become, if not commonplace, certainly not a rarity any more and bring a wonderful sense of warmth and sunshine to the table. All the new season's nuts seem to make their appearance now – brazils and pecans, walnuts and hazels, not forgetting chestnuts, fresh, dried and tinned. Fancy biscuit selections and exotic cakes – not just British Christmas cake but stollen and panforte di Verona from Europe – are available in profusion. Cranberries and cranberry sauces from America, and from the centre of England that most English of cheeses, Stilton, available sliced all the year round, can be bought in the great rounds it's made in.

All in all, a month to enjoy, but to start enjoying at the beginning using some of these ingredients for different dishes not just the ones of high days and holidays. You'll find here ideas

PREVIOUS PAGE

1 **Christmas Turkey and Stuffing**

2 **Melon with Cream Cheese Mousse**

3 **No Fat Christmas Pudding**

for chestnuts in a soup, smoked salmon made into little timbale mousses, recipes for fruit salads with the exotic fruits that don't have to wait for Christmas to be enjoyed. There's also that group of people for whom the carnivorous side of traditional Christmas eating isn't attractive, so I've included a number of recipes for vegetarian dishes of all sorts that are at least a match for their traditional counterparts. There's mincemeat for mince pies, a Christmas pudding without suet, and a grand raised pie – what's more, they will all find favour with the carnivores as well as with the vegetarians amongst your family and friends. Last but not least the spice of Christmas, the smell that almost defines Christmas celebrations, that of cloves, finds its way into dishes savoury and sweet, perfuming the air not just with its scent but with the sense of excitement that the coming of Yuletide always brings.

PRODUCE AT ITS BEST

Brussels sprouts ● *Cabbage* ● *Broccoli* ● *Onions* ● *Parsnips* ● *Chestnuts*
● *Cobnuts* ● *Walnuts* ● *Brazil nuts* ● *Filberts* ● *Hazelnuts* ● *Pecans*
● *Satsumas* ● *Clementines* ● *Kiwi fruit* ● *Dates* ● *Figs* ● *Dried fruit*
● *Beef* ● *Turkey* ● *Goose* ● *Tongue* ● *Smoked fish* ● *Stilton cheese*

STARTERS

CHESTNUT SOUP Ⓥ

Chestnut soup is a country house treat. Although chestnuts are commonplace at Christmas in stuffing and with sprouts, and they're eaten on the streets from vendors selling them roasted, there is no tradition outside the 'great houses' of turning them into soup. This is a great pity because they make the most delicious soup as they purée down into a smooth and almost velvety texture. The traditional way was to make it with a game stock from the carcasses of birds from previous meals but in fact I like it as a vegetarian soup. It has a lighter texture and a more delicate flavour that way. It's also improved served with herb croûtons: 5 mm (¼ in) cubes of bread fried lightly in olive oil and sprinkled with parsley and thyme before adding to the soup.

SERVES 4

450 g (1 lb) fresh chestnuts or 225 g (8 oz) dried	2 celery sticks, finely chopped
1 tablespoon olive oil	a small pinch of ground cloves
25 g (1 oz) butter	salt and freshly ground black pepper
225 g (8 oz) onions, chopped	900 ml (1½ pints) water
225 g (8 oz) potatoes, cut into 1 cm (½ in) dice	½ teaspoon freeze-dried thyme

Cut a slit in the base of each of the chestnuts and put into a pan of boiling water for 1 minute. Take the pan from the heat and remove the chestnuts one by one. You will find the skin, including the brown inner peel, will slip off fairly easily. Remove it from all the chestnuts. If you are using dried chestnuts soak them in warm water for 30 minutes. Discard the water from the pan. Melt the oil and butter in the pan and add all the vegetables. Turn until coated. Add the chestnuts and turn them as well. Add the cloves, season generously and cover with the water. Bring to the boil and simmer for 25 minutes until the chestnuts are cooked through and soft. Purée the mixture either in a liquidizer or food processor or, if you prefer, through a food mill. Add the thyme and check for seasoning before serving with herb croûtons.

SMOKED SALMON TIMBALES

This is a hot mousse highlighted by the flavour of smoked salmon. They're easy to make in specially designed metal moulds called timbales but you can also make them in teacups which produce an equally attractive though different shape. Teacups are also easier to get out of the pan when hot as they already have handles.

SERVES 4

1 tablespoon cooking oil (not olive)	1 teaspoon freeze-dried dill or a sprig of fresh dill
100 g (4 oz) smoked salmon	1 egg
100 g (4 oz) fresh salmon	salt and freshly ground black pepper
50 ml (2 fl oz) fromage frais	

Lightly oil the inside of four teacups or timbale moulds, line with cling film and oil lightly again, then use the slices of smoked salmon to form an edible lining. You may need to trim them – reserve the trimmings. Skin and remove any residual bones from the fresh salmon, cut into cubes and put it with the smoked salmon trimmings into a food processor. Add the fromage frais, herbs and egg and season generously. Process until a smooth mixture. Pour this into the smoked salmon-lined moulds and place these in a frying-pan which has 2.5 cm (1 in) of boiling water in it. Cover and simmer for 10 minutes, by which time the filling should have set and risen like a little pink cushion. If it is not completely set, cook for another 2–3 minutes with the lid on. Remove the cups from the boiling water and allow to stand for a moment. Invert each one on to a serving plate and remove the cup and the cling film which will help the salmon moulds to emerge easily. You can serve these as they are or surrounded by a lightly cooked tomato sauce or a little more fromage frais into which you've stirred another teaspoon of chopped fresh dill.

CELERIAC REMOULADE Ⓥ

Celeriac is the knobbly root of the celery plant. Although similar in flavour, it has firm, white flesh, not so crisp or stringy. It can be eaten raw or cooked and when coated with a remoulade sauce becomes a favourite winter salad of the French. Celeriac is also good cooked and mashed 50:50 with potatoes.

SERVES 4

450 g (1 lb) celeriac (about half a whole one)	1 teaspoon Dijon mustard
juice of 1 lemon	a small handful of fresh parsley, chopped
150 ml (5 fl oz) mayonnaise	

Cut away the hard outside skin of the celeriac and cut the flesh into matchsticks. You could do this with the grater attachment of a food processor. Put straight into a bowl of cold water with half the lemon juice added; this will prevent the celeriac from turning brown. Bring a pan of salted water to the boil and add the rest of the lemon juice. Tip in the celeriac and blanch in boiling water for 1 minute. Drain and run cold water over the celeriac until most of the heat is removed. Drain thoroughly. Mix the mayonnaise and mustard together and stir into the drained celeriac. Sprinkle with parsley, chill, and serve with other salads and French bread.

MELON WITH CREAM CHEESE MOUSSE Ⓥ

This is a perfect first course for Christmas lunch; if you want a first course that is. It comes in both a vegetarian and a fishy version. If you fancy the fishy version, add 50 g (2 oz) smoked salmon to your ingredients list. The only difficult bit of this recipe is that of learning the trick of how to cut the melons so that they present that marvellous deckle edge that makes it look as if they've been carved for hours by experts. The trick, as you'll discover, is very simple indeed and only requires a sharp knife and a steady hand.

SERVES 4

2 small ogen, galia or cantaloupe melons	juice of ½ lemon
100 g (4 oz) full fat soft cheese	salt
1 tablespoon snipped fresh chives	50 g (2 oz) smoked salmon (optional), cut into 1 cm (½ in) slices

ut the melons down on a firm work surface and, using a sharp knife, poke into the melon at the equator at an angle of 45°. Pull the knife out and put in again next to that cut joining at an angle of 90° so you produce a saw-toothed pattern of cutting. Proceed right the way round the equator of the melon and you'll find that the two halves will pull apart leaving the edges carved in an attractive pattern. Scoop out the seeds and you have the containers for the mousse. Put the full-fat soft cheese into a liquidizer or food processor, add the chives and the lemon juice, check for saltiness and add some if it's needed. If you're using the smoked salmon you need to add that at the same time. Process until the mixture is smooth then scoop ice-cream sized balls into the centre of each melon half. Place in attractive dishes and serve at once, garnished with more smoked salmon, if using.

MAIN COURSES

SPICED TONGUE

Tongue is one of those joints that everybody likes to eat, but seems so unprepossessing in its original state that very few of us cook it. This is a pity as it's actually very easy and not at all unpleasant. You can eat tongue hot or cold and there are a number of very unusual but quite delicious sauces from the eighteenth century for hot sliced tongue. One that's a particular favourite of mine is based on orange juice with dried fruit in it; the ideal accompaniment to the salty savouriness of the meat. This recipe, however, is for the classic cold rolled tongue which slices so wonderfully and provides such a pleasant contrast to the cold turkey that is left after Christmas lunch. I don't believe it's worth salting tongue yourself unless you are a real purist. Both butchers and supermarkets now sell them ready salted and it's quite the easiest way to approach the matter.

SERVES 6–8

1 × 2.7–3 kg (6–7 lb) ox tongue, ready salted or 'cured'	6 peppercorns
	2 bay leaves
4 juniper berries	1 cinnamon stick
4 allspice berries	

inse the tongue and put it into a bowl of fresh water for at least 2 hours to take off the excess salt. You then have two options for cooking, one in a conventional pan and one in a pressure cooker. Either way, place the tongue into the body of the pan without any trivet in it, even if you're using a pressure cooker. Add the spices and herbs. If you're using a conventional pan, cover the tongue with at least 2.5 cm (1 in) of water. If you're using a pressure cooker, put 4 cm (1½ in) of water into the bottom. Put the lid on and, if you're using a conventional pan, bring to the boil and simmer for 3 hours. You can do this in an oven, particularly in an Aga sort of oven, making sure that the water is only just above boiling point. If you're using a pressure cooker, bring to pressure, turn down and cook for 1 hour.

When the tongue is cooked either way, drain from the cooking liquid, which should be discarded with the herbs and spices. Allow to cool for 10 minutes and then, using a sharp knife and a table fork, remove the skin. You'll find that at one cut it will peel off effortlessly. Trim away any grizzly bits and remove the small bones that may have been left at the thick end of the tongue. Choose a soufflé dish or cake tin into which the tongue will just fit when rolled – this will probably be 15–20 cm (6–8 in) in diameter. Roll up the tongue and place it into the dish. Put a clean plate or cake tin bottom on top of the tongue and place a 1.75 kg (4 lb) weight on top. This can be scale weights or use tinned foods. Allow the tongue to be pressed until it's cool – about 1–1½ hours – and then, keeping the weights in place if possible, chill for at least 12 hours. A jelly will be pressed from the tongue and will set the whole joint into a firm and permanent shape.

To slice, remove the dish by running a knife around the edge and dipping the bottom into hot water for not more than 30 seconds and inverting over the carving dish or board. Cut the meat across into thin slices. The heel of the tongue, if you have any left after slicing, makes a wonderful potted meat mixed with a little butter and mace and puréed in a food processor.

CHRISTMAS TURKEY AND STUFFING

December is normally the only time we all cook whole turkeys. For the rest of the year, portions are widely available and much used, but the full scale roasting job of a 4.5–6.75 kg (10–15 lb) turkey normally is exclusively confined to Christmas time. Therefore, for all of us it's effectively a first time operation again as remembering the oven timings, stuffing techniques and the rest of it are fairly difficult over twelve months. There is always a great debate about the best way of cooking turkey and often some quite extraordinary and eccentric-appearing recipes work very well. I know of one from America that suggests you take a supermarket shopping bag (of the brown paper variety), butter it thoroughly, turn it inside out, pop the turkey into that and roast it in a medium oven. It's supposed to keep the turkey succulent and brings it out golden brown and delicious. I haven't tried it myself but know a number of people who have with success. However, there are more conventional ways that also work extremely well and my favourite is below.

The other issue is to stuff or not to stuff. For many years I thought the only acceptable stuffing was one placed in the crop end of the bird, leaving the after end open to allow the heat in to circulate and cook the turkey at an even level. However, the roasting method I now use over water makes sure that happens, so a stuffing in the larger end is once more possible. I still don't much reckon to a meat stuffing there, partly because of the heaviness of flavour and texture it provides and also because, unless every bit of that stuffing is cooked right through, it has all kinds of health implications. By the time sausage meat is cooked through, the rest of the turkey may well be past the normal edible condition. If you do stuff the larger cavity, don't stuff it rock hard because a certain amount of air circulation at the top end does help the cooking process.

I've recommended a stuffing here that has an unusual combination of ingredients through they are all Christmassy ones. It's based on brazil nuts which make a stuffing as interesting in texture as it is in flavour. It has another advantage too: if you have a vegetarian amongst your guests or family, a good helping of this baked in a separate dish and served with all the other traditional vegetables will be, I think you'll find, most acceptable and flavourful as well.

Cooking times are another vexed question. Although there's no scientific evidence for it, my own experience is that a fresh bird will cook quicker than even a properly defrosted frozen one. It is, however, quite certain that a frozen bird can be defrosted with advantage at least five days before you cook it, as a couple of days maturing after all the ice has gone improves both flavour and texture. The key way to test whether a turkey is cooked is to use a sharp skewer thrust into the largest portion of the thigh of the bird. If the juices run clear the turkey is cooked, whatever the time scale. If the juices still show any tinge of pink the bird needs another 15–20 minutes at least and a test again at the end of that time. The trick with turkey timings is that the heavier the bird the *shorter* amount of time per 450 g (1 lb) it needs to cook. Therefore even a big bird will not take a lot longer than a comparatively small one.

COOKING TIMES FOR TURKEY

20 minutes per 450 g (1 lb) for a 4.5 kg (10 lb) bird, 15 minutes for a 6.75 kg (15 lb) bird and 12 minutes for a 9 kg (20 lb) bird. All those weights are assumed with the stuffing in so it's important to estimate that even if you can't weigh the fully stuffed bird on your domestic scales.

SERVES 10 PLUS COLD CUTS

1 × 6.75 kg (15 lb) turkey	1 large onion, finely diced
900 ml (1½ pints) water	4 slices of white bread
50 g (2 oz) butter	grated rind and juice of 1 lemon
salt and freshly ground black pepper	25 g (1 oz) fresh parsley, finely chopped
	1 teaspoon freeze-dried thyme
FOR THE STUFFING	50 g (2 oz) butter, softened
450 g (1 lb) shelled brazil nuts	1 egg
2 celery sticks, finely diced	

To make the stuffing roughly chop the brazil nuts into peanut-sized pieces and mix with the celery and onion. Turn the bread into breadcrumbs using a food processor or grater and add those with the lemon juice and rind, herbs and softened butter and mix thoroughly. Add the egg and use that to bind the stuffing together. It should cohere reasonably well but not be a solid mass. On the day you're to roast the turkey or, at the earliest the night before, use the mixture to fill the large cavity three-quarters full. Any surplus should be rolled into balls and baked in a separate dish during the last 45 minutes of the turkey's cooking.

Pre-heat the oven to 180°C/350°F/Gas 4, 160°C fan, bottom of an Aga roasting oven. Place the turkey on a rack and place the rack in your roasting tin so that the turkey is at least 4–5 cm (1½–2 in) above the bottom of the tin. Put the water into the tin, coat the turkey with the butter as though you were buttering toast, salt and pepper it generously and cover with a large sheet of greaseproof paper, not tucking it in but leaving it more like a kind of tent. Roast in the oven for the appropriate length of time (15 minutes per 450 g (1 lb) in this case). Check whether it is cooked after approximately 3–3½ hours. It may need a few minutes longer up to the full time depending upon your oven and the solidity of any stuffing. When it's cooked remove from the oven, put the bird on its carving dish and allow to stand for 10–15 minutes before carving. Pour the liquid from the tin into a pan and reduce by a third by boiling rapidly. This makes giblet-style gravy in its own right. If you wish to thicken it you can use cornflour or arrowroot but not gravy browning.

CARVING THE TURKEY

To facilitate carving the turkey, before roasting it you might like to try removing the wishbone. You can do this with a sharp knife yourself or ask your butcher or poulterer to do it for you – a little notice will be required. You'll find that when carving the turkey, removal of the wishbone will allow you to carve the breast at 45° angles for slice after even slice without any of the usual knife slipping and hacking that so often takes place. The removal of the wishbone does not affect the cooking time or the ability to stuff the crop end of the bird if you so wish.

CHRISTMAS GOOSE

Before the turkey arrived from the New World and became a farmyard bird, goose reigned supreme as the British celebratory poultry, although it must be said that swan and peacock played a significant part in medieval and Tudor times. Although displaced for many years, goose is now making a comeback, particularly as the age pattern of the British population changes. Goose is essentially an adult taste, being rich and slightly gamy compared to the pale meat of turkey, but as more people have what is essentially an adult Christmas dinner with their children grown up and their palates developed, goose has become quite popular again. It's a very different proposition from turkey, not only in its taste and texture but also in the amount of meat it offers. A good-sized goose, which should be 3–4.5 kg (7–10 lb), will feed six people comfortably and eight people well but there will be little left for cold cuts afterwards. You can, though, get quite a lot of subsidiary benefits from a roast goose. Left-overs potted with some of the goose fat from the cooking make the basis of the confit of goose that's famous in the south-west of France, and even in a small scale like this can enliven cassoulets and other dishes. The giblets make an excellent basis for soup and the liver makes a terrific pâté, certainly when it's added to chicken or duck liver to increase the volume. Having said all that, goose is still worth buying and eating for a high holiday like Christmas as its generous flavour and richness do make for a very special occasion. It needs stuffing and saucing, however, to balance that richness, and I've got a combination here that includes some of the old allies of goose with a sauce that used to be enormously popular with meats of all sorts – Cumberland Sauce. You can make it in advance and keep it in jars in the fridge to eat with other Christmas meats as well.

SERVES 6–8 PEOPLE

750 g (1½ lb) Bramley apples	1 teaspoon freeze-dried or fresh sage
175 g (6 oz) fresh white breadcrumbs	salt and freshly ground black pepper
2 Jaffa-type oranges	1 × 3.5–4.5 kg (8–10 lb) goose
1 large onion, finely chopped	1 slice or crust of bread
½ teaspoon ground cloves	

To make the stuffing peel and core the Bramleys, cut them into walnut-sized pieces and cook them very gently in a non-stick pan with a little water until a rough purée – this will take about 15 minutes. Put the breadcrumbs in a bowl. Grate the rind from the oranges, peel them and chop up the flesh. Put that and the grated rind in to the bowl with the apples and the onion. Mix together thoroughly, add the herbs and season generously. Put the goose on a trivet or colander in the sink and pour over it a large kettle of boiling water, turning the goose carefully so that the water reaches all the parts. This will loosen the skin from the subcutaneous fat and when you roast the goose it will allow the fat to run out and prevent the bird being greasy. Allow it to dry out of the fridge for an hour or so.

Pre-heat the oven to 180°C/350°F/Gas 4, 160°C fan, middle of an Aga roasting oven. Stuff the goose loosely with the stuffing mixture in the large cavity and put a crust or piece of bread across the base to prevent any of the mixture running out while the goose is cooking. Place on a rack above your roasting tin so that the abundant fat that runs out may be collected and kept away from the goose. Cook in the oven for between 15–18 minutes per 450 g (1 lb). The goose should be cooked thoroughly and the skin dark golden brown. When it's cooked, take it out of the oven and pour away the goose fat. If you wish to keep it, it should be put into kilner-type jars and allowed to cool before sealing down. Serve with mashed potatoes, red and green cabbage and Cumberland sauce rather than gravy. The stuffing will have a certain fruity astringency that will go perfectly with this sweet spiced addition.

CUMBERLAND SAUCE Ⓥ

Cumberland Sauce is one of the few sauces or ketchups that is still, by and large, home-made. It's a very rich confection that's got quite a sweet and sour flavour. It's traditionally eaten with cold meats and is absolutely excellent in sandwiches, particularly those that contain rich ingredients like pâté. I also quite like using it in the sauces for things like game casserole as a replacement for redcurrant jelly, which of course it contains in substantial quantities.

SERVES 4

3 large oranges	2 teaspoons made English mustard
3 lemons (preferably unwaxed)	50 ml (2 fl oz) cider vinegar
175 g (6 oz) onions	a pinch of ground mace
1 tablespoon cooking oil	a pinch of ground ginger
350 g (12 oz) redcurrant jelly	a pinch of salt

Use a grater or fruit zester to remove the peel from the oranges and lemons. Squeeze the juice from the oranges and lemons, mix the peel into that and allow to stand for 30 minutes. Peel and very finely chop the onions – you can if you like liquidize it in a food processor or liquidizer. Cook it very gently in the oil in a non-stick pan for 10 minutes until translucent. Add the redcurrant jelly, the orange and lemon juice and peel and stir in the mustard, cider vinegar and spices and salt. Stir over a low heat until the redcurrant jelly is completely dissolved and then boil for 5–10 minutes until it begins to thicken. At this point, allow to cool for a few minutes then pour into sterilized jars (use a baby bottle sterilizing liquid for this). Seal down and allow to cool. It will keep in the fridge for months and is ideal not only with the goose but with tongue and other similar cold meats.

VEGETARIAN PIE Ⓥ

Vegetarians can feel particularly left out at Christmas time because so much of our traditional festive cooking revolves around meat and poultry. But there's no need for them to suffer, or for carnivores to suffer when eating with them either, because many of the vegetarian alternatives now are so delicious that they provide not only a vegetarian but a complete alternative to main course meat. This pie is delicious hot but also very good cold and makes an excellent contribution to a buffet table. In fact at a recent party I gave, all the carnivores made sure they got a slice of this as well as their own dishes until they were forcibly prevented. Although it's substantial it's also moist and melt–in–the–mouth.

SERVES 4

750 g (1½ lb) shortcrust pastry	1 tablespoon capers (optional)
225 g (8 oz) macaroni	100 ml (3½ fl oz) single cream
350 g (12 oz) spinach leaves	3 eggs
1 fennel bulb, cut into 5 mm (¼ in) dice	1 teaspoon vegetable concentrate
100 g (4 oz) pine nuts, fried until golden in a little oil	1 tablespoon cornflour mixed with 2 tablespoons water
salt and freshly ground black pepper	1 tablespoon caster sugar
½ red pepper, finely sliced	1 tablespoon ground cinnamon
100 g (4 oz) feta cheese, cut into small cubes	

Pre-heat the oven to 190°C/375°F/Gas 5, 170°C fan, top of an Aga roasting oven. Grease a 20–23 cm (8–9 in) spring-form pie or cake tin.

Roll out two-thirds of the pastry and line the tin, leaving the rest to make the lid. Cook the macaroni in plenty of boiling, salted water until *al dente*, then drain. Wash the spinach and discard any large stalks. Cook over a gentle heat, without adding any extra water, until soft. Drain. When the spinach is cool enough to handle squeeze out the excess water until it is quite dry and chop roughly.

To assemble the pie, put one-third of the macaroni into the lined tin, then the fennel and pine nuts, seasoning each layer as you go with salt and pepper. Add another third of the macaroni, followed by the spinach. Add the final layer of macaroni, then the pepper, feta and capers, if using. Beat the cream, eggs, vegetable concentrate and cornflour together, season to taste and pour into the pie. Roll out the pastry lid, press down the edges and trim. You can use left-over pastry to decorate. Sprinkle the top of the pie with the sugar and cinnamon. Bake for 1¼ hours. Serve immediately or cold.

MEDITERRANEAN MONKFISH

For a complete change from Christmas-style cooking, here's a fish dish from the very south of France, the Languedoc. It's the sort of dish that is eaten there in the run-up to Christmas, particularly on Christmas Eve. This dish made with salt cod or another fish was always the traditional meal to be followed, after Mass at midnight, by a table laden with what were known as the Treize Desserts, a mixture of thirteen different fruits, cakes, sweetmeats and nuts, to celebrate the beginning of the feast day itself. This is no abstemious dish, however. Monkfish is the most 'meaty' of all fish, having no conventional bones and cooking to a perfect clean white. It's therefore an ideal fish for people who aren't too keen on the idea, but over recent years its attractiveness has become apparent in its price so it's not a cheap option. Cooked like this, however, it's good enough to act as a serious alternative to one of the meat meals for the festive season.

SERVES 4

750 g (1½ lb) monkfish, skinned and filleted	salt and freshly ground black pepper
120 ml (4 fl oz) olive oil	225 g (8 oz) tinned Italian chopped tomatoes
juice of 1 lemon	½ teaspoon freeze-dried thyme
2 garlic cloves, thinly sliced	½ teaspoon freeze-dried marjoram
225 g (8 oz) onions, thinly sliced	½ teaspoon freeze-dried basil
225 g (8 oz) red peppers, de-seeded and thinly sliced	
225 g (8 oz) courgettes, sliced	

Pre-heat the oven to 190°C/375°F/Gas 5, 170°C fan, middle of an Aga roasting oven.

Marinate the fish in half the olive oil and the lemon juice. Fry the garlic and onions gently in the remaining olive oil for 5 minutes. Add the peppers and courgettes and cook a further 5 minutes. Season generously, add the tomatoes and cook the mixture for another 10 minutes. Season with the thyme and marjoram and put into a baking dish or gratin dish. Put the marinated fish on top, pour the marinade over, season the fish, cover with a piece of greaseproof paper or a couple of butter papers and bake in the oven for 35–40 minutes until the fish is cooked through. To serve, divide the fish into neat portions, stir the basil into the vegetable mixture and use as a bed on each plate for the fish. You can serve this on its own with French bread or with rice. Potatoes don't work with it terribly well. You can use other fish but the cooking time in the oven should be reduced according to the thickness of the fish you choose.

PUDDINGS

CHRISTMAS PUDDINGS

Christmas puddings eaten at this time of year are quite a recent development. As with so many of the Christmas 'traditions' that we currently enjoy, they were introduced by Prince Albert in the nineteenth century. Plum puddings, from which they derive, were eaten widely but not exclusively at Christmas time. So the coincidence of style and time is not, as one might expect from their taste and flavour, derived from the medieval period, but almost from living memory. In their original form, plum puddings had a great deal of suet in them, a relic of a time when they were made with meat as well; and indeed most modern Christmas puddings still maintain a significant proportion of suet in their mixture. There is a view that this makes for a particularly rich and delicious pudding at a time when self-indulgence is the norm, and there's no question if you want a long-matured pudding the traditional kind is best. I've included, however, an alternative which I've found very popular in recent years which has no suet in it, or indeed any other fat in it at all except for that which occurs naturally in the other ingredients. It's a lighter, moister version with a softer texture but one that's become for us a firm family favourite.

TRADITIONAL CHRISTMAS PUDDING

This recipe has, so legend recounts, been the Royal Family's favourite Christmas pudding from the time of the first Georges at the beginning of the eighteenth century. It's very simple and very rich, and in its original form it was made in huge quantities so this is a cut down version.

MAKES 2 × 750 g (1½ lb) PUDDINGS

175 g (6 oz) shredded suet	½ teaspoon salt
175 g (6 oz) soft brown or demerara sugar	1 teaspoon mixed spice
175 g (6 oz) seedless raisins	½ teaspoon freshly grated nutmeg
175 g (6 oz) stoned prunes	4 large eggs
175 g (6 oz) self-raising flour	150 ml (5 fl oz) milk
100 g (4 oz) chopped mixed peel	

Mix all the dry ingredients together. Beat the eggs and milk until frothy then stir into the dry ingredients until thoroughly mixed. Allow to stand in the basin in a cool place, not in the fridge, for 12 hours. Put into pudding basins and cover with a piece or greaseproof paper with a fold in it to allow for the rise. Tie round with string or use a heavyweight elastic band. Cook, covered, for 3 hours in a conventional pan with 4–5 cm (1½–2 in) of water, or for 1¼ hours in a pressure cooker. Check the water level from time to time. Allow to cool and store. They will keep without any deterioration in a cool place for up to a year, and are best left for at least a month for the flavours to mature.

Before eating, steam for an hour in a saucepan or 30 minutes in a pressure cooker and serve with any of the conventional accompaniments, although this is so rich that a little pouring cream is usually all I prefer.

NO-FAT CHRISTMAS PUDDING

This is the pudding that's become a firm favourite with everyone who uses it, not least because at the end of a rich Christmas dinner it provides all the old-fashioned flavour without the old-fashioned stodge. It won't keep, however, and shouldn't be made more than two to three weeks before it's needed at Christmas time.

SERVES 4

2 medium-size apples	450 g (1 lb) mixed fruit (sultanas, currants and raisins)
2 bananas	juice and grated rind of 1 lemon
50 g (2 oz) walnuts	1 teaspoon mixed spice
50 g (2 oz) almonds	1 teaspoon salt
50 g (2 oz) hazelnuts	450 g (1 lb) freshly made breadcrumbs, preferably wholemeal
4 eggs	50 g (2 oz) soft brown sugar
150 ml (5 fl oz) milk	

Grate the apples without peeling them and peel and roughly chop the bananas and nuts. Break the eggs and whisk them with the milk. Mix all the ingredients together and stir well. Put it into a 2.25-litre (4-pint) or two 1.2-litre (2-pint) basins, well greased with butter, and cover with greaseproof paper with a fold in it and secure with string or an elastic band. Steam for 3–4 hours (depending on size) in a conventional pan with about 5 cm (2 in) of water and a lid on, or for 1–1½ hours in a pressure cooker. Check the level of water at intervals during cooking. Remove and store until Christmas Day.

To re-heat, steam for an hour in a conventional pan, 25 minutes in a pressure cooker or 6–8 minutes in a microwave (check instructions on your particular model) before serving. Run a sharp knife around the pudding before inverting on to a serving dish.

MINCE PIE ROYALE

This is a version of the mince pie that I much prefer to the conventional ones which have far too much pastry and too little mince for my taste. It looks spectacular, is very easy to make and, I think, looks great on a large scale as well as in individual mince pies, so that's the recipe I give here. You can, of course, modify the whole process and make individual-sized mince pies if you prefer, in which case the cooking time needs to be reduced by a third. I also suggest you might like to use the fat-less mincemeat recipe you'll find as one of the preserve recipes for this month, although the method works perfectly well with conventional and shop-bought mincemeat.

SERVES 4

225 g (8 oz) good shortcrust pastry	2 egg whites
juice and grated rind of 1 orange	100 g (4 oz) caster sugar
225 g (8 oz) mincemeat	1 teaspoon cider vinegar

Pre-heat the oven to 200°C/400°F/Gas 6, 180°C fan, middle of an Aga roasting oven. Grease a 20 cm (8 in) flan tin.

Roll out the pastry and use to line the flan tin. Prick it with a fork and bake it blind in the oven for 10–15 minutes until pale gold. Remove and allow it to cool.

Add the grated rind and orange juice to the mincemeat and use that to fill the flan case. Whip the egg whites until thick and add the sugar a spoonful at a time, whipping until the meringue mixture goes glossy. Stir in the cider vinegar. This will turn the mixture into an Italian-style meringue that will go crisp on the outside but remain slightly chewy and marshmallowy in the centre. Pile the meringue mixture on to the pie and swirl round with the back of a spoon or fork until it completely covers the mincemeat and is in an attractive pattern. Bake in the same temperature oven for 25 minutes. The meringue topping will go gold and should set to a crisp casing but should not in any way be allowed to go dark brown or burn. Allow the pie to cool before removing from the tin and cutting and serving.

PINEAPPLE SURPRISE

With the exotic fruits that appear in our shops and greengrocers at Christmas, perhaps the most spectacular to look at is the one that was the favourite at Christmas time in the eighteenth century, the pineapple. As well as tasting good, the pineapple has another virtue and that is that it can be used for spectacular presentation. I've seen them turned into great turbans of spun sugar filled with ice-cream made from their own flesh and as the centrepieces of exotic flan bases. All a bit the province of the professional pastry chef and restaurant *maitre d'* perhaps, but this dish is equally spectacular in its own way. It makes an outstandingly splendid centrepiece for the end of a dinner party or Christmas celebration with the shells of the pineapple used as the dishes for a hot and scrumptious fruit salad.

SERVES 4

1 large pineapple with a big green plume	6 satsuma or clementine oranges
50 g (2 oz) butter	a pinch of ground cinnamon
50 g (2 oz) soft brown sugar	

Mince Pie Royale

sing a large, sharp knife, cut the pineapple, complete with green leaves, in half lengthways. Lay the pineapple pieces on their back and, using a grapefruit knife, cut round the edge of the flesh as though you were cutting out a grapefruit. Using a straight sharp knife, cut a noughts and crosses pattern into the middle of the flesh, cutting down to but not through the outside of the skin. Use a strong spoon to scoop out the pineapple centre. You'll find it will pop out in cubes without any difficulty. Do this to both halves of the pineapple, reserving the flesh. Place the empty shells head to tail on a large serving dish. Heat the butter in a large non-stick frying-pan, add the sugar and the pineapple cubes and allow to cook through for 2–3 minutes. Meanwhile, skin and peg the satsumas, removing any pips you can find. After 2 minutes, add the satsumas to the pineapple and spice with the cinnamon. Turn until the whole mixture is hot but not in any way collapsing or jammy. Pile back into the pineapple shells and serve immediately. This is wonderful hot and disgusting cold so make sure it is all eaten!

PRESERVES

BAKED CRANBERRY PRESERVE Ⓥ

Fresh cranberries
Granulated sugar

imply measure equal volumes of cranberries and sugar, (eg, a cup of cranberries and a cup of sugar or a jug of cranberries and a jug of sugar). Put them into an ovenproof pot with a tight fitting lid, stir and cook slowly. The cooking time will vary according to the quantities you choose to make. A pint measuring jug filled to the brim with cranberries and then with sugar will take 3 to 3½ hours or may be left overnight in the bottom of an Aga. When cooked, the cranberries are still whole but soft, and the sugar has dissolved into a clear thick conserve. Pour into sterilized jars and seal.

VEGETARIAN MINCEMEAT Ⓥ

This mincemeat is really a sophisticated version of the apple butters that are still made in New England at this time of the year. As it has no suet it's ideal for vegetarians but is also accordingly a much lighter confection. It keeps quite well and can be made up to six months in advance.

MAKES 1.5–1.75 kg (3–4 lb)

900 g (2 lb) cooking apples	300 ml (10 fl oz) freshly pressed apple juice
50 g (2 oz) slivered almonds	450 g (1 lb) mixed fruit (currants, sultanas and raisins)
100 g (4 oz) glacé cherries	½ teaspoon ground allspice
grated rind and juice of 1 lemon	½ teaspoon ground cloves
225 g (8 oz) Barbados or dark brown sugar	

eel and core the apples and chop the almonds and cherries with the lemon rind until finely chopped. Melt the sugar in the apple juice, put in the apples and cook until they begin to purée. Add all the other ingredients and stir together until completely mixed. Bring to the boil, stirring gently. Turn the heat down, cover and simmer for about 30 minutes until the mixture has become completely soft and there are no lumps left with the apple. Pour into clean sterilized jars and seal while warm. It will keep in a cool dark place for at least 6 months, maturing as it goes. Use as for traditional mincemeat or mixed with apples for an exotic apple pie.

BREAD

EMERGENCY CHRISTMAS BREAD

The one thing we always seem to run out of at Christmas time is bread and that is particularly the case now that long, sometimes ten day, holidays seem to be the norm, running from Christmas Eve until after New Year. After the rich dishes and confections of Christmas the simple pleasures of a little freshly-baked bread are very considerable by the middle of this period, but fresh yeast to make the bread with is usually in pretty thin supply. This recipe has another very basic advantage and that is that it can be made from a standing start to being sliced at the table within an hour. Unlike conventional bread, there are no difficulties involved in its being eaten while it's still warm. You can make it with white flour but my own preference is with wholemeal. This technique seems to bring out the nuttiness of brown flour in a unique way. The quantities make 2 small or 1 large loaf, traditionally moulded in a round bread shape. You can, if you wish to improve the rise, invert a large cake tin over the bread before you bake it. Make sure though that it's big enough to allow the bread to almost double in size, which it will as it cooks.

MAKES TWO SMALL OR ONE LARGE LOAF

450 g (1 lb) wholemeal flour (British flour is excellent for this)	2 teaspoons soft brown sugar (not demerara)
½ teaspoon salt	300 ml (10 fl oz) mixed milk and water
2 teaspoons baking powder	1 tablespoon plain yoghurt
1 teaspoon bicarbonate of soda	

re-heat the oven to 220°C/425°F/Gas 7, 190°C fan, top of an Aga roasting oven.

Put all the dry ingredients except the sugar together into a bowl (you can use a food processor to do this very quickly), and mix them thoroughly together. Add the sugar to the milk and water and stir until it's dissolved. Add the yoghurt to that and, when thoroughly mixed, put with the dry ingredients and knead and mix together until thoroughly blended. You may need to add a little more flour or a little more liquid at this stage because different flours absorb different amounts of liquid and you need to have a firm but not hard dough. Cut in half and shape it into two round balls and put these on a greased baking tray. Bake the bread for 30 minutes. Remove the tin if you've been using it and bake for another 5 to 10 minutes until the bread is cooked through and sounds hollow when tapped on the bottom. Cool on a wire tray for about 10 to 15 minutes. You can cut and eat them as soon a they are cool enough to handle. To eat the next day, they are best reheated gently in the oven for 10 to 15 minutes, or made into toast.

SPICE

CLOVES

Cloves are the flower of the clove tree, picked in bud and dried in the sun. Their hot, spicy flavour and aromatic scent embody the smells and flavours of Christmas. Pomander balls, pot-pourri, spiced beef, mince pies, mulled drinks, baked apples are but a few of the things that come to mind.

Whole cloves can be studded into meat, used in marinades or stocks. Studded into onions they make a powerful infusion in bread sauce, or cooked beans as in November's vegetarian baked bean recipe. Beware of their strength, a few go a long way. They make a welcome addition to poached and bottled fruit, or infused into a pot of tea.

Ground cloves add a spicy flavour to many baked confections: Christmas puddings, mince meat, eccles cakes, fruit breads and cakes. They also lend themselves as a good flavouring with carrots, sweet potatoes, white beans, even baked tomatoes and beef stews.

Oil is extracted from the cloves and used in perfumes, mouthwashes and as a very effective local anaesthetic for toothaches.

HOT EGG NOG

There is something innately soothing about a hot milky drink. The addition of egg yolks makes this drink creamy and nourishing. You could add a splash of liqueur to the drink just before serving if you like, but I prefer a few drops of vanilla essence.

MAKES 2 MUGS

300 ml (10 fl oz) milk	a few drops of vanilla essence
2 eggs	freshly grated nutmeg
2 teaspoons clear honey	

Heat the milk until scalding, but do not let it boil. Beat the eggs and strain through a sieve into a clean bowl. Add the honey. Pour the milk on to the eggs, whisking well to incorporate air and make the drink foamy. Add the vanilla essence or any other flavouring and pour into warmed mugs. Grate a little nutmeg on to each one before serving.

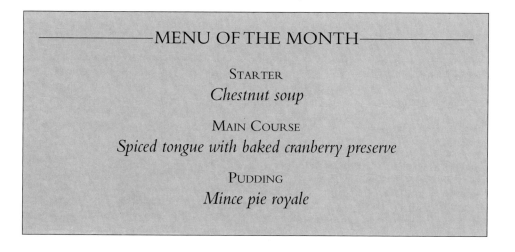

─────── MENU OF THE MONTH ───────

STARTER
Chestnut soup

MAIN COURSE
Spiced tongue with baked cranberry preserve

PUDDING
Mince pie royale

INDEX